SIFRA IN PERSPECTIVE

The Documentary Comparison of the Midrashim of Ancient Judaism

Number 146
SIFRA IN PERSPECTIVE
The Documentary Comparison of the
Midrashim of Ancient Judaism
by
Jacob Neusner

SIFRA IN PERSPECTIVE
The Documentary Comparison of the
Midrashim of Ancient Judaism

by
Jacob Neusner

Scholars Press
Atlanta, Georgia

SIFRA IN PERSPECTIVE
The Documentary Comparison of the Midrashim of Ancient Judaism

Library of Congress Cataloging in Publication Data

Neusner, Jacob, 1932-
   Sifra in the perspective : the documentary comparison of the
Midrashim of ancient Judaism / Jacob Neusner.
     p. cm. -- (Brown Judaic studies ; no. 146)
   Includes index.
   ISBN 1-55540-232-1 (alk. paper)
   1. Sifra--Criticism, interpretation, etc. 2. Bible. O.T.
Leviticus--Criticism, interpretation, etc., Jewish. I. Title.
II. Series.
BM517.S63N48 1988)
296.1'4--dc19   88-10073

Printed in the United States of America
on acid-free paper

For

THE OTTOLENGHI FAMILY
OF BOLOGNA, ITALY

EMILLIO AND NICOLETTE RUTH
AND THEIR SPLENDID SONS,
GUIDO, ALBERTO, AND EMANUELE
OTTOLENGHI

A token of thanks to
dear friends and gracious hosts

Choosing to carry forward the rich traditions
of Judaism in Italy,
this elegant family, the true nobility of Italian Judaism,
bears everyday witness to the faith of Israel, the Jewish People,
whether many, whether few,
and its remarkable strength
to persevere
and
to flourish
in the courts of that holy house that is constructed
in the Jewish heart and in the Jewish hearth,
wherever home takes place.

Contents

Preface

Defining the context in which Sifra, a document of the canon of the Judaism of the Dual Torah formed around the book of Leviticus, takes shape provides perspective on both Sifra and the canonical writings comparable to it. Comparing and contrasting one document with another allows us to determine in what ways a given writing is singular, and how that same writing shares traits common to an entire classification of documents, e.g., to a canon. The labor of classification through analysis of shared and identification of unique qualities further tells us in what ways a writing replicates traits of aesthetics (e.g., rhetoric), philosophy (e.g., logic), and even theology (e.g., topical program) with other writings of its larger genus. Then, too, we can find out how a document is particular as to its aesthetic, philosophical, and theological program and statement.

The purpose of establishing a well-examined context for each book of the canon is to permit the description, analysis, and interpretation of what no one canonical component wholly sets forth, but all of them adumbrate in one way or another: the Judaism beyond the texts. For in determining what is particular to a document, we also identify traits of rhetoric, modes of thought, and matters of doctrine shared among a variety of writings, even presupposed by all of them. The definition of those presupposed views and those premises of thought affords access to what no one text presents but what all texts represent. That is what is subject to inquiry when I speak of "the Judaism beyond the texts," and it is the goal, also, of the study of Sifra in its documentary context(s). The two appendices draw the reader abreast of debates on this matter and explain its urgency.[1]

The stakes of comparison and contrast in search of context therefore prove very considerable. When we know what one writing has in common with some other, we may hope to begin work on the presently troubling, and unsolved, problem of what the canonical writings as a group take for granted and present as a statement in common. The very conception, imposed from without to be sure, of the canon, that is, the corpus of recognized and authoritative writings of a religious system, rests, after all,

---

[1]The place of the issue in my own scholarly program for the next few years is spelled out in footnotes in Appendix One.

on the premise that the diverse writings form a cogent statement. To follow the unfolding of that statement – the canonical consensus, we may call it – requires us to move from one component to the next, all the time seeking not only contrast but also commonality. What writings take for granted, of course, is not a question accessible to solution in so systematic a way. But until we have established some basic facts about what is like and unlike between and among the documents of the canon, we are unlikely to make progress toward the solution of the more difficult question of the "Judaism" beyond any one document but common to, or presupposed by, all canonical writings.

Defining the theoretical basis for this book, Chapter One presents a reprise of my arguments concerning the correct basis for the comparison and contrast of midrash-compilations. Readers familiar with earlier studies will find the entire statement familiar, although it is much revised. Since the theoretical foundation of this book is the same as that for my comparative studies of Genesis Rabbah and Leviticus Rabbah, Pesiqta deRab Kahana and Pesiqta Rabbati and the other canonical writings, I find it important to repeat here, in abbreviated form, what has been said elsewhere, in the theory that people read one book at a time. In the context of the debates addressed in Chapter Five and in the two appendices, presenting a clear statement of the alternative position seems to me entirely in order.

Then, on the basis of what is set forth in Chapter One, I undertake two distinct exercises of documentary comparison, one for one species of writings in the canon of the Dual Torah, one for the other. Then I compare all species of the genus, canon of the Dual Torah. One species universally defined by all parties to study is that of "halakhic midrashim," by which is meant midrash-compilations of midrash-exegeses of legal passages of the Pentateuch. These are generally held to be Sifra and the two Sifrés, the one to Numbers, the other to Deuteronomy, as well as the Mekhilta attributed to R. Ishmael (a work that is next on my agenda). That characterization imputed by the word "halakhah," or law, is not entirely apt, since all the so-called halakhic midrashim cover important theological and narrative passages as well. But even to the naked eye, there are sufficient points in common among Sifra and the two Sifrés to justify deeming all three documents a single species, allowing us to compare and contrast them. The clear and self-evident points in common are the aesthetic and the philosophical, that is, rhetorical and logical conventions that operate among all three writings. These I treat in Chapters Two and Three.

To the naked eye, a second species into which our document falls is the one defined by the book of Leviticus. There is another important compilation of midrash-exegeses, Leviticus Rabbah, that permits us to compare and contrast the topical and propositional program (if any) of our document to those of another document of the same species: Leviticus-commentary. In that context, further, I draw upon two other documents that fall for other reasons into the same species as Leviticus Rabbah, which are Genesis Rabbah and Pesiqta deRab Kahana. All three form one taxon, Sifra a different taxon, when we compare the traits of program and even topic. That comparison forms the problem of Part Two, including only Chapter Four. In Chapter Five I deal with the definition of our document in context by asking about the ways in which Sifra is like, and unlike, other documents. I suggest why I find it singular among them all. Whether or not the same case can be made for each of the other midrash-compilations requires study. The methodical program of the book is very simple. In each study I present, first, the facts concerning Sifra, and then survey, as briefly as possible, the corresponding facts concerning the documents with which I compare Sifra. Relating established results to the problem of Sifra, Chapters Two, Three, and Four go over already available research covering the other documents. Chapter Five then concludes the work of comparison and contrast and takes up the issue of context: the Judaism to which all texts point.

This book forms a close companion to two books of mine, first, *The Making of the Mind of Judaism* (Atlanta: Scholars Press for Brown Judaic Studies, 1987), second, *Uniting the Dual Torah: Sifra and the Problem of the Mishnah* (Atlanta: Scholars Press for Brown Judaic Studies, 1988). As to the former, Chapter Five reviews in revised form some of the positions set forth in the introduction to *The Making of the Mind of Judaism,* which now seem to me fundamental to all further thought. As to the latter, while Chapter Four is separate, it covers some of the same material as I treat in *Uniting the Dual Torah* , particularly when in Chapter Four I set forth what I conceive to be the distinctive message of Sifra. But I write the book to be read on its own (just as is the case of the others). For that reason I review here the main theses presented in *The Making of the Mind of Judaism* and in *Uniting the Dual Torah.*

Let me focus on *Uniting the Dual Torah* in particular. The problem of the Mishnah, solved in one way by the authorship of Sifra, in a different way by the framers of the Talmud of Babylonia or Bavli (and their precursors as well) was posed by the character and standing of the Mishnah. From the moment of its promulgation as the basis for the law of Judaism, the Mishnah was represented as authoritative, therefore, in the context of Israel's life, as enjoying the standing, or falling into the classification, of *torah,* divine revelation, yet clearly not like The Torah revealed by God to Moses at Sinai. The proposition worked out by *Uniting the Dual Torah* is that there were two solutions to that problem, the one of

the successor-documents that undertook the exegesis, amplification, and
application of the Mishnah, the other presented by the authorship of
Sifra. The solution to that problem worked out by the successor-
authorities to the Mishnah, in Tosefta, ca. A.D. 300, the Talmud of the
Land of Israel or Yerushalmi, ca. A.D. 400, and the Talmud of Babylonia
or Bavli, ca. A.D. 600, was to treat the word or conception, *torah,* as a
common noun, signifying, among other things, process, status, or
classification. Then the Mishnah found ample place for itself within the
capacious classification, *torah.*

The solution to that problem worked out by the authorship of Sifra was
to treat the word, *torah,* as solely a proper noun, The Torah, but *also* to
insist that the Mishnah found a fully legitimate position within The Torah.
That solution required the authorship of the Mishnah to undertake a
profound and thorough-going critique of the logic of the Mishnah, both
as that logic dictated the correct joining of two or more sentences into a
cogent thought, and as that logic governed the formation of propositions
for analysis. In fact, the authorship of Sifra set forth a systematic critique
of the Mishnah in its principal definitive traits: its topical program and
arrangement, its principles of cogent discourse, and its logic of critical
analysis and probative demonstration of propositions. It furthermore set
forth a sizable portion of the Mishnah's contents, as these pertained to the
book of Leviticus, within its own definition of the correct topical program
and arrangement, its own principles of cogent discourse, and its own
logic of critical analysis and proof. The thesis of this book therefore is
that these two solutions came to full expression, one paramount in the
works of exegesis and amplification that adopted the Mishnah, the Oral
Torah, as the base-text, the other in the single work of exegesis and
amplification that adopted Scripture, in the particular form of the book of
Leviticus, as the base-text. In the prologue I explain the thesis of this book
and what I conceive to be at stake in it. In the shank of the book I made the
thesis stick. So at stake in the Tosefta and two Talmuds, on the one side,
and in Sifra on the other,[2] was how to unite the Dual Torah. That is what I
mean by "Sifra and the problem of the Mishnah."

The program of *Uniting the Dual Torah* therefore is a simple one. I
begin by spelling out the problem of the Mishnah as I conceive it to have
confronted the heirs and successors of the framers of that document. This
is covered in Chapters One and Two of that book. Chapter Three then
presents a sample of Sifra, specifically, six of the 277 chapters of the
writing. Chapter Four forms my theoretical statement and is the

---

[2] I shall deal with the standing of Sifré to Numbers and Sifré to Deuteronomy in
respect to the Mishnah in the companion-volume to this one, Sifra in Context. At
this point I have no need to claim for Sifra utterly unique traits or standing, though
I do maintain for our authorship a genuinely singular cast of mind.

centerpiece of the book. Chapters Five and Six of that book attend to formal questions of the order and organization of propositions and topics, on the one side, and the logic of cogent discourse on the other. These are fairly simple problems. Chapters Seven and Eight turn to the deep structure of logic: how we set forth and prove propositions. There I define the probative logic of hierarchical classification, comparison and contrast of like and unlike, that forms the foundation for all learning in antiquity; we call it *Listenwissenschaft*. I identify the particular traits of mind that characterize the Mishnah's framers' utilization of the logic of hierarchical classification and then show in detail the Sifra's authorship's sustained and stunning critique of the application of that logic.

In Chapter Eight of *Uniting the Dual Torah*, I show how that same authorship turned and rehabilitated *Listenwissenschaft* by showing the correct mode of defining classifications and comparing and contrasting categories in hierarchical order. In this way I lay forth the proposition of this book, that in order to re-present the Dual Torah in a single, whole statement, the authorship of Sifra set forth a sustained critique of practical reason. It was in their deep search into the Written Torah that they found the principles of probative logic for the demonstration of the unity of the two components of the Torah, oral and written. The underlying theological premise, of course, was that The Torah portrayed for humanity the workings of the mind of God, just as creation portrayed the workings of the hand of God. When, therefore, our authorship penetrated into the workings of the intellect revealed in The Torah, they entered into the mind of God.

The three books, this one, *The Making of the Mind of Judaism*, and *Uniting the Dual Torah*, therefore complement one another, but each makes its own statement to its own issue. Let me now place the two on Sifra into their proximate and broad context. Together they complete a trilogy of studies of Sifra, comprising the two studies and the following translation:

Sifra. An Analytical Translation. Atlanta: Scholars Press for Brown Judaic Studies, 1988. I. *Introduction and Vayyiqra Dibura Denedabah and Vayyiqra Dibura Dehobah.*

Sifra. An Analytical Translation. Atlanta: Scholars Press for Brown Judaic Studies, 1988. II. *Sav, Shemini, Tazria, Negaim, Mesora, and Zabim.*

Sifra. An Analytical Translation. Atlanta: Scholars Press for Brown Judaic Studies, 1988. III. *Aharé Mot, Qedoshim, Emor, Behar, and Behuqotai.*

The translation on which both studies rest is one that I call "form-analytical." In this analytical translation, now in print, I prepare the way to answer those questions, such as the ones treated here, that can be addressed on the basis of a form-analytical reading of a document when it is considered whole and complete, from beginning to end. The correct methodological approach to the study of any document on its own terms is dictated by established procedures in all humanistic learning in the West. First, we have to allow a document such as Sifra to speak for itself. Its authorship's own choices as to aesthetic and substantive questions alike must give its testimony. The choices of that authorship on how to express its ideas constitute the single authoritative commentary to the document.[3] That means that, in translating, the traits of the document demand attention on their own, without an *a priori* premise as to the origin, purpose, or character of the writing before us. The beginning of criticism is a translation that makes possible independent analysis, sustained inquiry into objective traits of evidence, analysis of the indicative characteristics of that evidence, and interpretation through comparison and contrast of the outcome of that analysis and inquiry. The methodological requirements of contemporary humanistic inquiry dictate the empirical approach taken in my translation of Sifra as of the two Sifrés and the other midrash-compilations produced in the formative age of the Judaism of the Dual Torah. Let me specify the larger context of this work of translation and phenomenological analysis.

With this trilogy on Sifra, I near the final part of a sustained project of midrash-studies. There is only one further document that seems to me urgently to require attention, and that is the Mekhilta attributed to R. Ishmael. Let me review what has now been completed, since this book and its companion rest upon prior research. After I systematically translated and analyzed nearly all of the successor-documents to the Mishnah of the Judaism of the Dual Torah produced in the formative age, that is, Tosefta (presented for the first time as a systematic commentary to the Mishnah and repository of relevant supplementary materials), and the two Talmuds (twenty-five tractates of the Yerushalmi, five, Berakhot,

---

[3]The conception that the medieval commentaries tell us the original meaning of an ancient document need not detain us. When my translations are criticized as ignorant for, e.g., ignoring what Rashi has to say about a passage in the Talmud of Babylonia, I marvel that my intent has registered. For that is not out of "ignorance" but entirely intentional. I began this mode of reading the rabbinic texts with the Mishnah, insisting that the Mishnah constitutes its own best exegesis, and that when people say things in one way and not in some other, that constitutes a signal as to their intent and meaning. I extended that same critical hermeneutics to principal documents of the rabbinic canon, and hope to complete the task. No one doubts that the received exegetical tradition contains points of interest, particularly as to the possible meanings of words and phrases.

Sukkah, Sotah, Sanhedrin, and Arakhin, in seven volumes, of the Bavli, with more planned later on) I turned to the midrash-compilations. In each case I translated, or retranslated, a document and then subjected it to a systematic study in the comparative method. In that way I have worked through the following midrash-compilations:

Judaism and Scripture: The Evidence of Leviticus Rabbah. Chicago: The University of Chicago Press, 1986. [First translation of Margulies' text].

Genesis Rabbah. The Judaic Commentary on Genesis. A New American Translation. Atlanta: Scholars Press for Brown Judaic Studies, 1985. I. *Genesis Rabbah. The Judaic Commentary on Genesis. A New American Translation. Parashiyyot One through Thirty-Three. Genesis 1:1-8:14.*

Genesis Rabbah. The Judaic Commentary on Genesis. A New American Translation. Atlanta: Scholars Press for Brown Judaic Studies, 1985. II. *Genesis Rabbah. The Judaic Commentary on Genesis. A New American Translation. Parashiyyot Thirty-Four through Sixty-Seven. Genesis 8:15-28:9.*

Genesis Rabbah. The Judaic Commentary on Genesis. A New American Translation. Atlanta: Scholars Press for Brown Judaic Studies, 1985. III. *Genesis Rabbah. The Judaic Commentary on Genesis. A New American Translation. Parashiyyot Sixty-Eight through One Hundred. Genesis 28:10-50:26.*

Sifré to Numbers. An American Translation. I. *1-58.* Atlanta: Scholars Press for Brown Judaic Studies, 1986

Sifré to Numbers. An American Translation. II. *59-115.* Atlanta: Scholars Press for Brown Judaic Studies, 1986. [III. *116-161*: William Scott Green].

The Fathers According to Rabbi Nathan. An Analytical Translation and Explanation . Atlanta: Scholars Press for Brown Judaic Studies, 1986.

Pesiqta deRab Kahana. An Analytical Translation and Explanation. I. *1-14.* Atlanta: Scholars Press for Brown Judaic Studies, 1987.

Pesiqta deRab Kahana. An Analytical Translation and Explanation. II. *15-28. With an Introduction to Pesiqta deRab Kahana.* Atlanta: Scholars Press for Brown Judaic Studies, 1987.

For Pesiqta Rabbati, see below, *From Tradition to Imitation. The Plan and Program of Pesiqta deRab Kahana and Pesiqta Rabbati.*

Sifré to Deuteronomy. An Analytical Translation. Atlanta: Scholars Press for Brown Judaic Studies, 1987. I. *Pisqaot One through One Hundred Forty-Three. Debarim, Waethanan, Eqeb, Re'eh.*

Sifré to Deuteronomy. An Analytical Translation. Atlanta: Scholars Press for Brown Judaic Studies, 1987. II. *Pisqaot One Hundred Forty-Four through Three Hundred Fifty-Seven. Shofetim, Ki Tese, Ki Tabo, Nesabim, Ha'azinu, Zot Habberakhah.*

Sifré to Deuteronomy. An Introduction to the Rhetorical, Logical, and Topical Program. Atlanta: Scholars Press for Brown Judaic Studies, 1987.

In addition to the analytical translations are the following monographic studies:

The Integrity of Leviticus Rabbah. The Problem of the Autonomy of a Rabbinic Document. Chico: Scholars Press for Brown Judaic Studies, 1985.

Comparative Midrash: The Plan and Program of Genesis Rabbah and Leviticus Rabbah. Atlanta: Scholars Press for Brown Judaic Studies, 1986.

From Tradition to Imitation. The Plan and Program of Pesiqta deRab Kahana and Pesiqta Rabbati. Atlanta: Scholars Press for Brown Judaic Studies, 1987. [With a fresh translation of Pesiqta Rabbati *Pisqaot* 1-5, 15.]

Canon and Connection: Intertextuality in Judaism. Lanham: University Press of America, 1986. *Studies in Judaism* Series.

Midrash as Literature: The Primacy of Documentary Discourse. Lanham: University Press of America, 1987. *Studies in Judaism* series.

Invitation to Midrash: The Working of Rabbinic Bible Interpretation. A Teaching Book. San Francisco: Harper & Row, 1988.

What Is Midrash? Philadelphia: Fortress Press, 1987.

Judaism and Scripture: The Evidence of Leviticus Rabbah. Chicago: The University of Chicago Press, 1986. [Systematic analysis of problems of composition and redaction.]

Judaism and Story: The Evidence of The Fathers According to Rabbi Nathan. Chicago: University of Chicago Press, 1989.

Other studies of Midrash-compilations, produced alongside the translations and analytical works listed above, are as follows:

The Foundations of Judaism. Method, Teleology, Doctrine. Philadelphia: Fortress Press, 1983-5. I-III. I. *Midrash in Context. Exegesis in Formative Judaism.* Second printing: Atlanta: Scholars Press for Brown Judaic Studies, 1988.

The Oral Torah. The Sacred Books of Judaism. An Introduction. San
   Francisco: Harper & Row, 1985. Paperback: 1987.

Editor: *Scriptures of the Oral Torah. Sanctification and Salvation in
   the Sacred Books of Judaism.* San Francisco: Harper & Row, 1987.

What has been the primary point of interest in these several studies of
midrash-compilations? The issue that has drawn me onward, from one
document to the next, and that accounts for the program of this book and
its companions as well, is simple to state. This, like so many of the titles
given above, is a work in the comparison of cogent documents with one
another. The premise, therefore, is that each of the documents is to be
read as an entity unto itself. In one study after another I have
demonstrated that a rabbinic document constitutes a text, not merely a
scrapbook or a random compilation of episodic materials. A text is a
document with a purpose, one that exhibits the traits of the integrity of the
parts to the whole and the fundamental autonomy of the whole from other
texts. I have shown that the documents I have analyzed, listed presently,
therefore fall into the classification of a cogent composition, put together
with purpose and intended as a whole and in the aggregate to bear a
meaning and state a message. I therefore disproved the claim that a
rabbinic document serves merely as an anthology or miscellany or is to be
compared only to a scrapbook, made up of this and that.

A document in the canon of Judaism thus does not merely define a
context for the aggregation of such already completed and mutually
distinct materials. Rather, a document constitutes a text. So at issue here
as in prior studies is what makes a text a text, that is, the textuality of a
document. At stake is how we may know when a document constitutes a
text and when it is merely an anthology or a scrapbook. The stake
therefore is what makes a text a text. Here as elsewhere I deal with the
textuality of a text, the issue of whether a given piece of writing hangs
together and is to be read on its own There is a second problem, awaiting
attention. It concerns what makes a group of texts into a canon, a cogent
statement all together. At issue is the relationship of two or more texts of a
single, interrelated literature to the world view and way of life of a religious
tradition viewed whole.

The problem of *Integrity of Leviticus Rabbah,* followed by
*Comparative Midrash. The Plan and Program of Genesis Rabbah and
Leviticus Rabbah,* the initial and also the most complete statements on
this matter, is whether or not a rabbinic document to begin with stands by
itself or right at the outset forms a scarcely differentiated segment of a
larger uniform canon. Since people rarely wonder why a given
composition should not be described by itself, let me spell out the basis
for the contrary view. The reason one might suppose that, in the case of

the formative age of Judaism, a document does not exhibit integrity and is not autonomous is simple. The several writings of the rabbinic canon of late antiquity, formed from the Mishnah, ca. A.D. 200, through the Talmud of Babylonia, ca. A.D. 600, with numerous items in between, share materials – sayings, tales, protracted discussions. Some of these shared materials derive from explicitly cited documents. For instance, passages of Scripture or of the Mishnah or of the Tosefta, cited verbatim, will find their way into the two Talmuds. But sayings, stories, and sizable compositions not identified with a given, earlier text and exhibiting that text's distinctive traits will float from one document to the next. But these floating materials form a negligible portion of any given document. More to the point, when we identify the paramount and definitive traits of a given document, they turn out to be singular to that document, as we shall see in Chapter Six is the case for Sifra.

It remains briefly to refer to further issues to be addressed in this chapter of my research. Forthcoming is the following work that addresses the broader issue of culture and theology in the Midrash-compilations:

Writing with Scripture: The Authority and Uses of the Hebrew Bible in the Torah of Formative Judaism. Philadelphia: Fortress Press, 1989. [With William Scott Green]. Professor Green is the source of the idea that people wrote with Scripture, which forms the *leit-motif* for the large-scale project now nearing its conclusion, as well as for the book he and I are writing together.

For late antiquity, I see few other Midrash-compilations of any consequence. As I said, in this line of work, my next project is planned as follows:

The Mekhilta Attributed to R. Ishmael. An Analytical Translation.

The Dating of Rabbinic Documents: The Case of the Mekhilta Attributed to R. Ishmael.

Beyond that work, for reasons set forth in the footnotes of Appendix One, I plan to return to work on the Mishnah in its political, philosophical, and jurisprudential context, with monographs completed or projected as follows:

The Economics of Judaism: The Initial Statement. Chicago, 1989: University of Chicago Press.

The Politics of Judaism: The Initial System in its Greco-Roman Philosophical Context.

The Initial Philosophy of Judaism: The Mishnah in its Second-Century Philosophical Context. [The Second Sophistic and the Sages of Judaism.]

The Mishnah in its Greco-Roman and Iranian Jurisprudential Context.
Late Antique Modes of Legal Codification and the Initial Code of
Judaism.

Jacob Neusner

April 26, 1988
Program in Judaic Studies
Brown University
Providence, Rhode Island 02912-1826 U.S.A.

Chapter One

Sifra In and Out of Context

I. DEFINING "MIDRASH": A REPRISE

Placing Sifra in context requires specification of the opposite: Sifra out of context. And that involves comparing Sifra to various other documents of its classification, which is to say, comparative midrash, the comparison of midrashim. When we know the ways in which this document is like and also unlike other documents, we may define the context of definition and also delineate the ways in which our document is singular, hence out of all relationship of context with others of its classification: midrash-compilations.

To begin with, therefore, we have to know what we mean by (a) midrash. The word *midrash* in the main is used in three ways. First of all, *midrash* refers to the processes of scriptural exegesis carried on by diverse groups of Jews from the time of ancient Israel to nearly the present day. Thus people say, "He produced a *midrash* on the verse," meaning, "an exegesis." A more extreme usage produces, "Life is a *midrash* on Scripture," meaning that what happens in the everyday world imparts meaning or significance to biblical stories and admonitions. It is difficult to specify what the word *midrash* in Hebrew expresses that the word *exegesis* in English does not. It follows that how "exegesis" in English differs from *midrash* in Hebrew, or why, therefore, the Hebrew will serve better than the more familiar English, I do not know. Some imagine that *midrash* for Jewish exegetes generically differs from *exegesis* for non-Jewish ones. What hermeneutics characterizes all exegeses produced by Jews, but no exegeses produced by non-Jews, who presumably do not produce *midrashim* on verses but do produce exegeses of verses of the same Hebrew Scriptures, no one has said. Accordingly, the first usage seems so general as to add up to nothing. That is to say, *midrash*, a foreign word, simply refers to the same thing – the activity or process or intellectual pursuit – as exegesis, an English word. The word *midrash* bears no more, or less, meaning than the word *exegesis*.

The other two usages will detain us considerably less, since they bear a precision lacking in the first. The word *midrash* further stands for [2] a compilation of scriptural exegeses, as in "that *midrash* deals with the book of Joshua." In that sentence, *midrash* refers to a compilation of exegeses, hence the statement means, "That compilation of exegeses deals with the book of Joshua." *Compilation* or composite in the present context clearly serves more accurately to convey meaning than *midrash.* I use both words in this book. The word *midrash,* finally, stands for [3] the written composition (e.g., a paragraph with a beginning, middle, and end, in which a completed thought is laid forth), resulting from the process of *midrash.* In this setting *a midrash* refers to a paragraph or a unit of exegetical exposition, in which a verse of the Hebrew Scriptures is subjected to some form of exegesis or other. In this usage one may say, "Let me now cite the *midrash,*" meaning, a particular passage of exegesis, a paragraph or other completed whole unit of exegetical thought, a composition that provides an exegesis of a particular verse. I use the word composition in this sense.

Accordingly the word bears at least three distinct, if related, meanings. If someone says "the *midrash* says," he may refer to [1] a distinctive *process* of interpretation of a particular text, thus, the hermeneutic, [2] a particular compilation of the results of that process, thus, a book that is the composite of a set of exegeses, or [3] a concrete unit of the working of that process, of scriptural exegesis, thus the write-up of the process of interpretation as it applies to a single verse, the exegetical composition on a particular verse (or group of verses). In the next four chapters we compare one *midrash* to another *midrash,* meaning, one compilation of exegeses, its plan and program, with another compilation of exegeses, its plan and program. *Comparative midrash* today may encompass three distinct activities. People may mean that they wish to compare [1] processes or methods of exegesis of Scripture (e.g., hermeneutics), [2] compilations of exegeses of Scripture (but this is uncommon), or [3] specific exegeses of a given verse of Scripture with other exegeses of the same verse of Scripture (this being the most commonplace activity of the genre). As is clear, what we compare here is compilations of exegeses of Scripture.

II. "COMPARATIVE MIDRASH": A REVIEW

What is it that we do when we compare one compilation to another? When we compare, we seek, first, perspective on the things compared, hence Sifra *in context.* Second, we look for the rule that applies to the unfamiliar thing among the things compared. The unknown thing is *like* something else, therefore falls under the rule governing the known thing to which it is likened, or it is *unlike* something else, therefore falls under the opposite (or, at least, another) rule. So comparison always entails the claim of likeness and requires the demonstration, at the same time, of difference: comparison and contrast at one and the same time. That accounts for the program of Chapters Two through Five. We compare, third, so as to discover the context for interpreting the things compared. How so? Through comparison we uncover traits that are unique to one thing and therefore also those that are shared among the things compared. That explains the purpose of Chapter Six.

In these three as well as in other ways the labor of comparison and contrast forms the foundation of all inquiry into the description, analysis, and interpretation of otherwise discrete and unintelligible data. Without [1] perspective, [2] knowledge of the applicable rule, and [3] a conception of the context, we understand only the thing itself – and therefore nothing at all. For not described, analyzed, and interpreted, the thing is not merely singular, requiring comparison with other things, but utterly unique – by definition. And what is unique, also by definition, is beyond all rational comprehension. The reason is that we understand what is not yet known by reference to metaphors supplied by the things already understood. Their perspective, the pertinent rule governing them, the understanding of them gained in knowledge of their context – these form the bridge between the known and the unknown. The work of comparison and contrast, classification and interpretation of discrete data, therefore defines all rational inquiry. The sole alternative, the claim of *a priori* understanding of things otherwise incompletely known, requires no attention. Why not? That claim lies outside of rational inquiry, for we have no way of falsifying, therefore verifying, *a priori* allegations concerning knowledge.

So we come to "comparative *midrash*" in particular. What, precisely, do we compare when we compare *midrash[im]*? The answer will derive from asking how properly to compare one thing with something else, in this case one *midrash* with another *midrash*. Do I mean comparing hermeneutics, one mode of exegesis of Scripture with some other, for example, comparing the methods of *midrash*/exegesis of Matthew with the methods of *midrash*/exegesis of the Essene writers of Qumran's library? Do I mean comparing the redactional and formulary plans and theological programs, the definitive traits of one compilation of exegeses/*midrashim* with another such compilation, for example, Matthew Chapter Two with an equivalent composition of the Habakkuk commentary or with an equivalent passage of the Sifré to Numbers? Or do I mean comparing the substantive results – the treatment of a given verse of Scripture/*midrash* in one compilation of exegeses/*midrashim* with the treatment of that same verse or theme of Scripture/*midrash* in another compilation of exegeses/*midrashim*?

Since the phrase, "comparative *midrash*," applies quite comfortably to all three types of comparison, the answer to my question cannot emerge from common usage. Common usage is confused. Here I propose to clarify and purify that usage. I maintain that the work of comparative *midrash*, should commence with [2] compilations, whole documents, and not [1] with modes of exegesis of Scripture occurring here, there, and everywhere, and also not with [3] discrete parts of documents. What should be compared at the outset is [2] whole to whole, document to document, and only later on [3] the constituent element of one document with the constituent element of another document, and last of all [1] the exegetical techniques, policies, or issues of one document with those of a second document. Why begin with the entirety of a composite of exegeses [2], rather than with [1] techniques or modes of exegesis, on the one side, or [3] the results of exegesis, on the other? The reason is simple. Comparison begins in the definition of things that are to be compared. That means we must know *that* things fall into a common genus, and only then shall we be able to ask *how* things are different from one another. We cannot be sure that a detail, e.g., the result of exegesis of a given verse of Scripture on the part of two or more parties, defines a common genus because the same verse is at hand. We all the more so cannot be certain that an approach to exegesis permits comparison of two or more principles. But we have the possibility of comparing something so concrete as a document with an equivalent thing, another document. Very little subjectivity enters into such a comparison.

The reason is that when we take up the outermost layer of an exegetical exercise, the document that presents exegeses, and not the mode or result – we describe the context that contains the other two layers of the same exercise. So, I maintain, on the basis of logic we first of all must determine the context – the two or more documents at hand – and their respective roles in imparting to the materials contained within those documents the characteristic and consistent preferences in matters of both style and viewpoint. Only when we know the impact of the documentary context upon the materials in a document can we take up an individual item from that document and set it into comparison and contrast with a discrete item drawn out of some other, also carefully delineated and defined, document. At the point at which we can define the traits distinctive to one documentary context we may ask about traits of an item that occur in other documentary contexts in which that item makes its appearance. Then we may inquire into the comparison and contrast of one detail, drawn from one document, with what we conceive to be a parallel or intersecting detail, drawn from another.

The documentary context stands first in line because it is what we know for sure. When we describe a document, we know as fact that [1] a given method of exegesis has yielded [3] a given exegetical comment on a verse of Scripture, the result of which is now in [2] *this particular document.*

Since we know the wonderfully simple facts of what is found in which document, we can begin the work of describing the traits imparted by [2] that document to the [3] exegetical result of [1] the exegetical method at hand. Traits characteristic of [2] the documentary setting likewise emerge without a trace of speculation. To state matters more concretely, if a document routinely frames matters in accord with one repertoire of formal conventions rather than some other, and if it arranges its formal repertoire of types of units of discourse in one way, rather than some other, and if its compilers repeatedly propose to make one point, rather than some other, we can easily identify those traits of the passage under study that derive from the larger documentary context. Accordingly, we begin with the document because it presents the first solid fact. Everything else then takes a position relative to that fact. What then are some of the documentary facts? Here are some: this saying or story occurs here, bears these traits, is used for this larger redactional and programmatic purpose, makes this distinct point in its context (or no point at all). One may readily test these allegations and determine their facticity. These facts therefore define the initial context of interpretation. The facts deriving from the documentary setting define the context in which a given trait shared or not shared among the two discrete items to be compared.

In laying emphasis on the document as the correct first point of comparison, I exclude as the appropriate point of departure for comparative studies two others, namely, [1] modes of exegesis, hence, comparative hermeneutics, and [3] results of exegesis, hence, comparison of the exegesis of a verse in one document, deriving from one period and group of authorities, with the exegesis of that same verse in some other document, deriving from a completely different sort of authorities and a much earlier or much later period. If we ignore as unimportant the characteristic traits of the documentary locations of an exegesis of a verse of Scripture or of a story occurring in two or more documents, or if we treat as trivial the traits characteristic of those locative points, we do not know the rule governing both items subject to comparison. We establish no context that imparts meaning to the work of comparison. We have no perspective on similarities and differences among two or more things that are compared with one another. These similarities and differences may prove merely adventitious. But we shall never know. Points of likeness may constitute mere accidents of coincidence, e.g., of internal logic of the statement of the verse of Scripture at hand. But we cannot tell.

If people in different places, times, or groups concur that a verse means one thing and not some other thing, it may be that that is because the meaning on which diverse groups concur is the only meaning the verse can yield. How do we know that that meaning, shared among diverse groups, is the only possible meaning? It is proved by the fact of broad concurrence among different groups (!). What is the upshot of this circular mode of reasoning? The claim that, because the items are alike – say the same thing, for example, about the same verse – therefore we know something we otherwise would not know about [1] hermeneutics, [2] documentary context, or [3] the history and meaning of the exegesis of the verse at hand, does not permit us to invoke processes of falsification or verification. Not knowing the context of likeness or difference, we also do not know the meaning of likeness or difference. That is why the definition of the context in which discrete data make their appearance demands attention first of all. But – I repeat – it is only first in sequence. Rightly done, comparative midrash in sequence also will take up questions of [1] shared or different techniques and also [3] shared or different exegetical results in discrete settings. These two define further points of interest. But we must start at the largest and most general stage of description, the one resting on no speculation as to the facts, that is, therefore, the stage of establishing context: defining the genus as a matter of context prior to comparing the species differentiated in that same context.

Comparison and contrast therefore depend, in strict logic, upon prior identification of appropriate commonalities. The genus comes before the species. When we know that in consequential ways things are alike, we then can discover in what ways they are not alike. We further can derive further insight from the points in common and the differences as well. We cannot ask how things differ if we do not know that there is a basis for the question of comparison and contrast. And the point of distinction between one thing and another thing must be shown to make a difference. If we do not ask the question concerning, in Jonathan Z. Smith's phrase, what difference a difference makes,[1] then we are comparing apples to Australians.

III. CORRECTING THE ERROR OF "COMPARATIVE MIDRASH"

The proponents of *comparative midrash* in its present formulation argue quite reasonably that they too begin with a premise of shared traits. Perhaps so, but then they select the wrong traits for comparison, and therefore they do not describe the right things at all. They describe and then compare [3] the results of exegesis of a given verse in one document with [3] the results of exegesis of that same verse in another document. But the context of description is not established. As a result their articles and

---

[1]Jonathan Z. Smith, "What a Difference a Difference Makes," in J. Neusner and E. S. Frerichs, eds., *"To See Ourselves as Others See Us." Christians, Jews, "Others" in Late Antiquity* (Atlanta: Scholars Press Studies in the Humanities, 1985), pp. 3-48.

books produce information of this sort: on a given verse, X says this and Y says something else. That, sum and substance is the result of their study of *comparative midrash*. What then defines that shared foundation that makes possible comparison and contrast? It is [3] the object of *midrash*, namely as verse of Scripture. So the proponents of *comparative midrash* invoke the continuity of Scripture in defense of comparing and contrasting only [3] the results of exegesis. They maintain that what one party says about a given verse of Scripture surely is comparable with what another party says about that same verse of Scripture. So they compare and contrast what two or more parties say about a given verse or story of Scripture. That seems to me entirely correct and proper, but only in its appropriate setting.

And what is that setting at which it is quite proper to undertake comparison of [3] results of exegesis and even [1] modes of exegesis? It is when we know the setting in which people reached one conclusion and not some other. That is to say, when we know the issues exegetes addressed and the intellectual and political and theological setting in which they did their work, then the fact that they said one thing and not something else will illuminate *what* they said and may further explain their rejection of what they did *not* say. Since, moreover, we deal not with the gist of what people said but with a given version in one set of words rather than some other, a message captured in particular language governed by conventions of form, comparison of modes of expression and conventions of language and form proceeds apace. So comparing what people said demands that we notice, also, the different ways in which they may (or may not) have said the same thing (or the opposite things). Formal traits, involving use of language and highly formalized expression, define part of the task of interpreting what is like and what is unlike.

Everything we propose to examine finds its original place in some document, rather than in some other (or in two or three documents and not in ten or twenty others). Have the framers or compilers of one document selected an item merely because that item pertains to a given verse of Scripture? Or have they chosen that item because it says what they wish to say in regard to a verse of Scripture they have identified as important? Have they framed matters in terms of their larger program of the formalization of language, syntax and rhetoric alike? Have their selection and formalization of the item particular relevance to the context in which they did their work, the purpose for which they composed their document, the larger message they planned to convey to those to whom they planned to speak? These questions demand answers, and the answers will tell us the *"what else,"* that is, what is important about what people say in common or in contrast about the verse at hand. Without the answers provided by analysis of circumstance and context, plan and program, of the several documents one by one and then in comparison and contrast with one another, we know only what people said about the verse. But we do not know why they said it, what they meant by what they said, or what we learn from the fact *that* they said what they said about the verse in hand. The answers to these questions constitute that "what-else?" that transforms catalogues of pointless facts into pointed and important propositions.

IV. THE DOCUMENTARY FOUNDATIONS OF COMPARISON

The question about the precipitant of exegesis, namely, whether it is the literary and theological context, as I maintain, or principally the verse subject to exegesis,[2] as proponents of *comparative midrash* in its present formulation hold, brings us to the crux of the matter. The premise of all that I have said (as well as the basis for the comparative study in Chapter five) is that Scripture serves a diversity of purposes and therefore cannot establish a single definitive plane of meaning, the frame of reference against which all other things constitute variables. Scripture constitutes the neutral background, not the variable. Exegetes tell us what verses of Scripture matter and what we should learn from those verses. Scripture dictates nothing but endures all things. What people tell us about the meaning of Scripture (points [1] and [3] in what has gone before) represents the outcome of the work of exegetes, not the inexorable result of the character or contents of Scripture. The issue for debate as I think it should be argued is this:

1. Does Scripture dictate the substance of exegesis?

2. Or do exegetes dictate the sense they wish to impart to (or locate in) Scripture?

If the former, then the ground for comparison finds definition in a verse of Scripture. What X said, without regard to circumstance or even documentary context, compared with what Y said, viewed also with slight attention to canonical context and concrete literary circumstance, matters.

If the latter, then canon and its components take pride of place, and what diverse persons said about a given verse of Scripture defines only a coincidence, unless proved on the basis of circumstance and context to constitute more than mere coincidence.

---

[2]That is the single most common mode of study of comparative midrash. The supposition is that traits of the verse subject to exegesis lead people to make one comment rather than some other. I cannot imagine a less likely possibility – in real life. But it is a common staple of research for those who compare midrashim.

So I think the question must be framed. The answer to the question lies spread across the surface of the reading of Scripture in the history of the scriptural religions of the West, the Judaisms and the Christianities in perpetual contention among and between themselves about which verses of Scripture matter, and what those that matter mean. That remarkably varied history tells the story of how diverse groups of believers selected diverse verses of the Hebrew Scriptures as particularly important. They then subjected those verses, and not other verses, to particular exegetical inquiry. The meanings they found in those verses answer questions they found urgent. Scripture contributed much but dictated nothing, system – circumstance and context dictated everything and selected what Scripture might contribute in *midrash*. In this context, *midrash* means the whole extant repertoire of exegeses of verses of Scripture we possess in [2] various compilations of exegeses of Scripture, made up of [3] compositions of exegesis of verses of Scripture, guided by [1] diverse hermeneutical principles of interpretation of Scripture.

Since in *midrash* as just now defined, the religious system comes first, prior to exegeses of particular verses of Scripture, all the more so prior to the hermeneutics that guides the work of exegesis, the documents that constitute the canon and contain the system form the definitive initial classification for comparative *midrash*. System must be compared to system, not detail to detail, and, therefore, to begin with, we compare [2] compilation of exegeses to the counterpart, thus document to document. That then accounts for the program of setting Sifra into documentary context as well. Comparison of the repertoires of verses people chose and those they ignored yields the governing insight. Before we know the answers, we have to understand the questions people addressed to Scripture. Why so? Because a group chose a repertoire of verses distinctive to itself, rarely commenting on, therefore confronting, verses important to other groups. When we deal with different groups talking about different things to different groups, what difference does it make to us that, adventitiously and not systematically, out of all systemic context, we discover that someone reached the same conclusion as did someone else, of some other group? What else do we know if we discover such a coincidence? Parallel lines never meet, and parallel statements on the same verse may in context bear quite distinct meaning.

Let me give a concrete instance, pertinent to the book of Leviticus in particular. Pharisees as represented in the synoptic Gospels and also in the Mishnah appear to have found especially interesting verses in Leviticus and Numbers; these same verses, we may readily stipulate, failed to attract much attention from the Evangelists. Evangelists found unusually weighty verses of Scripture that the Pharisees and their heirs tended to ignore. Accordingly, Scripture forms the neutral ground. It is the constant. Contending groups selected verses of Scripture important to the larger programs that, to begin with, brought them to the reading and interpretation of particular verses of Scripture. In context they may have reached the same conclusions as did other groups. But so what? Do we therefore learn what that verse of Scripture must mean? No one can imagine so. We learn little about Scripture, and little about the diverse groups whose views, on a given verse of Scripture, happened to coincide. What is neutral conveys no insight, only what is subject to contention. That is why the choice of a given verse of Scripture for sustained inquiry comes prior to inquiry into the meaning or message discovered in that verse of Scripture. And that choice derives not from the neutral repertoire of Scripture but the polemical program of the group that makes the choice. So we must describe the program and the system, and that means the canon, item by item: the documents in their canonical context, the exegeses of verses in their documentary context, then the results of exegesis.

This brings us back to Chapter Five, the comparison of documents by reference to their relationships to a single fixed point in common. Scripture itself forms the undifferentiated background. It is the form, not the substance, the flesh, not the spirit. The fact that a single verse of Scripture generates diverse comments by itself therefore forms a statement of a merely formal character. It is a sequence of facts that may or may not bear meaning. The stress in *comparative midrash* effected as comparison of conclusions reached about the same verse of Scripture or theme or topic or story in Scripture is on the formality that everyone is talking about the same thing. The upshot is long catalogues of information about what different people say about the same thing. What is at stake in making these lists, what syllogism or proposition we prove by compiling information, rarely, comes to expression. More often than not, the list is the thing.

That is why I maintain the position carried out in the earlier studies, listed in the Preface, as well as in this book. The correct thing to describe and compare first of all is [2] the document that contains the results of the exegesis of diverse verses of Scripture with [2] another such document. For comparison begins with the system as a whole, dealing with the system through its canon, so one whole document compared with another document, described in the way the first has been described. We have to describe documents one by one, then in relationship to one another: description first, then analysis through comparison and contrast. Description begins with the whole of the thing described, thus documents, one at a time, then documents in comparison with one another. Later on we turn to details of documents, their contents, viewed first in their respective documentary contexts, then alongside one another.

V. COMPARING WHOLE TO WHOLE:
THE CENTRALITY OF THE CANON AND ITS DOCUMENTS

All things depend upon the identification of appropriate classifications, or genera, for the species under study for purposes of comparison and contrast. The case of Sifra in particular involves, as I see it, two distinct genera. The taxonomic work in this book appeals to the genera of rhetoric and logic, on the one side (again: Chapters Two and Three), topic on the other (Chapter Four). The three criteria, rhetoric, topic, and logic, define the traits of any piece of writing. I distinguish rhetoric and logic by one set of traits, of a formal character, and topic by a different set of traits, of a substantive nature, and that accounts for my view that there are two genera to address. The genus, rhetoric, attends to formal traits of patterning words and sentences. The genus, logic, encompasses (for the purpose of this book) the simple question of how an authorship joins sentence to sentence to form an intelligible statement, not gibberish. The other genera is formed by the book of Leviticus and comments on that book, hence, the topical program. These then are the two genera in play here.

The work of analysis rests upon establishing the genus first, and only then the species. Comparing one species of one genus with another species of a different genus proves parlous indeed. For when we deal with a species distinct from the genus which defines its traits and establishes the context of those traits, we do not really know what we have in hand. Why not? The context of a definitive trait not having been established, we cannot know the sense and meaning of a given detail, indeed, even whether the detail by itself defines and distinguishes the species of which it is a part. It is the genus which permits us to describe and analyze the species of that genus. When, therefore, we propose to undertake a work of comparison and contrast, we must begin at the level of the genus, and not at any lesser layer. What that means is simple. The work of description, prior to analysis and so comparison and contrast, begins with the whole, and only then works its way down to the parts. The work of analysis, resting on such a labor of description, proceeds once more, as I have proposed, from the whole, the genus, to the parts, the species.

VI. THE TEXTUALITY OF A TEXT

When I frame matters in terms of the problem of the rabbinic document, I ask what defines a document as such, the text-ness, the textuality, of a text. How do we know that a given book in the canon of Judaism is something other than a scrapbook? The choices are clear.

One theory is that a document serves solely as a convenient repository of prior sayings and stories, available materials that will have served equally well (or poorly) wherever they took up their final location. In accord with that theory it is quite proper in ignorance of all questions of circumstance and documentary or canonical context to compare the exegesis of a verse of Scripture in one document with the exegesis of that verse of Scripture found in some other document. The other theory is that a composition exhibits a viewpoint, a purpose of authorship distinctive to its framers or collectors and arrangers. Such a characteristic literary purpose – by this other theory – is so powerfully particular to one authorship that nearly everything at hand can be shown to have been (re)shaped for the ultimate purpose of the authorship at hand, that is, collectors and arrangers who demand the title of authors. In accord with this other theory, context and circumstance form the prior condition of inquiry, the result, in exegetical terms, the contingent one.

To resort again to a less than felicitous neologism, I thus ask what signifies or defines the "document-ness" of a document and what makes a book a book. I therefore wonder whether there are specific texts in the canonical context of Judaism or whether all texts are merely contextual. In framing the question as I have, I of course lay forth the mode of answering it. We have to confront a single rabbinic composition, and ask about its definitive traits and viewpoint. But, as I said, that is why we have also to confront the issue of the "sources"[3] upon which the redactors of a given document have drawn. By "sources" I mean simply passages in a given book that occur, also, in some other rabbinic book. Such "sources" – by definition prior to the books in which they appear – fall into the classification of materials general to two or more compositions and by definition not distinctive and particular to any one of them. The word "source" therefore serves as an analogy to convey the notion that two or more sets of authors have made use of a single, available item. About whether or not the shared item is prior to them both or borrowed by one from the other at this stage we cannot speculate. These shared items, transcending two or more documents and even two or more complete systems or groups, if paramount and preponderant, would surely justify the claim that we may compare exegeses of verses of Scripture without attention to context. Why? Because there is no closed context defined by the limits of a given document and its characteristic plan and program.

---

[3]I use that word only because it is commonplace. In fact it is a misleading metaphor. In *Integrity* I pursued the possibility of characterizing the shared stories in such a way as to claim, as a matter of hypothesis, that they derive from a source, that is, a single common point of origin. The materials I examined in no way suggest that there was a single point of origin.

All the compilers of documents did is collect and arrange available materials.

Therefore we must ask about the textuality of a document – is it a composition or a scrap book? – so as to determine the appropriate foundations for comparison, the correct classifications for comparative study. Once we know what is unique to a document, we can investigate the traits that characterize all the document's unique and so definitive materials. We ask about whether the materials unique to a document also cohere, or whether they prove merely miscellaneous. If they do cohere, we may conclude that the framers of the document have followed a single plan and a program. That would in my view justify the claim that the framers carried out a labor not only of conglomeration, arrangement, and selection, but also of genuine authorship or composition in the narrow and strict sense of the word. If so, the document emerges from authors, not merely arrangers and compositors. For the same purpose, therefore, we also take up and analyze the items shared between that document and some other or among several documents. We ask about the traits of those items, one by one and all in the aggregate. In these stages we may solve for the case at hand the problem of the rabbinic document: do we deal with a scrapbook or a cogent composition? A text or merely a literary expression, random and essentially promiscuous, of a larger theological context? That is the choice at hand.

Since we have reached a matter of fact, let me state the facts as they are. I describe the relationships among the principal components of the literature with which we deal. The several documents that make up the canon of Judaism in late antiquity relate to one another in three important ways. First, all of them refer to the same basic writing, the Hebrew Scriptures. Many of them draw upon the Mishnah and quote it. So the components of the canon join at their foundations. Second, as the documents reached closure in sequence, the later authorship can be shown to have drawn upon earlier, completed documents. So the writings of the rabbis of the talmudic corpus accumulate and build from layer to layer. Third, as I have already hinted, among two or more documents some completed units of discourse, and many brief, discrete sayings, circulated, for instance, sentences or episodic homilies or fixed apophthegms of various kinds. So in some (indeterminate) measure the several documents draw not only upon one another, as we can show, but also upon a common corpus of materials that might serve diverse editorial and redactional purposes.

Now to the question of the peripatetic sayings, to which I made allusion in the preface. These are the materials shared among two or more compilations. The extent of this common corpus can never be fully known. We know only what we have, not what we do not have. So we cannot say what has been omitted, or whether sayings that occur in only one document derive from materials available to the editors or compilers of some or all other documents. That is something we never can know. We can describe only what is in our hands and interpret only the data before us. Of indeterminates and endless speculative possibilities we need take no account. In taking up documents one by one, do we not obscure their larger context and their points in common? In fact, shared materials proved for Leviticus Rabbah not many and not definitive. What is unique to that text predominates and bears the message of the whole. To date I have taken up the issue of homogeneity in a limited and mainly formal setting, for the matter of how sayings and stories travel episodically from one document to the next.[4] The real issue is not the traveling, but the unique, materials: the documents, and not what is shared among them. The variable – what moves – is subject to analysis only against the constant: the document itself.

VII. THE INTEGRITY OF A DOCUMENT IN THE CANON OF JUDAISM

To describe and analyze documents one by one violates the lines of order and system that have characterized all earlier studies of these same documents. Until now, just as people compared exegeses among different groups of a given verse of Scripture without contrasting one circumstance to another, so they tended to treat all of the canonical texts as uniform in context, that is, as testimonies to a single system and structure, that is, to Judaism. They made of the documents mere adventitious repositories of this and that. They treated as null the distinctive viewpoint of those who compiled documents, maintaining that they drew upon an undifferentiated mass of teachings and threw together without plan or program whatever happened to fall into their hands. What sort of testimonies texts provide varies according to the interest of those who study them. That is why, without regard to the source of the two expositions of the same verse, people would compare one *midrash,* meaning the interpretation of a given verse of Scripture, with another *midrash* on the same verse of Scripture. As I have argued, however, comparison cannot be properly carried out on such a basis. The hermeneutical issue dictated by the system overall defines the result of description, analysis, and interpretation.

Let me give a single probative example. From the classical perspective of the theology of Judaism the entire canon of Judaism ("the one whole Torah of Moses, our rabbi") equally and at every point testifies to the entirety of Judaism. Why so? Because all documents in the end

---

[4]This preparatory study is *The Peripatetic Saying. The Problem of the Thrice-Told Tale in Talmudic Literature* (Chico: 1985).

form components of a single system. Each makes its contribution to the whole. If, therefore, we wish to know what "Judaism" or, more accurately, "the Torah," teaches on any subject, we are able to draw freely on sayings relevant to that subject wherever they occur in the entire canon of Judaism. Guided only by the taste and judgment of the great sages of the Torah, as they have addressed the question at hand, we thereby describe "Judaism." And that same theological conviction explains why we may rip a passage out of its redactional context and compare it with another passage, also seized from its redactional setting. In the same way *comparative midrash* as presently practiced moves freely across the boundaries of systems and documents alike. But the theological *apologia* for doing so has yet to reach expression; and there can be no other than a theological *apologia.* In logic I see none; epistemologically there never was one.

In fact documents stand in three relationships to one another and to the system of which they form a part, that is, to Judaism, as a whole. The specification of these relationships constitutes the principal premise of this inquiry and validates the approach to *comparative midrash* I offer here.

1. Each document is to be seen all by itself, that is, as autonomous of all others.

2. Each document is to be examined for its relationships with other documents universally regarded as falling into the same classification, as Torah.

3. And, finally, in the theology of Judaism (or, in another context, of Christianity) each document is to be allowed to take its place as part of the undifferentiated aggregation of documents that, all together, constitute the canon of, in the case of Judaism, the "one whole Torah revealed by God to Moses at Mount Sinai."

Simple logic makes self-evident the proposition that, if a document comes down to us within its own framework, as a complete book with a beginning, middle, and end, in preserving that book, the canon presents us with a document on its own and not solely as part of a larger composition or construct. So we too see the document as it reaches us, that is, as autonomous.

If, second, a document contains materials shared verbatim or in substantial content with other documents of its classification, or if one document refers to the contents of other documents, then the several documents that clearly wish to engage in conversation with one another have to address one another. That is to say, we have to seek for the marks of connectedness, asking for the meaning of those connections. It is at this level of connectedness that we labor. For the purpose of comparison is to tell us what is like something else, what is unlike something else. To begin with, we can declare something unlike something else only if we know that it is like that other thing. Otherwise the original judgment bears no sense whatsoever. So, once more, canon defines context, or, in descriptive language, the first classification for comparative study is the document, brought into juxtaposition with, and contrast to, another document.

Finally, since the community of the faithful of Judaism, in all of the contemporary expressions of Judaism, concur that documents held to be authoritative constitute one whole, seamless "Torah," that is, a complete and exhaustive statement of God's will for Israel and humanity, we take as a further appropriate task, if one not to be done here, the description of the whole out of the undifferentiated testimony of all of its parts. These components in the theological context are viewed, as is clear, as equally authoritative for the composition of the whole: one, continuous system. In taking up such a question, we address a problem not of theology alone, though it is a correct theological conviction, but one of description, analysis, and interpretation of an entirely historical order.

In my view the various documents of the canon of Judaism produced in late antiquity demand a hermeneutic altogether different from the one of homogenization and harmonization, the ahistorical and anti-contextual one definitive for *comparative midrash* as presently practiced. It is one that does not harmonize but that differentiates. It is a hermeneutic shaped to teach us how to read the compilations of exegeses first of all one by one and in a particular context, and second, in comparison with one another.

To do the work I have defined, therefore, I have to prove that the document at hand rests upon clear-cut choices of formal and rhetorical preference and principles of logical coherence, so it is cogent from the viewpoint of form and mode of expression and medium of thought. I have to demonstrate that these formal choices prove uniform and paramount. Then, I proceed to survey all of Sifra to find out whether or not every chapter of the entire document finds within a single cogent taxonomic structure suitable classification for its diverse units of discourse. If one taxonomy serves all and encompasses the bulk of the units of discourse at hand, I may fairly claim that Sifra does constitute a cogent formal structure, based upon patterns of rhetoric uniform and characteristic throughout. In this way I answer the question, for the documents under study, of whether or not we deal with texts exhibiting traits of composition, deliberation, proportion, and so delivering a message on their own.[5]   Since we do, then Sifra demands description, analysis, and interpretation first of all on its own, as an autonomous statement.   The document, established as a document unto itself, then requires comparison and contrast with other compositions of its species of the rabbinic genus, that is to say, to be brought into connection with, relationship to, other rabbinic compositions of its type.   And on that basis, comparison becomes possible.

---

[5]In connection with Sifra I am ignoring one consideration that seemed important elsewhere.   My next step for Genesis Rabbah and Leviticus Rabbah was to ask whether the framers of the document preserved a fixed order in arranging types of units of discourse, differentiated in accord with the forms I identified.   In both documents I am able to show that, in ordering materials, the framers or redactors paid much attention to the formal traits of their units of discourse.   They chose materials of one formal type for beginning their sustained exercises of argument or syllogism, then chose another formal type for the end of their sustained exercises of syllogistic exposition.   This seems to me to show that the framers or redactors followed a set of rules which we are able to discern.

Part One

COMPARISONS OF RHETORIC AND LOGIC AMONG SPECIES OF THE GENUS, MIDRASH-COMPILATIONS

THE SPECIES: "HALAKHIC MIDRASHIM"

Chapter Two

Rhetorical Comparison

I. DEFINING AND COMPARING FORMS

In all the writings of the canon of the Judaism of the dual Torah the highly formalized modes of composition convey ideas. Fixed literary structures dictate to the authorships of nearly all documents the repertoire of choices available for saying whatever it is that they wish to say. What this means is that individual preferences, personal modes of forming sentences for instance, rarely come into play. Thoughts are set forth in a few well-defined ways, and not in the myriad diverse ways in which, in a less formalized literature, people say their piece. That fact vastly facilitates the comparison of document to document, since the range of rhetorical choices is limited to the forms and literary structures paramount in the documents subject to description and analytical comparison, and that range is remarkably circumscribed. Not only so, but the work of comparison is made still more reliable by the very extrinsic character of forms and structures; identifying them is not a matter of taste and judgment.

Once we have defined a form or structure, we know whether or not it is present by appeal to some few facts that are readily accessible to the naked eye. Consequently, there can be irrefutable proof that one set of forms or literary structures, and not another, predominates in a given document, and that proof can even take the form of the statistics which describe the total number of units of thought subject to description and the proportion of those units of thought that fall into the several defined categories of form or structure, as against the proportion of those that do not. Defining these rhetorical conventions therefore sets forth the first step in describing the documents, one by one, and then comparing them to one another. For the forms or literary structures paramount in one differ from those found useful in another, and hence the work of comparison and contrast commences in the simplest and most extrinsic matter. Only when we have established the distinctive traits of documents by appeal to such external matters, in which matters of taste and judgment do not figure, do we move on to substantive differences of topic and even proposition, in which they do – if we let them.[1]

Let me begin with simple definitions. A form or literary structure is a set of rules that dictate those recurrent conventions of expression, organization, or proportion, that are *extrinsic* to the message of the author. The conventions at hand bear none of the particular burden of the author's message, so they are not idiosyncratic but systemic and public. A form or literary structure imposes upon the individual writer a limited set of choices about how he will convey whatever message he has in mind. Or the formal convention will limit an editor or redactor to an equally circumscribed set of alternatives about how to arrange received materials. These conventions then form a substrate of the literary culture that preserves and expresses the world-view and way of life of the system at hand.[2] When we can define the form or literary structures, we also can ask about the program of thought – recurrent modes of analysis and exercises of conflict and resolution – that dictate the content of the commentary. For how I think and what the syntax of my language and thought permits me to say dictates what I shall think and why I shall think it: this, not that.

How are we to recognize the presence of such structures? On the basis of forms that merely appear to be patterned or extrinsic to particular meaning and so entirely formal, we cannot allege that we have in hand a fixed, form or literary structure. Such a judgment would prove subjective. Nor shall we benefit from bringing to the text at hand recurrent syntactic or grammatical patterns shown in *other* texts, even of the same canon of literature, to define conventions for communicating ideas. Quite to the contrary, we find guidance in a simple principle: *A text has to define its own structures for us.* Authors do so simply by repeatedly resorting to a severely circumscribed set of linguistic patterns and literary conventions and to no others. These patterns, we shall soon see, not only dictate formal syntax and principles of composition but also define the deep structure of logical analysis and the modes of proof for particular propositions of argument. On the basis of inductive evidence alone, therefore, a document will testify that its authors adhere to a fixed canon of literary forms. It will show that these forms guide the authors to the propositions for, or against, which they choose to argue: the program of the book, not only its plan. If demonstrably present, these forms present an author or editor with a few choices on how ideas are to be organized and expressed in intelligible – again, therefore, public – compositions.

---

[1]But we do not have to let them.

[2]It is that ongoing and definitive trait that later pseudepigraphs imitate when they wish to improve the received text with their additional materials and ideas. The uniformity of the final version of the text testifies to the power of the initial literary structure.

So internal evidence and that alone testifies to the form or literary structures of a given text.

The adjective "recurrent" therefore constitutes a redundancy when joined to the noun "structure." For – to state matters negatively – we cannot know that we have a structure if the text under analysis does not repeatedly resort to the presentation of its message through that disciplined structure external to its message on any given point. And, it follows self-evidently, we do know that we have a structure when the text in hand repeatedly follows recurrent conventions of expression, organization, or proportion *extrinsic* to the message of the author. The form or literary structures or patterns find definition in entirely formal and objective facts: the placement of the key-verse subject to discussion in the composition at hand, the origin of that verse. No subjective or impressionistic judgment intervenes.

For Sifra, as was the case for the prior documents I have analyzed, we had best move first to the analysis of a single *pisqa*. We seek, within that *pisqa* to identify the recurrent arrangements of words in a fixed manner, e.g., syntactic form, characteristic and repeated patterns of questions, use of fixed formulas that impose one pattern of making statements rather than some other. These are the patterns or forms that hold the whole together. For this purpose I shall try to describe what I conceive to be the underlying and repeated structures of formulation or pattern. These I do one by one, simply experimenting with the possibility that a way of forming ideas will recur and so constitute a pattern. The description of course is inductive: I say what I see. Reader can check every step and form their own judgments. The second step then is to see whether what I have identified exemplifies formations beyond itself or forms a phenomenon that occurs in fact only once or at random.

II. THE REPERTOIRE OF FORMS OF SIFRA: TYPES AND PROPORTIONS

1. Introduction

Let me begin by describing what is apparent to the naked eye. Only then shall we take up the detailed analysis of specific texts. First comes the simple form, in which a verse, or an element of a verse, is cited, and then a very few words explain the meaning of that verse. Second is the complex, in which a simple exegesis is augmented in some important way, commonly by questions and answers, so that we have more than simply a verse and a brief exposition of its elements or of its meaning as a whole. The authorship of the Sifra time and again wishes to show that prior documents, Mishnah or Tosefta, cited verbatim, require the support of exegesis of Scripture for important propositions, presented in the Mishnah and the Tosefta not on the foundation of exegetical proof at all. In the main, moreover, the authorship of Sifra tends not to attribute its materials to specific authorities, and most of the pericopae containing attributions are shared with Mishnah and Tosefta. As we should expect, Sifra contains a fair sample of pericopae which do not make use of the forms common in the exegesis of specific Scriptural verses and, mostly do not pretend to explain the meaning of verses, but rather resort to forms typical of Mishnah and Tosefta. When Sifra uses forms other than those in which its exegeses are routinely phrased, it commonly, though not always, draws upon materials also found in Mishnah and Tosefta. It is uncommon for Sifra to make use of non-exegetical forms for materials peculiar to its compilation. As a working hypothesis, to be corrected presently, the two forms of rhetorical patterning of language in Sifra are two, simple and complex.

Every example of a complex form, that is, a passage in which we have more than a cited verse and a brief exposition of its meaning, may be called "dialectical," that is, moving or developing an idea through questions and answers, sometimes implicit, but commonly explicit. What "moves" is the argument, the flow of thought, from problem to problem. The movement is generated by the raising of contrary questions and theses. There are several subdivisions of the dialectical exegesis, so distinctive as to be treated by themselves. But all exhibit a flow of logical argument, unfolding in questions and answers, characteristic, in the later literature, of the Talmud. One important subdivision of the stated form consists of those items, somewhat few in number but all rather large in size and articulation, intended to prove that logic alone is insufficient, and that only through revealed law will a reliable view of what is required be attained. The polemic in these items is pointed and obvious; logic (DYN) never wins the argument, though at a few points flaws in the text seem to suggest disjunctures in the flow of logic.

Since Sifra is a composite document, with what I think is an early stratum of simple exegeses and a later, and much larger, stratum of dialectical ones, the purposes of the ultimate formulators of the dialectical materials and of the final redactors is revealed in particular in these dialectical constructions. It is to apply rigorous logic to the exegesis of Scripture and to demonstrate that revelation, not logic alone, is necessary for the discovery of the law. In doing so, the formulators and redactors of the late second and early third century probably made use of the inherited, simple form, spinning out their theses by presenting ideas in that uncomplicated form and then challenging those ideas in various ways but in equally simple, disciplined forms and formulaic usages. The final redaction also drew abundant materials from completed, free floating pericopae also utilized in the redaction of Mishnah and Tosefta. So far as we now can discern, these shared materials are prior to ultimate redaction to the work of compiling both Sifra and Mishnah and Tosefta. But they are, normally though not always, primary to the editorial and redactional purposes of Mishnah and Tosefta and secondary to those of Sifra.

The rhetorical plan of Sifra leads us to recognize that the exegetes, while working verse by verse, in fact have brought a considerable program to their reading of the book of Leviticus. It concerns the interplay of the Oral Torah, represented by the Mishnah, with the Written Torah, represented by the book of Leviticus. That question demanded, in their view, not an answer comprising mere generalities. They wished to show their results through details, masses of details, and, like the rigorous philosophers that they were, they furthermore argued essentially through an inductive procedure, amassing evidence that in its accumulation made the point at hand. The syllogism I have identified about the priority of the revelation of the Written Torah in the search for truth is nowhere expressed in so many words, because the philosopher-exegetes of the rabbinic world preferred to address an implicit syllogism and to pursue or to test that syllogism solely in a sequence of experiments of a small scale. Sifra's authorship therefore finds in the Mishnah and Tosefta a sizable laboratory for the testing of propositions. We have therefore to ask, at what points do Sifra and Mishnah and Tosefta share a common agenda of interests, and at what points does one compilation introduce problems, themes, or questions unknown to the other? The answer to these questions will show that Sifra and Mishnah and Tosefta form two large concentric circles, sharing a considerable area in common. Sifra, however, exhibits interests peculiar to itself. On the criterion of common themes and interests, Mishnah and Tosefta and Sifra exhibit a remarkable unity. If I had to compare the rhetorical program of Sifra's authorship with that of their counterparts in our document, I should say that the latter group has taken over and vastly expanded the program selected by the former. More to the point, the two documents intersect, but, for Sifré to Deuteronomy, the rhetorical intersection covers only a small segment of the whole plan governing the formulation of the document. In that sense, we have to say that our authorship has made choices and has not simply repeated a restricted program available to all rabbinic authorships and utilized at random by each.

2. The Forms of Sifra Chapter 14

We now address a particular chapter of Sifra and out of its details form a theory of the repertoire of forms on which our authorship has drawn.

14. Parashat Vayyiqra Dibura Denedabah: Parashah 7

XIV:I

1. A. ["If his offering to the Lord is a burnt-offering of birds, he shall choose [bring near] his offering from turtledoves or pigeons. The priest shall bring it to the altar, pinch off its head, and turn it into smoke on the altar; and its blood shall be drained out against the side of the altar. He shall remove its crop with its contents and cast it into the place of the ashes, at the east side of the altar. The priest shall tear it open by its wings, without severing it, and turn it into smoke on the altar, upon the wood that is on the fire. It is a burnt-offering, an offering by fire, of pleasing odor to the Lord" (Lev. 1:14-17)]:

   B. "[The priest] shall bring it [to the altar]":

   C. What is the sense of this statement?

   D. Since it is said, "he shall choose [bring near] his offering from turtledoves or pigeons," one might have supposed that there can be no fewer than two sets of birds.

   E. Accordingly, Scripture states, "[The priest] shall bring it [to the altar]" to indicate, [by reference to the "it,"] that even a single pair suffices.

Reduced to its simplest syntactic traits, the form consists of the citation of a clause of a verse, followed by secondary amplification of that clause. We may call this commentary form, in that the rhetorical requirement is citation plus amplification. Clearly, the form sustains a variety of expressions, e.g., the one at hand: "what is the sense of this statement...since it is said...accordingly Scripture states . . . ." But for our purposes there is no need to differentiate within the commentary-form.

2. A. "The priest shall bring it to the altar, pinch off its head":

   B. Why does Scripture say, "The priest...pinch off..."?

   C. This teaches that the act of pinching off the head should be done only by a priest.

   D. But is the contrary to that proposition not a matter of logic:

   E. if in the case of a beast of the flock, to which the act of slaughter at the north side of the altar is assigned, the participation of a priest in particular is not assigned, to the act of pinching the neck, to which the act of slaughter at the north side of the altar is not assigned, surely should not involve the participation of the priest in particular!

   F. That is why it is necessary for Scripture to say, "The priest...pinch off...,"

   G. so as to teach that the act of pinching off the head should be done only by a priest.

3. A. Might one compose an argument to prove that one should pinch the neck by using a knife?

   B. For lo, it is a matter of logic.

   C. If to the act of slaughter [of a beast as a sacrifice], for which the participation of a priest is not required, the use of a correct utensil is required, for the act of pinching the neck, for which the participation of a priest indeed is required, surely should involve the requirement of using a correct implement!

D.   That is why it is necessary for Scripture to say, "The priest...pinch off . . . ."

4. A.   Said R. Aqiba, "Now would it really enter anyone's mind that a non-priest should present an offering on the altar?

    B.   "Then why is it said, 'The priest...pinch off...'?

    C.   "This teaches that the act of pinching the neck must be done by the priest using his own finger [and not a utensil]."

5. A.   Might one suppose that the act of pinching may be done either at the head [up by the altar] or at the foot [on the pavement down below the altar]?

    B.   It is a matter of logic:

    C.   If in the case of an offering of a beast, which, when presented as a sin-offering is slaughtered above [at the altar itself] but when slaughtered as a burnt-offering is killed below [at the pavement, below the altar], in the case of an offering of fowl, since when presented as a sin-offering it is slaughtered down below, surely in the case of a burnt-offering it should be done down below as well!

    D.   That is why it was necessary for Scripture to make explicit [that it is killed up by the altar itself:] "The priest shall bring it to the altar, pinch off its head, and turn it into smoke on the altar."

    E.   The altar is explicitly noted with respect to turning the offering into smoke and also to pinching off the head.

    F.   Just as the offering is turned into smoke up above, at the altar itself, so the pinching off of the head is to be done up above, at the altar itself.

The form at hand is to be characterized as a dialectical exegetical argument, in which we move from point to point in a protracted, yet very tight, exposition of a proposition. The proposition is both implicit and explicit. The implicit proposition is that "logic" does not suffice, a matter vastly spelled out in *Uniting the Dual Torah*. The explicit proposition concerns the subject-matter at hand. We may identify the traits of this form very simply: citation of a verse or clause plus a proposition that interprets that phrase, then "it is a matter of logic" followed by the demonstration that logic is insufficient for the determination of taxa.

XIV:II

1. A.   "...pinch off its head":

    B.   The pinching off of the head is done at the shoulder.

    C.   Might one suppose that it may be done at any other location?

    D.   It is a matter of logic. Lo, I shall argue as follows:

    E.   Here an act of pinching off the neck is stated, and elsewhere we find the same [Lev. 5:8: "He shall bring them to the priest, who shall offer first the one for the sin-offering, pinching its head at the nape without severing it"].

    F.   Just as pinching off at the neck in that passage is to be done at the nape of the neck, so pinching off at the neck in the present context is to be done at the nape of the neck.

    G.   Perhaps the analogy is to be drawn differently, specifically, just as the pinching stated in that other passage involves pinching the neck without dividing the bird [Lev. 5:8: "without severing it"], so the importance of the analogy is to yield the same rule here.

    H.   In that case, the priest would pinch the neck without severing it.

    I.   Accordingly, [the ambiguous analogy is such as to require] Scripture to state, "...pinch off its head."

We have an example of the dialectical exegesis of the limitations of logic for definition of taxa.

2.   A.   "[turn it into smoke on the altar;] and its blood shall be drained out":

     B.   Can one describe matters in such a way?

     C.   Specifically, after the carcass is turned into smoke, can one drain out the blood?

     D.   But one pinches the neck in accord with the way in which one turns it into smoke:

     E.   Just as we find that the turning of the carcass into smoke is done up to the head by itself and then the body by itself, so in the act of pinching the neck, the head is by itself and the body is by itself.

3.   A.   And how do we know that in the case of turning a carcass into smoke, the head is done by itself?

     B.   When Scripture says, "The priest [shall tear it open by its wings, without severing it,] and turn it into smoke on the altar" (Lev. 1:17),

     C.   lo, the turning of the body into smoke is covered by that statement.

     D.   Lo, when Scripture states here, "pinch off its head, and turn it into smoke on the altar," it can only mean that the head is to be turned into smoke by itself.

     E.   Now, just as we find that the turning of the carcass into smoke is done up to the head by itself and then the body by itself, so in the act of pinching the neck, the head is by itself and the body is by itself.

Nos. 2, 3 present in a rather developed statement the simple exegetical form. The formal requirement is not obscured, however, since all we have is the citation of a clause followed by secondary amplification. This version of commentary-form obviously cannot be seen as identical to the other; but so far as the dictates of rhetoric are concerned, there is no material difference, since the variations affect only the secondary amplification of the basic proposition, and in both cases, the basic proposition is set forth by the citation of the verse or clause followed by a sentence or two of amplification.

XIV:III

1.   A.   "...and its blood shall be drained out [against the side of the altar]":

     B.   all of its blood: he takes hold of the head and the body and drains the blood out of both pieces.

This is commentary-form.

2. A.   "...against the side of the altar":
    B.   not on the wall of the ramp up to the altar, and not on the wall of the foundation, nor on the wall of the courtyard.
3. A.   It is to be on the upper half of the wall.
    B.   Might one suppose it may be on the lower half of the wall?
    C.   It is a matter of logic: in the case of the sacrifice of a beast, which, if done as a sin-offering, has its blood tossed on the upper part of the wall, and if done as a burnt-offering, has its blood tossed on the lower part of the wall,
    D.   in the case of the sacrifice of a bird, since, if it is offered as a sin-offering, the blood is tossed at the lower half of the wall, should logic not dictate that if it is offered as a burnt-offering, its blood should be tossed on the lower part of the wall as well?
    E.   That is why it is necessary for Scripture to frame matters in this way:
    F.   "The priest shall bring it to the altar, pinch off its head, and turn it into smoke on the altar; and its blood shall be drained out against the side of the altar,"
    G.   the altar is noted with respect to turning the carcass into smoke and also with reference to the draining of the blood.
    H.   Just as the act of turning the carcass into smoke is done at the topside of the altar, so the draining of the blood is done at the topside of the altar.

This is the dialectical exegetical form. Now we come to a third usage.

4. A.   How does the priest do it?
    B.   **The priest went up on the ramp and went around the circuit. He came to the southeastern corner. He would wring off its head from its neck and divide the head from the body. And he drained off its blood onto the wall of the altar [M. Zeb. 6:5B-E].**
    C.   **If one did it from the place at which he was standing and downward by a cubit, it is valid. R. Simeon and R. Yohanan ben Beroqah say, "The entire deed was done only at the top of the altar" [T. Zeb. 7:9C-D].**

What we have now is the verbatim-citation of a passage of the Mishnah or of the Tosefta, joined to its setting in the exegetical framework of Sifra by some sort of joining-formula. We shall call this formal convention Mishnah-citation-form. Its formal requirement is simply appropriate joining language.

XIV:IV

1. A.   "He shall remove its crop [with its contents and cast it into the place of the ashes, at the east side of the altar]":
    B.   this refers to the bird's crop.
    C.   Might one suppose that one should extract the crop with a knife and remove it surgically?
    D.   Scripture says, "...with its contents."
    E.   He should remove it with its contents [including the innards, or, alternatively, the feathers].

F.   Abba Yosé b. Hanan says, "He should remove the intestines with it.

A variation on commentary-form, we have secondary development at C, might one suppose? I am not inclined to think a sizable catalogue of variations on commentary-form will materially advance our inquiry.

3. The Forms of Sifra Chapters 164 and 243

We have now formed the thesis that Sifra's authorship appealed to three basic forms for the composition of any thought or proposition it might wish to set forth. These are [1] commentary-form; [2] dialectical-exegetical form; and [3] citation-form. The simple catalogue at hand conforms to the introductory theoretical statement. Let us now test the thesis by reference to two further chapters.

164. Parashat Zabim Pereq 3

CLXIV:I

1. A.   "And whoever sits on anything on which he who has the discharge has sat will be unclean [shall wash his clothes and bathe himself in water and be unclean until the evening]" (Lev. 15:6).
    B.   I know only that this is the case if he sits on it and [actually] touches it. [That is to say, if the Zab is in direct contact with the chair, then he imparts uncleanness to it.]
    C.   How do I know that [if the Zab sits on] ten chairs, one on the other, and even [if he sits] on top of a heavy stone, [what is underneath is clean]? [If the chair bears the weight of the Zab, even though the Zab is not touching the chair, the chair is made unclean.]
    D.   Scripture says, "And he who sits on the utensil on which the Zab has sat will be unclean" –
    E.   In any place in which the Zab sits and imparts uncleanness, the clean person sits and becomes unclean.
    F.   I know only that when the Zab sits on it, and the Zab is there [that it is unclean]. How do I know that I should treat the empty as the full one?
    G.   Scripture says, "Utensil" – to treat the empty like the full.
    H.   I know only that this [rule concerning transmission of the Zab's uncleanness merely through applying the burden of his weight, even without his actually being in contact with the object] applies to the chair. How do I know that it applies to the saddle?
    I.   And it is logical:
    J.   If we have found that Scripture does not distinguish between the one who carries and the one who is carried in respect to sitting, so we should not distinguish between the one who is carried and the one who carries with respect to the saddle.
    K.   But what difference does it make to me that Scripture did not distinguish between carrying and being carried in respect to the chair?
    L.   For it did not distinguish touching it and carrying it.
    M.   Should we not distinguish between carrying and being carried with reference to the saddle,
    N.   for lo, it has indeed distinguished touching it from carrying it?

0.   Scripture [accordingly is required] to state, "A utensil" – to encompass even the saddle.

2. A.   R. Hananiah b. Hanina says, "If in a manner in which uncleanness has not descended upon it, [that is, if a Zab carries a saddle, in which case uncleanness does not descend on the saddle such as to make a man who carries the saddle unclean], uncleanness has gone forth from it, [for the one who carries the saddle made unclean by the Zab is made unclean and has to wash his clothing],

   B.   "in a manner in which uncleanness has descended upon it [if a Zab rides upon it, he makes it unclean], should not uncleanness go forth from it? [If, it must follow, the chair bears the weight of the Zab, even though the Zab is not touching the chair, the chair is made unclean.]"

   C.   No. For why does the law impart a strict rule on the saddle that is carried, for lo, the law has applied a strict rule in connection with a Zab who himself is carried.

   D.   But should we impose a strict rule on the saddle that bears weight, for lo, the law imposes a lenient rule on the Zab who bears weight [for if the Zab carries an object without actually touching it, he does not impart uncleanness to that object]?

   E.   [The proposed logical argument does not serve, but] Scripture says, "[And he who sits] on the utensil [on which the Zab has sat will be unclean]" –

   F.   thus encompassing the saddle.

No. 1 is an interesting variation: I know X, how about Y? In basic structure, what we have is a citation of a clause followed by secondary amplification, hence commentary-form as before. That classification is further justified by D. Then E-F moves onward, a secondary expansion of the former; what we see, therefore, is how commentary-form permits an authorship to pile on case after case in a sustained and fully coordinated statement. But the form in its complex and developed utilization is not vastly different from its primitive version: verse, some words of amplification. But at Iff., we shift into the "it is logical-"form. This dialectical exegesis is autonomous of the foregoing, in that it can be fully understood without what has come before; and what has come before hardly requires the dialectical exegesis for a full and exhaustive account ot the message that the prior materials wish to set forth. No. 2 carries forward the second form. No. 2 goes through the same question from a different perspective, and in the end the proposed proof fails, because the argument from hierarchical classification proves flawed, as anticipated.

CLXIV:II

1. A.   "[And whoever touches] the flesh of the Zab [shall wash his clothes and bathe himself in water and be unclean until evening]" (Lev. 15:7) –

   B.   The flesh of the Zab, and not the excrement which is on him, and not the entangled hair which is on him,

C.   and not the chains, and not the finger–rings and not the earrings, even though they do not stick out [but are imbedded in the flesh].

D.   Or might [I think that] I should encompass the hair and the fingernails?

E.   Scripture says, "It is unclean."

2. A.   "[And whoever touches] the flesh of the Zab [shall wash his clothes and bathe himself in water and be unclean until evening]" (Lev. 15:7) –

B.   not a bone that separates from him or flesh that separates from him.

C.   It is an argument *a fortiori* that that which separates from a clean person should be clean.

D.   Then how shall I deal with the verse, "[...anyone who touches a person who was killed or who died naturally,] or human bone, or a grave, [shall be unclean seven days]" (Num. 19:16)?

E.   This refers to a limb that separates from a living person [thus rejecting the proposed argument *a fortiori*].

T. Zab. 5:2 A, to M. Zab. 5:4–5, has dealt with things deemed connected to the Zab, so that, if one touches such connected parts, it is as if he touched the Zab. Included there are hair and fingernails (T. Zab. 5:2 A/B). Now our task is to specify things which are not deemed connected, and, not surprisingly, we specify that those things which wash away, B, and those things which are not part of his body but are merely ornamental, C, are not deemed connected. If one touched these things, it is not as if he touched the flesh of the Zab. But D–E then exclude from the list of unconnected objects those things which we take to be integral to the person's body. No. 2 goes on to its own interests. This utilization of the exegetical form has its own dynamic. Now following our initial proposition, A-B, we have a secondary development, C. This then yields the methodical analysis, with which the next chapter will deal: I exclude this and I include that. What I call an exclusionary/inclusionary exercise, which is repeated countless times, has its own formulary traits. In the context of form-analysis of the most basic patterns in the arrangements of words, however, the secondary expansion of methodical analysis changes nothing about the classification of No. 1: commentary, pure and simple. No. 2 invokes the dialectical exegetical form.

CLXIV:III

1. A.   If these rules are stated in connection with the Zab, [Lev. 15:7–8], why are they stated in connection with the bed [Lev. 15:4–6], and if they are said in connection with the bed, why are they said in connection with the Zab?

B.   But the reason is that there are rules pertaining to the Zab which do not pertain to the bed, and there are rules pertaining to the bed which do not pertain to the Zab.

C.   The Zab imparts uncleanness to the bed, but the bed does not impart uncleanness to the Zab.

D.   Things which are connected to the Zab are clean, and things which are connected to bed are unclean.

E. Lo, since there are rules applying to the Zab which do not apply to the bed, and rules applying to the bed which do not apply to the Zab, Scripture has to state the rule in connection with the Zab.

We find ourselves in new territory. We have no citation of a verse, and also no exegetical dynamic at all. Rather we find an effort to generalize in respect to two distinct taxa. True, the repetition of Scripture is accounted for. The appeal is to a logic of classification, however, pointing out that were we to treat the items within the same taxon, we should err. D refers to things not integral to the body. But we find ourselves in a different world from the formal structures we have identified to this point. The form serves a taxonomic purpose: there are traits/rules pertinent to one thing but not another, and hence we may identify the form as a taxonomic one.

CLXIV:IV

1. A. "And if one who has the discharge spits on one who is clean, [then he shall wash his clothes and bathe himself in water and be unclean until the evening]" (Lev. 15:8) –
   B. Might I think that even if he spit, but the spit did not touch him [the clean person], [the person in whose direction the spit was sent] should be unclean?
   C. Scripture says, "On the clean person" – [that he is clean] until it actually will touch him.
   D. I know only that this applies to his spit.
   E. How do I know that this applies to his phlegm, slaver, and snot?
   F. Scripture says, "And if he will spit."

This is commentary-form. The subdivision, were we to classify the diverse utilizations of the form, is marked by an interest in exclusion (B), then inclusion (E). Hence the methodical-analytical logic, with which we shall be occupied presently, imposes its requirements upon the formal repertoire. But the base-syntax remains identical.

CLXIV:V

1. A. "Any means for riding that one with a discharge has mounted shall be unclean. [Whoever touches anything that was under him shall be unclean until evening; and whoever carries such things shall wash his clothes, bathe in water, and remain unclean until evening]":
   B. Might one suppose that even if the Zab should ride upon what is used for lying or sitting, uncleanness would inhere in this wise?
   C. Scripture says, "means for riding,"
   D. not what is used for lying or sitting.
2. A. I shall eliminate these [from the present category], but I shall not eliminate the bit.
   B. Scripture says, "...means for riding,"
   C. what is used in particular for riding.

Once more the methodical-analytical logic imposes its requirements upon the formal repertoire.

3. A. **What is used in particular for riding?**

   B. **The Askelon girth, Median mortar, pack saddle of a camel, and horsecloth.**

   C. **R. Yosé says, "The horse cloth is susceptible to uncleanness as a seat, because people stand on it in the arena, but the saddle of the female camel is susceptible to uncleanness [only as an ordinary chair or bed] [M. Kel. 23:2].**

The citation-form bears no joining-language of any kind.

4. A. I know only that this is the case if he is riding on it and [actually] touches it. [That is to say, if the Zab is in direct contact with the saddle, then he imparts uncleanness to it.]

   B. How do I know that [if the Zab sits on] ten saddles, one on the other, and even [if he sits] on top of a heavy stone, [what is underneath is clean]? [If the saddle bears the weight of the Zab, even though the Zab is not touching the saddle, it is made unclean.]

   C. Scripture says, "Any means for riding that one with a discharge has mounted shall be unclean" –

   D. so long as the saddle bears the greater part of his weight.

While the fact is not clear, what we have is a citation of a Mishnah-rule. The joining language is "how do I know that...," followed by Mishnah-language or a case drawn from the Mishnah.

243. Parashat Emor Pereq 19

CCXLIII:I

1. A. ["And the Lord said to Moses, Bring out of the camp him who cursed, and let all who heard him lay their hands upon his head and let all the congregation stone him. And say to the people of Israel, whoever curses his God shall bear his sin. He who blasphemes the name of the Lord shall be put to death; all the congregation shall stone him; the sojourner as well as the native, when he blasphemes the Name, shall be put to death. He who kills a man shall be put to death. he who kills a beast shall make it good, life for life. When a man causes a disfigurement in his neighbor, as he has done so shall it be done to him, fracture for fracture, eye for eye, tooth for tooth, as he has disfigured a man, so shall he be disfigured. He who kills a beast shall make it good; and he who kills a man shall be put to death. You shall have one law for the sojourner and for the native, for I am the Lord your God. So Moses spoke to the people of Israel, and they brought him who had cursed out of the camp and stoned him with stones. Thus the people of Israel did as the Lord commanded Moses" (Lev. 24:15-23).]

   B. "And the Lord said to Moses, Bring out of the camp him who cursed":

   C. This teaches that the court meets inside, but the place of stoning is outside.

2. A. "and let [all] who heard him lay their hands upon his head":

   B. this refers to the witnesses.

3. A. "and let [all] who heard him lay their hands upon his head":

   B. this refers to the judges.

4. A. "their hands":

   B. the hand of every single individual.

5. A. "their hands upon his head":

   B. They place their hands upon him and say to him, "Your blood be on your own head, for you caused this thing to him."

6. A. "and...stone him":

   B. and not his garments.

7. A. "let all the congregation":

   B. But does the entire congregation actually stone him?

   C. Why then does it say "congregation"?

   D. This refers to the witnesses,

   E. who stone him in the presence of the entire congregation.

8. A. Might one suppose that the instruction was only provisional?

   B. Scripture says, "And say to the people of Israel, [whoever curses his God shall bear his sin]" –

   C. this is to be the practice for all generations.

9. A. "whoever ['a man, a man'] [curses his God shall bear his sin]":

   B. this serves to gentiles, who also are put to death for blasphemy, just like Israelites.

   C. But they are put to death only with a sword,

   D. for the only form of the death penalty assigned to the children of Noah is execution with the sword.

10. A. "'whoever curses his God [shall bear his sin]':

    B. "What is the point of Scripture here?

    C. "Since it is said, 'if he also pronounces the name Lord, he shall be put to death' (Lev. 24:16),

    D. "one might have supposed that liability to the death penalty should be incurred only by reason of pronouncing the Ineffable Name alone.

    E. "How do we know that all euphemisms are encompassed as well?

    F. "Scripture says, 'whoever curses his God [shall bear his sin],'" the words of R. Meir.

    G. And sages say, "**For fully pronouncing the Ineffable Name, one is liable to the death penalty [M. San. 7:5A],**

    H. "and as to other euphemisms, one is subject only to an admonition."

11. A. "[whoever curses his God] shall bear his sin":

    B. R. Judah says, "Here we find a reference to 'bearing sin,' and elsewhere we find a reference to 'bearing sin' [namely, at Lev. 22:9:he shall not eat anything that died or was torn by beasts thereby becoming unclean...they shall keep my charge, lest they incur sin thereby and die for it, having committed profanation'].

    C. "Just as 'bearing sin' mentioned there involves the penalty of extirpation, so 'bearing sin' mentioned here involves extirpation."

12. A. He who blasphemes the name of the Lord shall be put to death; all the congregation shall stone him; the sojourner as well as the native, when he blasphemes the Name, shall be put to death":

B.   The entire congregation are to be to him as parties to the quarrel.
C.   "sojourner":
D.   this is the proselyte.
E.   "the sojourner as well as...":
F.   this serves to encompass the wives of proselytes.
G.   "native"·
H.   this is the native.
I.   "as well as the native":
J.   this serves to encompass the wives of native-born Israelites.

13. A.   "when he blasphemes the Name":
B.   Said R. Menahem b. R. Yosé, "This serves to encompass the one who curses his father or his mother, that liability should be incurred only if he curses them by invoking the divine name."

We have another sequence of essentially ad hoc amplifications. The commentary-form appears here in its purest version: clause, amplification, clause, amplification. I see no implicit program or unstated proposition of any kind. There is, therefore, no predicting how this passage will have been treated, e.g., by inclusions or exclusions, by appeals to parallel passages, or by theorems about correct logic. If Sifra's authorship planned to present an essentially exegetical study of the book of Leviticus, then the entire document would look like this. Now that we have identified a highly limited repertoire of forms utilized in the test-chapters, let us turn to the document as a whole and determine whether or not the entire writing in fact is so restricted as now appears to be the case.

III. THE FORMAL CONVENTIONS OF SIFRA: CATALOGUE OF TYPES

For this illustrative survey of the types and proportions of forms in Sifra I catalogue the exempla of Chapters 1-20, 70-80, 110-115, 160-173, and 256-260 – 56 out of 277 chapters of Sifra or in excess of 20% of the whole. Since my translation has shown the uniform and formally coherent character of the document, that sample is very sizable indeed. Not only so, but I have taken my sample from different parts of the document. Furthermore, since most of the selections are only parts of *parashiyyot* we examine all of Parashat Zabim. Examining a complete *parashah* gives us a different kind of sample, namely, one of the thirteen whole *parashiyyot* into which the document is divided. This survey of a complete *parashah* moreover permits us to determine whether or not there is a fixed order in the types of forms that are used, e.g., attention to commentary-form, followed by citation-form, followed by dialectical-exegetical form addressed to the taxonomic critique of the Mishnah's logic, or some other fixed order. To see the results graphically, the groupings of types of forms for Chapters 160-173 tell the story. Hence these illustrations cover the range of materials in Sifra to test whether there is a limited and fixed pattern of formal preferences characteristic of the document as a whole. This purposive sample quite adequately serves the purpose of the present study.

1. Instances of the Use of [1] Commentary-Form

I:I [But this encompasses a sustained argument on the problem of classification.]

I:II [Citation + how on the basis of Scripture do we know...might one suppose...how on the basis of Scripture do I know....]

I:III

I:IV

II:I.3 [Sustained exercise of exclusion and inclusion.]

II:II

II:III

II:IV

III:II

III:III [Inclusion, exclusion.]

III:IV

III:V

III:VI [Citation + "might one suppose + verse]

III:X.1

IV:III

V:IV

V:V [V:V2ff. forms an exemplary demonstration of the inclusionary exegesis, e.g., I know...but how do I know that even if....]

V:VI

VI:I [But the commentary-form serves as a prologue to the sustained dialectical argument.]

VI:II [This, not that; sustained work of exclusion and inclusion.]

VI:IV

VI:V [I know only...how do I know...?]

VI:VII [Citation plus an analytical statement of Simeon that bears strong resemblance to Mishnah-statements.]

VII:I.2

VII:II

VII:III [+ debate of Aqiba and Tarfon.]

VII:IV [Include, exclude.]

VII:V [How do you know...it is possible to suppose...but how do we know...I shall concede...but how do I know...: sustained and sizable exercise of inclusion.]

VII:VI

VII:VII

VII:VIII.1

[VIII:I Serves as a prologue to VIII:II, list 2]

VIII:III

VIII:IV

VIII:V

VIII:VI

VIII:VII

IX:I

IX:II

IX:III

IX:V

IX:VI [Exclusion, inclusion.]

IX:VII [Might one argue...?]

IX:VIII

IX:IX.2

X:I

X:II

X:IV [I know only...how do I know....]

X:VI:1

XI:II [Citation plus might one suppose..., repeated in this and the following entries of the same chapter.]

XI:III

XI:IV

XII:II

XIII:I [Might one suppose...? Scripture says....]

XIII:II

XIV:I.1 [What is the sense of this statement? Since it is said..., one might have thought.... Accordingly, Scripture states....

XIV:II.3

XIV:IV

XV:I.1, 2

XV:II

XV:V

XV:VI

XVI:II

XVII:I.1

XVII:III

XVIII:I.1-2

XVIII:V

XIX:II

XIX:III [I know only..how do I know....]

XX:I

XX:II

XX:III

LXX:I.1, 8 [But the entire chapter is highly propositional and the formal appearance of commentary is not indicative of the rhetorical program at hand.]

LXX:I:I.1-3, 8-23 [how do we know...?]

LXXII:I.1-22 [Sequence of glosses of phrases, without a proposition to unify the whole.]

LXXIII:I.113 [As above.]

LXXIV:I-10

LXXVI:I.1-3, 5-6 ["I know only...how do I know...might I encompass...?"]

LXXVII:I.1-15 [Scripture defines generative categories. But that proposition is shown only implicitly; logical classification unaffected by Scripture is simply not attempted. The form is wholly exegetical within the definition operative here.]

LXXVIII:I.7-8 ["I know only...how do I know...?"]

LXXIX:I.1 [As above.]

LXXX:I.1, 3-5 [As above.]

CX:I.1, 2, 3ff. [This is a protracted and well-composed amplification: "what is the point of Scripture? Since it is said..., I might infer...Scripture says...might one suppose....Scripture says...might one suppose...Scripture says...or perhaps the intent is to specify.... A classic presentation of inclusionary exegesis.]

CXI:I.1-7 [As above, another splendid example of inclusionary form.]

CXII:II.1

CXIII:II

CXV:I,1-6. ["Might one suppose...? Scripture says... But should I then eliminate...? Scripture says...."]

CLXI:II [This is the first commentary-form in Parashat Zabim. The function is inclusionary: I know only that...how do I know...Scripture says.... This is followed immediately by a citation of the Mishnah.]

CLXII:I [This is a sustained exclusionary exercise: I shall eliminate these but not...I know that the law covers only...how do I know...might I then encompass under the law...might I exclude....]

CLXII:II [Precisely as above.]

CLXII:III [Precisely as above.]

CLXIII:I.3-6

CLXIII:II

CLXIII:III.1.A-N [Exclusionary/inclusionary form.]

CLXIV:I.1 ["I know only...how do I know"]

CLXIV:III

CLXIV:IV [Inclusionary exercise.]

CLXIV:V.1 [Exclusionary.]

CLXV:V [How do we know that....]

CLXVII:V [The sequence of types of forms in CLXVII shows no interest in a fixed ordering of types of forms, such as is evinced in other midrash-compilations. We have, in sequence, dialectical-exegetical form, citation-form, then commentary-form, and the three forms may occur elsewhere in other sequence entirely. Hence there is no sustained interest in ordering the forms in one way rather than in some other, so far as the present illustrative selections suggest.]

CLXVIII:II.1-5

CLXVIII:III [This is a fine instance of an exclusionary exercise: citation of verse...this exludes...then should I exclude...Scripture says....]

CLXIX:I.1: I know only...how do I know...Scripture says...on this basis have they said + Mishnah-citation.]

CLXIX:I.2-4 [Same as above]

CLXIX:II.1 [Citation of Scripture + this teaches + is not the opposite logical + I know that this is...how do I know...Scripture says....She who... Scripture says + Mishnah-citation. All three forms occur, promiscuously, as needed by the program of Scripture.]

CLXIX:II.2-3

CLXIX:IV.1 [Here we have a sustained and dialectical exegesis, phrase and proposition by phrase and proposition, but there is no demonstration of the limitations of taxonomy without Scripture. We have a variety of arguments that derive from the substance of the matter under discussion. In the end Scripture is invoked, but not in a polemical setting.]

CLXIX:IV.3

CLXX:I [Here we have another excellent illustration of the workings of an exclusionary study: citation of a phrase + excluding + then might I exclude + Scripture says....]

CLXX:III [Citation of verse + might one suppose + No–substantive argument + might one suppose + Scripture says.... I know only....Scripture says....I know only...how do I know...Scripture says . . . .]

CLXXI:I.1-2

CLXXI:II

CLXXII:I [Might one suppose...then how shall I interpret...Scripture is explicit...Then I know only...how do I know? Scripture says...Then I know only...how do I know...Scripture says . . . .]

CLXXII:II [As above. What we do see is that a particular form will dominate for a sizable stretch of discussion, then give way to another form, which will take over for another sizable passage. But this is not the same thing as ordering the types of forms in some fixed sequence. The formalization of discourse plays a far less important redactional role than it does in, e.g., Leviticus Rabbah, where we find a fixed order of types of forms, and where that fixed order dictates the character of discourse.]

CLXXIII:I [This goes over precisely what we find at CLXX, form and program alike.]

CLXXIII:II [Potpourri of miscellanies tied to the cited verses in sequence.]

CCLVI:I,.-13 [Systematic citation of clauses and amplification or gloss thereof.]

CCLVII:I.1-17 [Sequence of ad hoc clarifications of minor matters.]

CCLVIII:I.115 [Ad hoc clarifications, just as above; some of the entires are exclusionary, some inclusionary, but there is no clear pattern, other than the intent to work through clauses of the base-verse.]

CCLXIX:I [How do we know...might one suppose...Scripture says...might one suppose...Scripture says...."]

CCLXIX:II [As above, sequence of ad hoc clarifications of cited clauses.]

CCLX:I.1-6 [Citation of clause + this teaches that.... Citation of clause + might this refer to...? When Scripture says., lo, that is covered...etc. This same pattern runs throughout.]

2. Instances of the Use of [2] Dialectical-Exegetical Form

The one trait of the listed items that is hidden by the catalogue is the sheer immensity of the discussions. They tend to run on for many lines, while the commentary-form, listed item by item, is ordinarily brief and succinct. So the proportion of the document as a whole filled by the proof that classification without reference to the taxa ordained by Scripture can never serve is understated in this catalogue.

III:I

III:VII

III:VIII

III:IX

IV:I

IV:II [The comparison between the sustained and interesting discussion at IV:I-II with the abbreviated entry at IV:III shows the under-representation of the dialectical-exegetical form in this catalogue.]

V:I

V:II-III

VI:I

VI:III

VIII:I+II

X:III

X:V

XII:I

XII:III

XIII:III

XIV:I.3

XIV:II.1-2

XIV:III

XV:I.3

XV:III

XV:IV

XVI:I

XVII:II

XVIII:I.3

XVIII:II

XVIII:IV

XIX:III.2 [Simeon proposes that logic proves the required proposition, but the proof is rejected.]

LXX:II.9 [The entire composition is highly propositional.]

LXXV:I [This is a classic discourse on the argument of analogy, comparison, and contrast.]

LXXVIII:I.2-3

CXII:I [As excellent an example of the exposition of the taxonomic limitations of logic as CX and CXI are classic statements of inclusionary/exclusionary exegesis.]

CXII:II.6 [In the context of a Mishnah-citation, we ask whether logic proves the proposition at hand and show that that is not so. Here is a case in which the citation-form is paramount and definitive, the resort to "is it not logical" secondary. The example is complex and classic for its own reasons.]

CXIII:I [The process of extension and restriction is at stake, but the argument and its form derive from dialectical-exegetical considerations.]

CXIV:I.1-4, 7-11, 13 [Here again we have the mixture of proof that logic does not supply valid taxonomic definition and citation of Mishnah or Tosefta. But while the forms are interspersed, the composition as a whole never directs against the cited Mishnah-passage the critique that taxa derive solely from Scripture. The joining language, "in this connection sages have ruled," is neutral and diverts attention from the critique of taxonomy not dictated by Scripture's taxa.]

CXV:I.7-8

CLX:II

CLX:III

CLX:IV.1

CLX:IV:3 [The opening parashah of Parashat Zabim presents a mixture of citations and refutations of logic undirected by Scripture. There is no commentary-form whatever.]

CLXI:I

CLXI:III

CLXI:IV

CLXII:IV [We have concluded at CLXII:I-III a sustained exclusionary-inclusionary operation and now turn to a citation of a verse followed by "and is not the contrary logical?" But the proposition at hand has no bearing on anything that was said before. By working our way through the clauses of the verse, we order the types of forms and discourse that are followed. There is no autonomous order of types of forms, independent of what are deemed to be the requirements of Scripture.]

CLXIII:I.1-2

CLXIV:I.2

CLXIV:II

CLXV:I

CLXV:II

CLXVI:I.1-2

CLXVI:II

CLXVII:I

CLXVII:III

CLXVII:IV

CLXIX:II.1 [Citation of Scripture + this teaches + is not the opposite logical + I know that this is...how do I know...Scripture says....She who... Scripture says + Mishnah-citation. All three forms occur, promiscuously, as needed by the program of Scripture.]

CLXIX:III

CLXX:II

3. Instances of the Use of [3] Citation-Form

Our special interest here is to note whether or not a passage of the Mishnah is cited in the setting of proof that taxonomy uncorrected by Scripture cannot accomplish its purpose. If we find such passages, then we shall note explicit criticism of Mishnaic logic in Sifra. If not, we shall note that where the form described above, 2., avoids criticism of the Mishnah or the Tosefta, cited verbatim.

VII:I.1 [Verse plus Tosefta-citation without joining language.]

VII:VIII.2

VII:X

VII:IX [Mishna-Tosefta not cited verbatim, but the issue is at Tosefta and is simply tacked on to the base-verse.]

IX:IV

IX:IX

X:VI.2

XI:I

XIV:III.4 [How does the priest do it + Tosefta-citation.]

XVII:I.2

XVIII:I.3

XVIII:III.1, 6 [In this connection sages have ruled....]

XIX:I

XX:I.2

XX:IV

LXX:I.2-7

LXXI:I.4-7, 24

LXXIV:I.11 [But the basic trait of the chapter as a whole is narrowly exegetical. The materials at hand are simply tacked on.]

LXXV:II

LXXVI:I.4 ["How do I know that + Tosefta citation.]

LXXVIII:I.1, 5-6, 8-11

LXXIX:I.2-11

LXXX:I.2, 6 [On this basis sages have ruled....]

(CXI:I.2. [This serves to encompass + language used in Mishna This is not an appropriate example of citation-form, since what is cited is not a fully spelled-out pericope of the Mishnah or the Tosefta, but only a standard phrase thereof.])

CXII:II.2-8 [Might one suppose that + citation of Mishnah-pericope.]

CXIV:I.5, 11-12 ["In this connection sages have ruled...."]

CLX:I

CLX:IV.2 ["On this basis...."]

CLXI:II.1 [Following commentary-form for inclusionary purposes, we have a conclusion, "The intent is..., then: that is + Mishnah-citation.]

CLXII:IV.1.R-U, 2.

CLXIII:III.1.O-U [Follows a sustained e x p o s i t i o n i n exclusionary/inclusionary form.]

CLXIV:V.3 [Tacked on to exclusionary exercise.]

CLXV:III

CLXV:IV

CLXVII:II

CLXVIII:I

CLXVIII:II.6

CLXIX:I.1: I know only...how do I know...Scripture says...on ˙ this basis have they said + Mishnah-citation.]

CLXIX:I.2-4 [Same as above]

CLXIX:II.1 [Citation of Scripture + this teaches + is not the opposite logical + I know that this is...how do i know...Scripture says....She who...Scripture says + Mishnah-citation. All three forms occur, promiscuously, as needed by the program of Scripture.]

CLXIX:IV.2 [Proof of a proposition plus "in this connection sages have said."]

CLXXI:I.3-4 [The proposition proved by Scripture is then amplified through the detail provided by the Mishnah and the Tosefta.]

CCLVI:I.1 [How do we know that + Tosefta-citation.]

4. Instances of the Use of [4] Taxonomic-Form: Miscellanies

II:I [There are thirteen passages in the Torah in which + catalogue.]

III:X.3 [A rule pertains to a beast that does not apply to....]

5. Proportions of Types of Forms in Sifra

One fact is now proven beyond all doubt. A simple formal program, consisting of three types of forms, served for every statement in the illustrative material I have now surveyed, and I think it highly likely that that same tripartite formal plan served the entire document. An author of a pericope could make use of one or more of three forms but of no other forms at all. Since, as we shall see in the following sections of this chapter, a sizable repertoire of other forms were utilized by other authorships, we may state with finality that our authorship made choices about the formal plan of its document. In a moment, we shall note that these choices corresponded to the authorship's polemical purpose in framing the document. What were these three forms? Counting each entry as a single item presents a gross and simple picture of the proportions of the types of forms we have catalogued. Since numerous entries in each of the catalogues encompass more than a single item, the understatement of the numbers of examples in any one catalogue will be balanced by understatements of the numbers of examples in the other catalogues. Overall, my count is as follows:

Form	Number of entries	Percentage of the whole
Commentary	121	55%
Dialectical	57	26%
Citation	42	19%
	220	100%

The rough proportions of forms can stand considerable refinement, but we may say with some certainty that Sifra's authorship planned to produce a commentary to the book of Leviticus, and that commentary would encompass as two major, though not ubiquitous, concerns first the demonstration that if we wish to classify things, we must follow the taxa dictated by Scripture rather than relying solely upon the traits of the things we wish to classify; and, second, the citation of passages of the Mishnah or the Tosefta in the setting of Scripture. In *Uniting the Dual Torah: Sifra and the Problem of the Mishnah,* I have spelled out what I conceive to be the purpose of our authorship. It suffices to state with considerable finality that the forms of the document admirably expressed the polemical purpose of the authorship at hand. What they wished to prove was that a taxonomy resting on the traits of things without reference to Scripture's classifications cannot serve. They further wished to restate the Oral Torah in the setting of the Written Torah. And, finally, they wished to accomplish the whole by rewriting the Written Torah. The dialectical form accomplished the first purpose, the citation-form the second, and the commentary-form the third. Let us now compare our document's formal program and plan with those of other documents.

Having shown the presence of a restricted range of choices, I still have not proved that this particular authorship made choices distinctive to itself. I have demonstrated only that, in a given rabbinic writing, a fair amount of formalization or patterning of discourse has characterized the expression at hand. That does not delineate the limns of this particular document nor does it establish a prima facie case, on superficial, rhetorical grounds, that I deal with a systematic statement of an authorship. To the contrary, we may conceive that the formal patterns before us were general to rabbinic writings, not particular to the authorship of a single document (or closely aligned group of documents). Accordingly, a brief set of comparisons is now required, to show that this authorship not only conformed to the requirement that all speech be public and formal, not private and idiosyncratic in form, but also made its own choices as to the particular formalized modes of rhetoric that that authorship would utilize. For that purpose, to be sure, only a complete survey of the results of the form analysis of all rabbinic writings suffices. Having undertaken form-analysis of most of the canonical documents of the Judaism of the dual Torah, I should not find onerous such a systematic and complete survey. Though the results are in hand, however, readers may concur that a brief overview suffices. And for a preliminary result, a comparison with the results of my studies of other documents' formal characteristics will validate the simple claim at hand, that in Sifra, as in every other rabbinic compilation of midrash-exegeses I have studied, we deal with a consensual authorship, not merely with a random sample of the kinds of writings (formalized to be sure) that occur here, there, and everywhere in the rabbinic canon. To state matters simply, what we see is not merely how people happened to say things, but choices people made in how they wished to say things: this, not that.

IV. THE REPERTOIRE OF FORMS OF SIFRÉ TO NUMBERS

Let me begin with a catalogue of the forms of Sifré to Numbers.

1. Extrinsic Exegetical Form

The form consists of the citation of an opening verse, followed by an issue stated in terms extrinsic to the cited verse. That is to say, no word or phrase of the base-verse (that is, the cited verse at the beginning) attracts comment. Rather a general rule of exegesis is invoked. C then introduces a broad range of items not at all subject to attention in the verse at hand. The formal traits: [1] citation of a base-verse from Numbers, [2] a generalization ignoring clauses or words in the base-verse, [3] a further observation without clear interest in the verse at hand. But the whole is linked to the theme of the base-verse – and to that alone. So an extrinsic exegetical program comes to bear. We shall call this the extrinsic exegetical form. The types of this form are specified as the exercise unfolds. A subdivision of this form is form C: Syllogistic argument on the meaning of words or phrases, in which the base-verse of Numbers occurs as one among a set of diverse items. Here is that syllogistic form:

I.III

1. A.   R. Judah b. Beterah says, "The effect of a commandment stated in any context serves only [1] to lend encouragement.

  B.   "For it is said, 'But command Joshua and encourage and strengthen him' (Deut. 3:28).

  C.   "Accordingly, we derive the lesson that strength is granted only to the strong, and encouragement only to the stout of heart."

  D.   R. Simeon b. Yohai says, "The purpose of a commandment in any context is only [2] to deal with the expenditure of money, as it is said, 'Command the children of Israel to bring you pure oil from beaten olives for the lamp, that a light may be kept burning continually outside the veil of the testimony in the tent of meeting, Aaron shall keep it in order from evening to morning before the Lord continually; it shall be a statute for ever throughout your generations' (Lev. 24:2). 'Command the people of Israel that they put out of the camp every leper and every one having a discharge, and every one that is unclean through contact with the dead' (Num. 5:1-2). 'Command the children of Israel that they give to the Levites from the inheritance of their possession cities to dwell in, and you shall give to the Levites pasture lands round about the cities' (Num. 35:2). 'Command the people of Israel and say to them, "My offering, my food for my offerings by fire, my pleasing odor you shall take heed to offer to me in its due season"' (Num. 28:2). Lo, we see in all these cases that the purpose of a commandment is solely to bring about the expenditure of money.

  E.   "There is one exception, and what is that? It is this verse: 'Command the people of Israel and say to them, "When you enter the land of Canaan, this is the land that shall fall to you for an inheritance, the land of Canaan in its full extent"' (Num. 34:2).

  F.   "You must give encouragement to them in the matter of the correct division of the land."

  G.   And Rabbi [Judah the Patriarch] says, "The use of the word, 'commandment' in all passages serves only for the purpose of [3] imparting an admonition [not to do a given action], along the lines of the following: 'And the Lord God commanded the man, saying, "You may freely eat of every tree of the garden, but of the tree of the knowledge of good and evil you shall not eat"' (Gen. 2:16)."

2. Intrinsic Exegetical Form

In what I call the intrinsic-exegetical form(s), the verse itself is clarified. In the first instance, the exegesis derives from the contrast with another verse that makes the same point. But the formal trait should not be missed. It is that the the focus is on the base-verse and not on a broader issue. We may call this an intrinsic exegetical form, in that the focus of exegesis is on the verse, which is cited and carefully spelled out. We shall know that we have it when the base-verse is cited, clause by clause or in other ways, and then given an ample dose of attention. The simplest example gives us the verse plus a simple declarative sentence that states the meaning. A somewhat more elaborate version will explain the purpose of a passage, thus: Citation of base-verse plus "For what purpose is this passage presented?" In a still more complex version, we find the assertion that "the passage means X, but what about possibility Y?" In this form we have the citation of a word or clause in the base-verse, followed by a declarative sentence explaining the purpose and meaning of the cited passage. Then we ask, "You say this, but perhaps it means that." Then we proceed to justify the original statement. Here is a fine example of the dialectical exegesis of an intrinsic character.

I:II

1. A.   "Command" (Num. 5:2):

    B.   The commandment at hand is meant both to be put into effect immediately and also to apply for generations to come.

    C.   You maintain that the commandment at hand is meant both to be put into effect immediately and also to apply for generations to come.

    D.   But perhaps the commandment is meant to apply only after a time [but not right away, at the moment at which it was given].

    E.   [We shall now prove that the formulation encompasses both generations to come and also the generation to whom the commandment is entrusted.] Scripture states, "The Lord said to Moses, 'Command the people of Israel that they put out [of the camp every leper and every one having a discharge, and every one that is unclean through contact with the dead. You shall put out both male and female, putting them outside the camp, that they may not defile their camp, in the midst of which I dwell.'] And the people of Israel did so and drove them outside the camp, as the Lord said to Moses, *so the people of Israel did"* (Gen. 5:1-4). [The verse itself makes explicit the fact that the requirement applied forthwith, not only later on.]

    F.   Lo, we have learned that the commandment at hand is meant to be put into effect immediately.

    G.   How then do we derive from Scripture the fact that it applies also for generations to come? [We shall now show that the same word used here, *command*, pertains to generations to come and not only to the generation at hand.]

    H.   Scripture states, "Command the children of Israel to bring you pure oil from beaten olives [for the lamp, that a light may be kept burning continually outside the veil of the testimony in the tent of meeting, Aaron shall keep it in order from evening to morning before the Lord continually; it shall be a statute for ever throughout your generations]" (Lev. 24:2).

    I.   Lo, we here derive evidence that the commandment at hand is meant both to be put into effect immediately and also to apply for generations to come, [based on the framing of the present commandment].

    J.   How, then, do we drive evidence that all of the commandments that are contained in the Torah [apply in the same way]? [We wish now to prove that the language, *command*, always bears the meaning imputed to it here.]

    K.   R. Ishmael maintained, "Since the bulk of the commandments stated in the Torah are presented without further amplification, while in the case of one of them [namely, the one at hand], Scripture has given details, that commandment [that has been singled out] is meant both to be put into effect immediately and also to apply for generations to come. Accordingly, I apply to all of the other commandments in the Torah the same detail, so that in all cases the commandment is meant both to be put into effect immediately and also to apply for generations to come."

Yet another intrinsic-exegetical form, and the most interesting, yields a dialectical exegesis. It consists of a sequence of arguments about the meaning of a passage, in which the focus is upon the base-verse, and a sequence of possibilities is introduced to spell out the meaning of that verse. At issue is not the power of logic but the meaning of the base-verse, but that issue is pursued through an argument of many stages. Here is the first example of Sifré to Numbers:

I:IV

1. A. "[The Lord said to Moses, 'Command the people of Israel that] they put out of the camp [every leper and every one having a discharge, and every one that is unclean through contact with the dead']" (Num. 5:1-2).

B. Is it from the [innermost] camp, of the Presence of God, or should I infer that it is only from the camp of the Levites?

C. Scripture states, "...they put out them of the camp." [The sense is that they are to be put outside of the camp of the Presence.]

D. Now even if Scripture had not made the matter explicit, I could have proposed the same proposition on the basis of reasoning [that they should be put outside of the camp of the Presence]:

E. If unclean people are driven out of the camp that contains the ark, which is of lesser sanctity, all the more so should they be driven out of the camp of the Presence of God, which is of greater sanctity.

F. But if you had proposed reasoning on that basis, you would have found yourself in the position of imposing a penalty merely on the basis of reason [and not on the basis of an explicit statement of Scripture, and one does not impose a penalty merely on the basis of reason].

G. That is why it is stated: "...they put out of the camp."

H. Making that matter explicit in Scripture serves to teach you that penalties are not to be imposed merely on the basis of logic [but require explicit specification in Scripture]. [That is, Scripture made a point that reason could have reached, but Scripture made the matter explicit so as to articulate a penalty applicable for violating the rule.]

I. [Rejecting that principle,] Rabbi says, "It is not necessary for Scripture to make the matter explicit, since it is a matter of an argument *a fortiori:*

J. "If the unclean people are driven out of the camp that contains the ark, which is of lesser sanctity, all the more so should they be driven out of the camp of the Presence of God, which is of greater sanctity.

K. "Then why it is stated: '...they put out of the camp every leper and every one having a discharge, and every one that is unclean through contact with the dead'?

L. "[By specifying that all three are put out of the camp,] Scripture thereby served to assign to them levels or gradations [of uncleanness, with diverse rules affecting those levels, as will now be spelled out. Since we know that that rule applies to the ostracism of the leper, the specification that the others also are to be put out of the camp indicates that a singular rule applies to each of the category. If one rule applied in common, then the specification with respect to the leper alone would have sufficed to indicate the rule for all others.]"

M.   [We review the distinctions among several gradations of uncleanness affecting human beings, inclusive of the three at hand: the leper, the one having a discharge, and the one unclean through contact with the dead.] "The Lord said to Moses, 'Command the people of Israel that they put out of the camp every leper and every one having a discharge, and every one that is unclean through contact with the dead'" (Num. 5:1-2).

N.   Shall I then draw the conclusion that all three of those listed [the leper, the one affected by a discharge, the one unclean with corpse-uncleanness] are to remain in the same locale [in relationship to the Temple]?

O.   With respect to the leper, Scripture states explicit, "He shall dwell by himself; outside of the camp shall be his dwelling" (Lev. 13:46).

P.   Now the leper fell into the same category as the others, and he has been singled out from the general category, thereby serving to impose a single rule on the category from which he has been singled out.

Q.   [And this is the rule applicable to the leper and hence to the others from among whom he has been singled out:] Just as in the case of the leper, who is subject to a most severe form of uncleanness, and who also is subjected to a more severe rule governing ostracism than that applying to his fellow, so all who are subject to a more severe form of uncleanness likewise are subject to a more severe rule of ostracism than that applying to his fellow.

R.   On this basis sages listed distinctions that apply to those that are unclean [since a different rule applies to each of them, in descending order of severity, as is now spelled out]:

S.   To any object that one affected by a flux imparts uncleanness, a leper imparts uncleanness. A leper is subject to a more severe rule, however, in that a leper imparts uncleanness through an act of sexual relations.

T.   To any object that one unclean with corpse-uncleanness imparts uncleanness, one affected by a flux imparts uncleanness. But a more severe rule affects one affected by a flux, in that he imparts uncleanness to an object located far beneath a rock in the deep [imparting uncleanness to that deeply-buried object merely by the application of the pressure of his weight, while one unclean with corpse-uncleanness does not impart uncleanness merely by pressure of his weight alone].

U.   To any object that one unclean by reason of waiting for sunset after immersion imparts uncleanness one unclean by corpse-uncleanness imparts uncleanness. A more severe rule applies to one unclean by corpse-uncleanness, for he imparts uncleanness to a human being [which is not the case of one who is unclean by reason of waiting for sunset after his immersion].

V.   What is made unfit by one who has not yet completed his rites of atonement following uncleanness and purification is made unfit by one who awaits for sunset to complete his process of purification. A more strict rule applies to one awaiting sunset for the completion of his rite of purification, for he imparts unfitness to food designated for priestly rations [while the one who has completed his rites of purification but not yet offered the atonement-sacrifice on account of his uncleanness does not impart unfitness to priestly rations that he may touch].

Another example of the working of dialectical exegesis, and the dominant one in Sifra, involves the moving demonstration of the fallacy of logic uncorrected by the exegesis of Scripture for taxonomic purposes. This is another moving, or dialectical, exegetical form, but while the basic trait is familiar – a sequence of shifts and turns in the possibility of interpretation, all of them subjected to close logical scrutiny, the purpose is different. And the purpose comes to expression not in content, particular to diverse passages, but in form. The formal indicator is the presence of the question, in one of several versions: is it not a matter of logic? That is the never-failing formal indicator. From that clause we invariably move on to a set of arguments of a highly formalized character on taxonomic classification: what is like, or unlike? What is like follows a given rule, what is unlike follows the opposite rule, and it is for us to see whether the likenesses or unlikenesses prevail. (When Ishmael's name occurs, they prevail, and when Aqiba's occurs, they do not. But these seem rather conventional.) The argument is formalized to an extreme, and there are very few variations among our document's exempla of this form, though one – the matter of length – should not be missed. The exegesis of the verse at hand plays no substantial role, beyond its initial introduction. What is critical is the issue of the reliability of logic. The base-verse before us contributes virtually nothing and in no way serves as the foundation for the composition at hand.

Another important intrinsic exegetical form in Sifré to Numbers presents the Scriptural basis for a passage of the Mishnah. In this form what we have is simply a citation of the verse plus a law in prior writing (Mishnah, Tosefta) which the verse is supposed to sustain. The formal traits require [1] citation of a verse, with or without comment, followed by [2] verbatim citation of a passage of the Mishnah or the Tosefta. Here is an example of the working of that form in Sifré to Numbers:

I:IX

1. A.   "[You shall put out both male and female, putting them outside the camp,] that they may not defile their camp, [in the midst of which I dwell]":

    B.   On the basis of this verse, the rule has been formulated:

    C.   **There are three camps, the camp of Israel, the camp of the Levitical priests, and the camp of the Presence of God. From the gate of Jerusalem to the Temple mount is the camp of Israel,**

from the gate of the Temple mount to the Temple courtyard is the camp of the Levitical priesthood, and from the gate of the courtyard and inward is the camp of the Presence of God [T. Kelim 1:12].

Yet another intrinsic exegetical form involves linking a law stated in apodictic form to a verse of Scripture. This is a somewhat less well-framed entry. Here we have a statement of a rule, in which the Mishnah or Tosefta is not cited verbatim. That is the undefined side. But the rule that is presented is not intrinsic to the verse at hand, in that the verse does not refer in any way to the case or possibility framed as the issue. In that case we do not have a clear-cut exegesis of the verse in its own terms. But we also do not have an example of the linking of Scripture to the Mishnah. An example of this type follows:

Sifré to Numbers

II:I

1.   A.   "[And the Lord said to Moses, 'Say to the people of Israel, When a man or woman commits any of the sins that men commit by breaking faith with the Lord, and that person is guilty,] he shall confess his sin which he has committed, [and he shall make full restitution for his wrong, adding a fifth to it, and giving it to him to whom he did the wrong.']" (Num. 5:5-10).

      B.   But [in stressing, "his sin," Scripture makes it clear that he does not have to make confession] for what his father did.

      C.   For if one said to him, "Give me the bailment that I left with your father," and he says, "You left no bailment," [and the other says,] "I impose an oath on you," and the first says, "Amen,"

      D.   [and if] after a while the [son] remembers [that a bailment indeed had been left and must be handed over] –

      E.   should I conclude that the son is liable [to make confession, not merely to hand over the bailment]?

      F.   Scripture says, " he shall confess his sin which *he* has committed," but he does not make confession for what his father did.

The proof-text serves for a proposition given in apodictic form. The point is that the son does not confess the father's sin, though he has to make up for it. Scripture then yields the stated law by its stress. We derive laws from the verses at hand to cover further such situations.

We now turn to the comparison of the formal repertoire of Sifra with that of Sifré to Numbers. The rhetorical program of Sifré to Numbers is substantially larger than that of the authorship of Sifra, and it is also different from the one guiding the authorship of Sifré to Deuteronomy. Let me present my formulation of that program as I gave it in my *Sifré to Numbers* (Atlanta: Scholars Press for Brown Judaic Studies, 1986).

I cannot find a counterpart in our document among the rhetorical forms I have identified. But those propositional compositions which merely cite, in a context established by a generalization, a verse of Deuteronomy do run parallel to what, in Sifré to Numbers, I called the syllogistic argument on the meaning of words or phrases, in which the base-verse of Numbers occurs as one among a set of diverse items. I do not find Sifra's commentary-form to constitute a counterpart, since the ordinary purpose of commentary-form in Sifra is not to develop a generalization. It is rather to identify the sense of a passage by asking what is included or excluded within the rule of the passage, as numerous examples in my catalogues have already indicated. However, comparison of commentary-form, as designated earlier, with the extrinsic exegetical form of Sifré to Numbers will show more graphically that, while formally similarl in basic structure and purpose, the two types of patterns in fact bear no important traits in common. Here is an example drawn from Sifré to Numbers (noting in italics the type of phrase without counterpart in Sifra):

Sifré to Numbers

I:III

1.   A.   R. Judah b. Beterah says, "The effect of a commandment stated in any context serves only [1] to lend encouragement.

        B.   *"For it is said, 'But command Joshua and encourage and strengthen him' (Deut. 3:28).*

        C.   *"Accordingly, we derive the lesson that strength is granted only to the strong, and encouragement only to the stout of heart."*

        D.   *R. Simeon b. Yohai says, "The purpose of a commandment in any context is only [2] to deal with the expenditure of money, as it is said, 'Command the children of Israel to bring you pure oil from beaten olives for the lamp, that a light may be kept burning continually outside the veil of the testimony in the tent of meeting, Aaron shall keep it in order from evening to morning before the Lord continually; it shall be a statute for ever throughout your generations' (Lev. 24:2). 'Command the people of Israel that they put out of the camp every leper and every one having a discharge, and every one that is unclean through contact with the dead' (Num. 5:1-2). 'Command the children of Israel that they give to the Levites from the inheritance of their possession cities to dwell in, and you shall give to the Levites pasture lands round about the cities' (Num. 35:2). 'Command the people of Israel and say to them, "My offering, my food for my offerings by fire, my pleasing odor you shall take heed to offer to me in its due season"' (Num. 28:2). Lo, we see in all these cases that the purpose of a commandment is solely to bring about the expenditure of money.*

        E.   *"There is one exception, and what is that? It is this verse: 'Command the people of Israel and say to them, "When you enter the land of Canaan, this is the land that shall fall to you for an inheritance, the land of Canaan in its full extent' (Num. 34:2).*

        F.   *"You must give encouragement to them in the matter of the correct division of the land."*

G.　*And Rabbi [Judah the Patriarch] says, "The use of the word,*
　　'commandment' in all passages serves only for the purpose of [3]
　　imparting an admonition [not to do a given action], along the lines of
　　the following: 'And the Lord God commanded the man, saying, "You
　　may freely eat of every tree of the garden, but of the tree of the
　　knowledge of good and evil you shall not eat"' (Gen. 2:16)."

It is perfectly clear that Sifra's citation and amplification has no
relationship to the extrinsic exegetical form before us.

2.　Intrinsic Exegetical Form

The verse itself is clarified. In the first instance, the exegesis derives
from the contrast with another verse that makes the same point. But the
formal trait should not be missed. It is that the the focus is on the base-
verse and not on a broader issue. We may call this an intrinsic exegetical
form, in that the focus of exegesis is on the verse, which is cited and
carefully spelled out. We shall know that we have it when the base-verse is
cited, clause by clause or in other ways, and then given an ample dose of
attention. Here we do have an exact formal counterpart, a rhetorical
pattern shared by the authorships of all three documents – Sifra and the
two Sifrés. It is the smallest, and also the most widely shared, building
block of formal expression I can identify in the diverse compilations of
scriptural exegesis. It consists, as is clear, of a verse plus a simple
declarative sentence that states the meaning. A subdivision will give us the
citation of base-verse plus "For what purpose is this passage presented?"
Here is an example in Sifré to Numbers:

Sifré to Numbers

I:I

1.　A.　"The Lord said to Moses, 'Command the people of Israel that they put
　　　out of the camp [every leper and every one having a discharge, and
　　　every one that is unclean through contact with the dead]'" (Num. 5:1-2).

　　B.　For what purpose is this passage presented?

　　C.　Because it is said, "But the man who is unclean and does not cleanse
　　　himself, [that person shall be cut off from the midst of the assembly,
　　　since he has defiled the sanctuary of the Lord, because the water for
　　　impurity has not been thrown upon him, he is unclean]" (Num. 19:20).

　　D.　Consequently, we are informed of the penalty [for contaminating the
　　　sanctuary]. But where are we informed of the admonition not to do
　　　so?

　　E.　Scripture accordingly states, "Command the people of Israel that they
　　　put out of the camp every leper and every one having a discharge, and
　　　every one that is unclean through contact with the dead" (Num. 5:1-2).

　　F.　Lo, here is an admonition that unclean persons not come into the
　　　sanctuary ["out of the camp"] in a state of uncleanness. [Consequently,
　　　the entire transaction – admonition, then penalty – is laid forth.]

Here we do find ourselves on familiar ground, but only in part. We have numerous counterparts to B: "For what purpose is this passage presented?" But it is unusual indeed for a different verse, selected from some other passage altogether, to be introduced by Sifra's authorship in response to the question of B. Still, intrinsic exegetical form as followed in Sifré to Numbers and the commentary-form of Sifra bear strong affinities and in some measure serve the same purpose in the same way.

Another variation will have the citation of a word or clause in the base-verse, followed by a declarative sentence explaining the purpose and meaning of the cited passage. Then we ask, "You say this, but perhaps it means that." Then we proceed to justify the original statement. The dialectical mode – moving from point to point – is common to both compositions, but the particular rhetorical pattern that follows is not shared with our document.

Sifré to Numbers

I:II

1. A. "Command" (Num. 5:2):

    B. The commandment at hand is meant both to be put into effect immediately and also to apply for generations to come.

    C. You maintain that the commandment at hand is meant both to be put into effect immediately and also to apply for generations to come.

    D. But perhaps the commandment is meant to apply only after a time [but not right away, at the moment at which it was given].

    E. [We shall now prove that the formulation encompasses both generations to come and also the generation to whom the commandment is entrusted.] Scripture states, "The Lord said to Moses, 'Command the people of Israel that they put out [of the camp every leper and every one having a discharge, and every one that is unclean through contact with the dead. You shall put out both male and female, putting them outside the camp, that they may not defile their camp, in the midst of which I dwell.'] And the people of Israel did so and drove them outside the camp, as the Lord said to Moses, *so the people of Israel did*" (Gen. 5:1-4). [The verse itself makes explicit the fact that the requirement applied forthwith, not only later on.]

    F. Lo, we have learned that the commandment at hand is meant to be put into effect immediately.

    G. How then do we derive from Scripture the fact that it applies also for generations to come? [We shall now show that the same word used here, *command*, pertains to generations to come and not only to the generation at hand.]

    H. Scripture states, "Command the children of Israel to bring you pure oil from beaten olives [for the lamp, that a light may be kept burning continually outside the veil of the testimony in the tent of meeting, Aaron shall keep it in order from evening to morning before the Lord continually; it shall be a statute for ever throughout your generations]" (Lev. 24:2).

I. Lo, we here derive evidence that the commandment at hand is meant both to be put into effect immediately and also to apply for generations to come, [based on the framing of the present commandment].

J. How, then, do we drive evidence that all of the commandments that are contained in the Torah [apply in the same way]? [We wish now to prove that the language, *command*, always bears the meaning imputed to it here.]

K. R. Ishmael maintained, "Since the bulk of the commandments stated in the Torah are presented without further amplification, while in the case of one of them [namely, the one at hand], Scripture has given explicit details, that commandment [that has been singled out] is meant both to be put into effect immediately and also to apply for generations to come. Accordingly, I apply to all of the other commandments in the Torah the same detail, so that in all cases the commandment is meant both to be put into effect immediately and also to apply for generations to come."

At stake here is the demonstration of propositions, and that is rarely the upshot of the appearance of the commentary-form in Sifra.

The authorship of Sifré to Numbers also will present, in a fixed rhetorical pattern, a sequence of arguments about the meaning of a passage, in which the focus is upon the base-verse, and a sequence of possibilities is introduced to spell out the meaning of that verse. At issue is not the power of logic but the meaning of the base-verse, but that issue is pursued through an argument of many stages.

Sifré to Numbers

I:IV

1. A. "[The Lord said to Moses, 'Command the people of Israel that] they put out of the camp [every leper and every one having a discharge, and every one that is unclean through contact with the dead']" (Num. 5:1-2).

B. Is it from the [innermost] camp, of the Presence of God, or should I infer that it is only from the camp of the Levites?

C. Scripture states, "...they put out them of the camp." [The sense is that they are to be put outside of the camp of the Presence.]

D. Now even if Scripture had not made the matter explicit, I could have proposed the same proposition on the basis of reasoning [that they should be put outside of the camp of the Presence]:

E. If unclean people are driven out of the camp that contains the ark, which is of lesser sanctity, all the more so should they be driven out of the camp of the Presence of God, which is of greater sanctity.

F. But if you had proposed reasoning on that basis, you would have found yourself in the position of imposing a penalty merely on the basis of reason [and not on the basis of an explicit statement of Scripture, and one does not impose a penalty merely on the basis of reason].

G. That is why it is stated: "...they put out of the camp."

H.   Making that matter explicit in Scripture serves to teach you that penalties are not to be imposed merely on the basis of logic [but require explicit specification in Scripture]. [That is, Scripture made a point that reason could have reached, but Scripture made the matter explicit so as to articulate a penalty applicable for violating the rule.]

I.   [Rejecting that principle,] Rabbi says, "It is not necessary for Scripture to make the matter explicit, since it is a matter of an argument *a fortiori:*

J.   "If the unclean people are driven out of the camp that contains the ark, which is of lesser sanctity, all the more so should they be driven out of the camp of the Presence of God, which is of greater sanctity.

K.   "Then why it is stated: '...they put out of the camp every leper and every one having a discharge, and every one that is unclean through contact with the dead'?

L.   "[By specifying that all three are put out of the camp,] Scripture thereby served to assign to them levels or gradations [of uncleanness, with diverse rules affecting those levels, as will now be spelled out. Since we know that that rule applies to the ostracism of the leper, the specification that the others also are to be put out of the camp indicates that a singular rule applies to each of the category. If one rule applied in common, then the specification with respect to the leper alone would have sufficed to indicate the rule for all others.]"

M.   [We review the distinctions among several gradations of uncleanness affecting human beings, inclusive of the three at hand: the leper, the one having a discharge, and the one unclean through contact with the dead.] "The Lord said to Moses, 'Command the people of Israel that they put out of the camp every leper and every one having a discharge, and every one that is unclean through contact with the dead'" (Num. 5:1-2).

N.   Shall I then draw the conclusion that all three of those listed [the leper, the one affected by a discharge, the one unclean with corpse-uncleanness] are to remain in the same locale [in relationship to the Temple]?

O.   With respect to the leper, Scripture states explicit, "He shall dwell by himself; outside of the camp shall be his dwelling" (Lev. 13:46).

P.   Now the leper fell into the same category as the others, and he has been singled out from the general category, thereby serving to impose a single rule on the category from which he has been singled out.

Q.   [And this is the rule applicable to the leper and hence to the others from among whom he has been singled out:] Just as in the case of the leper, who is subject to a most severe form of uncleanness, and who also is subjected to a more severe rule governing ostracism than that applying to his fellow, so all who are subject to a more severe form of uncleanness likewise are subject to a more severe rule of ostracism than that applying to his fellow.

R.   On this basis sages listed distinctions that apply to those that are unclean [since a different rule applies to each of them, in descending order of severity, as is now spelled out]:

S.   To any object that one affected by a flux imparts uncleanness, a leper imparts uncleanness. A leper is subject to a more severe rule, however, in that a leper imparts uncleanness through an act of sexual relations.

T.   To any object that one unclean with corpse-uncleanness imparts uncleanness, one affected by a flux imparts uncleanness. But a more severe rule affects one affected by a flux, in that he imparts uncleanness to an object located far beneath a rock in the deep [imparting uncleanness to that deeply-buried object merely by the application of the pressure of his weight, while one unclean with corpse-uncleanness does not impart uncleanness merely by pressure of his weight alone].

U.   To any object that one unclean by reason of waiting for sunset after immersion imparts uncleanness one unclean by corpse-uncleanness imparts uncleanness. A more severe rule applies to one unclean by corpse-uncleanness, for he imparts uncleanness to a human being [which is not the case of one who is unclean by reason of waiting for sunset after his immersion].

V.   What is made unfit by one who has not yet completed his rites of atonement following uncleanness and purification is made unfit by one who awaits for sunset to complete his process of purification. A more strict rule applies to one awaiting sunset for the completion of his rite of purification, for he imparts unfitness to food designated for priestly rations [while the one who has completed his rites of purification but not yet offered the atonement-sacrifice on account of his uncleanness does not impart unfitness to priestly rations that he may touch].

I am at a loss to identify, in Sifra, compositions that form a counterpart to this interesting exposition. In many ways this kind of writing places us within the orbit of Sifré to Deuteronomy, which contains highly propositional compositions indeed. Where we have this sort of sustained exposition in Sifra, in general one of two purposes will be served. Either we shall show the limitations of taxonomy attempted outside the framework of Scripture. Or we shall discover the inclusionary and exclusionary intent of Scripture. Those two methodical inquiries of analysis cover most of the examples of sustained propositional discourse in Sifra.

Dialectical exegesis pointed toward proving the fallacy of logic uncontrolled by exegesis of Scripture is common in Sifra and in Sifré to Numbers. The formal indicator is the presence of the question, in one of several versions: is it not a matter of logic? That is the never-failing formal indicator. From that clause we invariably move on to a set of arguments of a highly formalized character on taxonomic classification: what is like, or unlike? The exegesis of the verse at hand plays no substantial role, beyond its initial introduction. What is critical is the issue of the reliability of logic. The base-verse before us contributes virtually nothing and in no way serves as the foundation for the composition at hand. Formally, items in this pattern can readily have found a comfortable home in the other Sifré, our Sifré, as much as in Sifra. So too the variation, which gives us simply a citation of the verse plus a law in prior writing (Mishnah, Tosefta) which the verse is supposed to sustain, is common among all three writings. The formal traits require [1] citation of a verse, with or without comment, followed by [2] verbatim citation of a passage of the Mishnah or the Tosefta. What I called citation-form in Sifra in no important way differs from the following pattern:

Sifré to Numbers

I:IX

1. A.   "[You shall put out both male and female, putting them outside the camp,] that they may not defile their camp, [in the midst of which I dwell]":

   B.   On the basis of this verse, the rule has been formulated:

   C.   **There are three camps, the camp of Israel, the camp of the Levitical priests, and the camp of the Presence of God. From the gate of Jerusalem to the Temple mount is the camp of Israel, from the gate of the Temple mount to the Temple courtyard is the camp of the Levitical priesthood, and from the gate of the courtyard and inward is the camp of the Presence of God [T. Kelim 1:12].**

I find in Sifré to Numbers also a few items that in form do not pretend to provide an exegesis of Scripture at all. All are narratives. These stories fall entirely outside of the formal range of both Sifrés. They present stunning proof that the two documents' authorships proposed an exegetical program, defined very narrowly. Sifra has no counterparts, so far as I see matters.

No form in the pages of Sifra, Sifré to Numbers, and Sifré to Deuteronomy, serves an other-than-exegetical task – not one. The document contains only exegetical materials; these exceptions prove the rule. When comparison and contrast to Genesis Rabbah and Leviticus Rabbah go forward, that fact will take on meaning. We see the precision of definition that governed the work of our authorships: this, not that. They knew not only what they wanted, but also what they did not want.

V. THE REPERTOIRE OF FORMS OF SIFRÉ TO DEUTERONOMY: TYPES AND PROPORTIONS

Sifré to Deuteronomy presents a far more propositional composition than either Sifra or Sifré to Numbers. Our classification of the patterns of rhetoric in that document therefore draws attention to the manner in which propositions are set forth, a classification that, in general, cannot serve in Sifra at all. I may state very simply the results of already published research. Nine recurrent patterns prove dominant in Sifré to Deuteronomy. We distinguish among them by the presence of propositions, explicit, and then implicit, and how these are argued or proved:

1. **Propositions Stated Explicitly and Argued Philosophically (By Appeal to Probative Facts)**

    1. The Proposition and its Syllogistic Argument
    2. The Proposition Based on the Classification of Probative Facts
    3. The Proposition Based on the Recurrent Opinions of Sages
    4. The Narrative and its Illustrated Proposition: Parable
    5. Narrative and its Illustrated Proposition: Scriptural Story

2. **Propositions Stated Implicitly but Argued Philosophically (As Above)**

    6. The (Implicit) Proposition Based on Facts Derived from Exegesis
    7. The Priority of Exegesis and the Limitations of Logic

3. **Facts That Do Not Yield Propositions beyond Themselves**

    8. Exegetical Form with No Implicit Proposition. This is one form with a clear counterpart in Sifra.

4. **Facts That Do Not Yield Propositions Particular to the Case at Hand**

    9. Dialectical Exegesis with No Implicit Proposition Pertinent to the Case at Hand but with Bearing on Large-Scale Structural Issues. This form is the same as our dialectical-exegetical one.

Let me now review the catalogue just now given and spell out the formal traits of the patterns I have identified.

I. PROPOSITIONS STATED EXPLICITLY AND ARGUED PHILOSOPHICALLY

1. **The Proposition and its Syllogistic Argument**

This form is made up of simple sentences, in one way or another, which set forth propositions and demonstrate them by amassing probative facts, e.g., examples. The patterning of the individual sentences of course varies. But the large scale rhetoric, involving the presentation of a proposition, in general terms, and then the amassing of probative facts (however the sentences are worded), is essentially uniform. What we have are two or more sentences formed into a proposition and an argument, by contrast to those that are essentially singleton sentences, rather than components of a more sustained discourse. These items ordinarily deal with matters of proper conduct or right action, hence *halakhic* issues. There is a two-layer discourse in them, since, at the superficial level, they yield only a detail of a law, that is, thus and so is the rule here; but at the deep layer of thought, they demonstrate a prevailing and global proposition, that applies – it is implied – throughout, and not only to a single case. Overall, rhetorical analysis draws our attention to modes of stating a middle level proposition, affecting a variety of verses and their cases, in the present list. Then we move onward, to the low level proposition, that pertains only to a single case, and, finally, we turn to a global proposition, that affects a broad variety of cases, left discrete, but homogenizes them. These distinctions are meant to explain the classification system represented here. The absence of a counterpart in Sifra hardly requires proof.

2. The Proposition Based on the Classification of Probative Facts

The prevailing pattern here is not vastly changed. This is different from the foregoing only in a minor matter. In this case we shall propose to prove a proposition, e.g., the meaning of a word, by classifying facts that point toward that proposition. In the foregoing, the work of proof is accomplished through listing proofs made up of diverse facts. The difference between the one and the other is hardly very considerable, but I think we can successfully differentiate among the formal patterns through the stated criterion. However, one may reasonably argue that this catalogue and the foregoing list essentially the same formal patterns of language or argument. In many of these instances, we have a complex development of a simple exegesis, and it is at the complexity – the repeated use of a simple pattern – that the propositional form(s) reach full exposure. Sifra's authorship has no use for such a pattern.

3. The Proposition Based on the Recurrent Opinions of Sages

This is another variation, in that the nature of the evidence shifts, and, it follows, also the patterning of language. Here we shall have the attributive constantly present, e.g., X says, and that does form an important rhetorical indicator. We may say flatly that this form is not characteristic of our authorship and accomplishes none of their goals. It is a commonplace in the Mishnah, inclusive of tractate Avot, and in the Tosefta; large-scale compositions in the Yerushalmi and the Bavli follow the same pattern; and other large-scale compositions will be drawn together because a sequence of simple declarative sentences on diverse topics, whether or not related in theme, bears the same attributive. The omission of this pattern here therefore is noteworthy and constitutes a decision for one pattern and against another. I know of no material equivalent in Sifra.

4-5. The Narrative and Its Illustrated Proposition: The Scriptural Story. Also: The Parable as Illustration of an Established Proposition

The construction in which a proposition is established and then illustrated in a narrative, whether parable, scriptural story, or other kind of narrative, is treated in a single rubric. The formal-structural uniformity justifies doing so. We may find varieties of patterns of sentences, e.g., parables as against stories. But the narrative is always marked by either, "he said to him...he said to him...," for the story, or counterpart indications of a select pattern of forming and arranging sentences, for the parable.[3] The authorship of Sifré to Deuteronomy has resorted to a very limited repertoire of patterns of language, and "narrative," a gross and hardly refined, classification, suffices. For narratives, viewed as an encompassing formal category, do not play a large role in defining (therefore differentiating) the rhetorical-logical program of our authorship. Sifra's authorship scarcely presents stories of this kind.

II. PROPOSITIONS STATED IMPLICITLY BUT ARGUED PHILOSOPHICALLY

6. Implicit Propositions

These items involve lists of facts, but lack that clear statement of the proposition that the facts establish. What we have here are complexes of tightly joined declarative sentences, many of them (in the nature of things) in that atom-pattern, "commentary-form," but all of them joined into a much larger set of (often) highly formalized statements. Hence I characterize this form as an implicit proposition based on facts derived from exegesis. For obvious reasons, there is no counterpart in Sifra.

III. FACTS THAT DO NOT YIELD PROPOSITIONS BEYOND THEMSELVES

7. Exegetical Form with No Implicit Proposition

This simple exegetical form presents a single fact, a discrete sentence, left without further development and without association or affinity with surrounding statements – once more, "commentary-form." The form is as defined: clause + phrase. In Sifra this is the single most common pattern, as we saw. But in Sifré to Deuteronomy that same form in the propositional compositions rarely occurs without development, and if I had to specify the one fundamental difference between non-propositional exegetical form (such as we find in Sifra and Sifré to Numbers and in some

---

[3]Further differentiation, to identify the diverse forms of narrative, is not required here. For The Fathers According to Rabbi Nathan, I have carried out that work of differentiation, in my *Judaism and Story*.

measure in Sifré to Deuteronomy) and all other forms, it is in the simplicity of the one as against the complexity of the other. Or, to state matters more bluntly, excluding narrative, the sole rhetorical building block of any consequence in Sifra, Sifré to Numbers, and Sifré to Deuteronomy is the simple exegetical one, consisting of clause + phrase = sentence.

But then the differences from one document to the other have to be specified. What differentiates Sifra and Sifré to Numbers from Sifré to Deuteronomy? In the last-named document, what happens is that all other forms develop the simple atom into a complex molecule, but the "exegetical form with no implicit proposition" remains at the atomic level (if not an even smaller particle than the atom) and never gains the molecular one. These therefore constitute entirely comprehensible sense units, that is, on their own, simple sentences, never formed into paragraphs, and define the lowest rhetorical form of our document. The other rhetorical forms build these simple sense units or sentences into something more complex. That fact of rhetoric accounts, also, for our having – willy-nilly – to appeal to considerations of logical cogency in our analysis of rhetoric and form.

IV. FACTS THAT DO NOT YIELD PROPOSITIONS PARTICULAR TO THE CASE AT HAND

8. Dialectical Exegesis with No Implicit Proposition Pertinent to the Case at Hand but with Bearing on Large-Scale Structural Issues

Here we deal with the same pattern that, in Sifra, we have called dialectical-exegetical form. The purpose of the form in Sifra is limited to the two purposes of, first, exclusionary-inclusionary inquiry, and, second, the critique of non-scripturally-based taxonomy, while in Sifré to Deuteronomy a variety of propositions will be served. This form is made up of a series of closely joined thought-units or sentences. Hence they present us with two or more sentences that constitute joined, propositional paragraphs. But their rhetorical traits are so much more particular, and their net effect so much more distinctive, that I treat them as a quite distinct rhetorical phenomenon. Moreover, these are the most patterned, the most formed, of all formal compositions at hand. They require sustained exposition of a proposition, not a simple proposition plus probative facts. They all make two points, as I have already pointed out, one at the surface, the other through the deep structure. Strictly speaking, as sustained and complex forms, all of these items conform most exactly to the fundamental definition of a rhetorical form, language that coheres to a single pattern. And the pattern is one of both rhetoric and also logic.

Two such patterns are, first, the systematic analytical exercise of restricting or extending the application of a discrete rule, ordinarily signified through stereotype language; second, the demonstration that logic without revelation in the form of a scriptural formulation and exegesis produces unreliable results. There are other recurrent patterns of complex linguistic formation matched by sustained thought that conform to the indicative traits yielded by these two distinct ones. The form invariably involves either the exercise of generalization through extension or restriction of the rule to the case given in Scripture, or the demonstration that reason unaided by Scripture is not reliable. The formal traits are fairly uniform, even though the intent – the upshot of the dialectical exegesis – varies from instance to instance. Very often these amplifications leave the base-verse far behind, since they follow a program of their own, to which the base-verse and its information is at best contributory. One of the ways in which this formalization of language differs from the foregoing is that the exegesis that is simple in form always is closely tied to the base-verse, while the one which pursues larger-scale structural issues very frequently connects only very loosely to the base-verse. Another persistent inquiry, external to any given verse and yielding, in concrete terms, no general rule at all, asks how to harmonize two verses, the information of which seems to conflict. The result is a general proposition that verses are to be drawn into alignment with one another. Here, we see, we are entirely at home. Sifra and Sifré to Deuteronomy have in common the usage of the dialectical-exegetical form for pretty much the same purposes. So much for Sifré to Deuteronomy. Sifra bears affinities of patterning of language with both Sifrés, but also differs in noteworthy ways from each of them. The three have traits in common and also traits particular to themselves. In form-analytical terms they form three species of a single genus, as comparison with the Rabbah-compilations will now show us.

VI. ANOTHER GENUS ALTOGETHER: THE FORMS OF THE RABBAH-COMPILATIONS, GENESIS RABBAH, LEVITICUS RABBAH, AND PESIQTA DERAB KAHANA

To show that the two Sifrés together with Sifra form three species of one genus of form, we turn to a counterpart set of documents, which have their own shared preferences. We begin with Genesis Rabbah. The atom of formal composition in Genesis Rabbah is what I call the exegetical form. But how it is used in the construction of molecules – sustained propositional thought – differentiates one document from the next.

I find three formal patterns in Genesis Rabbah. One juxtaposes a given verses of the book of Genesis with a verse chosen from some other biblical writing; the second focuses upon a verse of the book of Genesis, read by itself; the third makes use of a verse of the book of Genesis in establishing a proposition of a syllogistic character. There is no counterpart to any of this in Sifra, since Sifra's authorship deals with verses in Leviticus and rarely invokes verses from other books, except in the context of demonstrating propositions. To state matters differently, the citation of a verse from some book other than Leviticus never forms part of the established formal or structural pattern of a pericope of Sifra. But it is constant in the Rabbah-compilations.

All three formal patterns aim at conveying propositions, and the formal traits dictate whether the topic at hand is (I) the interplay of the base-verse with some other verse, (II) the meaning of the base-verse, or (III) the proof of a proposition abstracted from the context established by the base-verse (that is, the book of Genesis) in particular. Our formal criterion for differentiating the first two forms is the placement of a verse, e.g., at the beginning or at the end of a passage. The criterion for identifying form III is no more subjective, since anyone can tell that verses derive from a variety of books of Scripture and equally serve as proof for a proposition distinct from them all. Form I has absolutely no counterpart in the formal repertoire of Sifré to Deuteronomy. Form II has corresponding forms, and so does form III. So what differentiates the formal repertoire of Genesis Rabbah from that of Sifré to Deuteronomy is clear; one authorship has made use of a form the other authorship has not found useful. Let me briefly describe the forms to which I have alluded, for a closer look will now show that forms I and II have no substantial equivalent in our document, though form III does.

Form I: when a verse from a biblical book other than Genesis occurs at the beginning of the passage, a single formal pattern follows: exposition of that other verse, which I have called the intersecting-verse, followed by juxtaposition of the intersecting-verse with a verse of the book of Genesis.

I. THE INTERSECTING-VERSE/BASE-VERSE FORM

1. Attribution + joining language + intersecting-verse.
2. Exposition of the intersecting-verse.
3. Reciprocal exposition of the base-verse and the intersecting-verse.

Form **II**: when a verse from the book of Genesis occurs at the beginning of the passage, then the focus of discourse will rest upon the exposition of that verse alone. The difference from Sifra is self-evident.

II. EXEGESIS OF A VERSE OF SCRIPTURE

A. Citation of the base-verse (which will always be a verse chosen from the larger passage subject to interpretation, not a verse chosen from some other book of the Scripture).

B. Comment of a given rabbi. The comment is formulated in diverse ways.

C. Secondary, miscellaneous materials will be appended. Sifra exhibits no counterpart.

Form **III**: when a given syllogism comes to expression at the beginning of a passage, followed by a broad range of verses, made up ordinarily as a list exhibiting fixed syntactic preferences, then the focus of discourse will require proof of the syllogism, not exposition of the verses cited in evidence for the facticity of that syllogism.

III. SYLLOGISTIC COMPOSITION

A. Statement of a syllogism or proposition.

B. Verses of Scripture that prove or illustrate that syollogism, listed in a catalogue of relevant evidence.

C. Secondary expansion: miscellanies (e.g., stories) on the syllogism, providing further illustration.

We have counterparts or parallels to this form, commonly in Sifré to Deuteronomy, only very rarely in Sifra. The formal requirement invariably is the composition of a list, a repertoire of facts ordinarily formulated in a single syntactic pattern. A syllogistic composition makes a point autonomous of the verse at hand. In this type of composition, the point of interest is in not the exposition of a verse but the proposition that is subject to demonstration, the proofs of course deriving from various verses of Scripture.

Leviticus Rabbah is made up of thirty-seven *parashiyyot*, and each *parashah* is comprised of from as few as five to as many as fifteen subdivisions. These subdivisions in the main form cogent statements. Some of the *pisqaot* of Sifré to Deuteronomy form cogent demonstrations of a single proposition; most do not. A taxonomy of units of discourse of Leviticus Rabbah proves congruent to that of Genesis Rabbah. The first (form **I**) is familiar: (1) a verse of the book of Leviticus will be followed by

(2) a verse from some other book of the Hebrew Scriptures. The latter (2) will then be subjected to extensive discussion. But in the end the exposition of the intersecting-verse will shed some light, in some way, upon (1) the base-verse, cited at the outset. The second form (form **II**) is the exegetical one, in which a verse of Leviticus is cited and then explained. The sustained analysis and amplification makes no reference to an intersecting-verse but to numerous proof-texts, or to no proof-texts at all The third form (form **III**) is simply the citation of a verse of the book of Leviticus followed by an exegetical comment, corresponding to form **II** in Genesis Rabbah. Form **IV** represents a miscellany, no formal traits at all being discernible by me.

In the intersecting-verse/base-verse pattern we have an intersecting-verse, then the base-verse, then interpretation of the latter in terms of the form. So the base-verse is read in light of the intersecting-verse, which itself is not unpacked. In form **II**, the verse-by-verse exegetical construction, the base-verse is cited and then subjected to systematic amplification in some way or other. The form is characterized by the preliminary citation of the base-verse (not much of a formalization of syntax or composition, to be sure). It corresponds, overall, to the exegetical-form of Sifré to Deuteronomy. I find in Leviticus Rabbah no sustained formal counterpart to the methodical-analytical syntactic pattern of Sifré to Deuteronomy, and, it follows, none whatsoever to the formal preferences of the authorship of Sifra.

Another important difference between the rhetorical programs of Leviticus Rabbah and Sifré to Deuteronomy and Sifra is that the former follows a rigid pattern in ordering its rhetorical types, always placing at the head of a sustained unit of thought (corresponding to our *pisqa*) the intersecting-verse/base-verse form, following with its other forms. There is in Sifré to Deuteronomy simply no single form that always stands at the head of a sustained exposition of a verse or set of verses. That is to say, the framer of a passage intended for use in Leviticus Rabbah ordinarily began with a base-verse/intersecting-verse construction. He very commonly proceeded with an intersecting-verse/base-verse construction (a distinction important in my analysis of Leviticus Rabbah). These would correspond to both sorts of form **I** in Genesis Rabbah. The upshot is that Leviticus Rabbah much more strictly follows a clear program in laying out types of forms of units of discourse, nearly always preferring to place form **I** prior to form **II**, and so on down. Does this careful ordering of types of forms represent a clear choice? I think it can be shown that it does, simply by pointing out a contrary fact.

The organizers of Genesis Rabbah, by contrast, did not so conscientiously follow a similar program. What would the authorities who ordered Leviticus Rabbah choose for the secondary amplification of their composition? First, as is clear, the framer would take a composition in form **I**. Then he would provide such exegeses of pertinent verses of Leviticus as he had in hand. He would conclude either with form **III** (parallel in Genesis Rabbah: form **II**) or form **IV** constructions, somewhat more commonly the latter than the former. When we observe that Genesis Rabbah does not appear so carefully arranged in the order of types of forms of units of discourse, that judgment now appears to rest upon the comparison of two documents, Leviticus Rabbah and Genesis Rabbah. It no longer sets upon foundations of impression and rough and ready guesswork. Thus Leviticus Rabbah consists of two main forms of units of discourse, first in position, expositions of how verses of the book of Leviticus relate to verses of other books of the Hebrew Bible, second in position, exposition of verses of the book of Leviticus viewed on their own, and, varying in position but in any event very often concluding a construction, miscellaneous materials. We have already noted the indifference of Sifra's authorship to the order of types of forms.

We come now to the closest companion of Leviticus Rabbah, which is Pesiqta deRab Kahana. Pesiqta deRab Kahana's authorship resorted to three rhetorical patterns:

1. The Propositional Form

The implicit syllogism is stated through the intervention of an contrastive-verse into the basic proposition established by the base-verse. This form cites the base-verse, then a contrastive-verse. Sometimes the base-verse is not cited at the outset, but it is always used to mark the conclusion of the *pisqa*. The sense of the latter is read into the former, and a syllogism is worked out, and reaches intelligible expression, through the contrast and comparison of the one and the other. There is no pretense at a systematic exegesis of the diverse meanings imputed to the contrastive-verse, only the comparison and contrast of two verses, the external or intersecting and the base-verses, respectively. The base-verse, for its part, also is not subjected to systematic exegesis. This represents, therefore, a strikingly abstract and general syllogistic pattern, even though verses are cited to give the statement the formal character of an exegesis. But it is in no way an exegetical pattern. The purpose of this pattern is to impute to the base-verse the sense generated by the intersection of the base-verse and the contrastive-verse. This form corresponds to the intersecting-verse/base-verse form of Genesis Rabbah and Leviticus Rabbah; and there is no counterpart in Sifré to Deuteronomy.

2. The Exegetical Form

The implicit syllogism is stated through a systematic exegesis of the components of the base-verse on their own. This of course corresponds in a general way to our exegetical form.

3. The Syllogistic List

The syllogism is explicit, not implicit, and is proven by a list of probative examples. This clearly corresponds to our propositional form in which a syllogism is proven by a list of pertinent cases, one of them involving a verse from the book of Deuteronomy.

The nature of these rhetorical preferences also suggests that the order in which these types of forms occur will be as just now given, first the syllogism generated by the intersection of the contrastive- and base-verses, then the syllogism repeated through a systematic reading of the base-verse on its own, finally, whatever miscellanies the framers have in hand (or later copyists insert). There is no ordering of types of rhetorical patterns in Sifré to Deuteronomy. There is a further important difference. The propositions I can identify in Sifré to Deuteronomy overall are episodic. They are many, and they surely do not dominate the composition as a whole. And, as we shall presently see, I find no sustained propositional program whatever in Sifra. By contrast, Leviticus Rabbah's authorship makes thirty-seven propositional statements. Along these same lines Pesiqta deRab Kahana consists of twenty-eight syllogisms, each presented in a cogent and systematic way by the twenty-eight *pisqaot*, respectively. Each *pisqa* contains an implicit proposition, and that proposition may be stated in a simple way. It emerges from the intersection of an external verse with the base-verse that recurs through the *pisqa*, and then is restated by the systematic dissection of the components of the base-verse, each of which is shown to say the same thing as all the others. Each *pisqa* of Pesiqta deRab Kahana is made up of from four to twenty subdivisions, and each subdivision is made up of from one to fifteen of the same. The *pisqaot* then make each its own point. One definitive (I think, generative) trait of Pesiqta deRab Kahana's *pisqaot* and of Leviticus Rabbah's *parashiyyot* is the cogency of the *pisqa*, viewed whole, and we cannot remotely suggest a counterpart trait in our composition.

VII. THE COMPARISON: ALIKE AND NOT ALIKE

By focusing upon the gross and blatant traits of formalization, examining a rough-and-ready mixture of rhetorical and logical traits, I have specified what I believe at the level of large-scale composition and formation of sustained units of thought, beyond the level of discrete sentences, the specific options were. This brings us back to our original question, which we may answer very succinctly indeed. Does a prevailing, miscellaneous rhetorical repertoire circulate more or less promiscuously among the authorships of diverse documents? In that case, the formal plan of our document (as of all the others) is random and not indicative. Or can we show that one authorship has made choices different from those effected by another authorship? In that case, the formal plan of our document also bespeaks deliberation. The answer is that Sifra's authorship appeals to three forms: simple, complex, and mishnaic. In the simple form, with its many variations, we always have a citation of a passage of the book of Leviticus followed by amplification. In the complex form we have a sustained demonstration concerning the requirements of taxonomy. In citation-form we have a joining of a Mishnah- or Tosefta-passage to Scripture. And that covers, in gross definition to be sure, the entire formal program of Sifra.

So too various other documents' authorships make choices as to form and even as to the ordering of forms and the cogency of their sustained units of thought. Some documents choose one set of forms and order them quite deliberately, making a single point in a given sustained unit of thought. Others choose other forms and do not make a single point in a sustained unit of thought, e.g., treatment of a single theme or set of verses. Among the authorships that have chosen a limited repertoire of forms and ordered types of forms with great care so as to establish a single, encompassing proposition (not merely so as to discuss from various viewpoints a shared theme) are those of Leviticus Rabbah and Pesiqta deRab Kahana. Other authorships – that of Sifré to Deuteronomy, for instance – chose a set of forms that differed, in part if not entirely, from the choices made by the authorships of Leviticus Rabbah and Pesiqta deRab Kahana, and that authorship has also taken no interest in the order of the types of forms that they have chosen. The compositors of Sifré to Deuteronomy furthermore, had no large-scale propositional program in mind in the composition of sustained units of thought, which, in scale, are substantially smaller than those in Leviticus Rabbah and Pesiqta deRab Kahana. One may both group Sifra and the two Sifrés in accord with indicative traits, differentiating all three from Genesis Rabbah, Leviticus Rabbah, and Pesiqta deRab Kahana, and, moreover, differentiate Sifra and the two Sifrés from one another. But to do so would carry us far afield and is not required for the important, but simple, proposition at hand. Let me state the conclusion very briefly.

The several documents exhibit important differences of rhetoric, the ordering of rhetorical patterns, and the sustained cogency of a given large-scale composition. Some documents' authorships do not take an interest in the order of rhetorical patterns, other authorships exhibit keen concern for that matter. Sifra falls into the former category; its authorship clearly found little interest in the order of types of forms. No message that they wished to convey emerged from that consideration. Some documents' authorships join a large number of individual units of thought to establish a single proposition, and that sustained mode of argumentation and demonstration characterizes every single principal division of those documents. That is not the case for Sifra. Other authorships are quite content to make one point after another, with no interest in establishing out of many things one thing. That surely characterizes Sifra's authorship, along with that of Sifré to Numbers. These differences entirely suffice to show us that people made choices and carried them out, doing one thing, not another, in the formation of the units of thought in accord with a fixed rhetorical pattern and in the ordering of units of thought in accord with the diverse rhetorical patterns and in the composing, within a single composite, of a carefully framed proposition to be established by these ordered patterns of a limited sort. Some people did things that way, other people did things in a different way. So the differences are systematic and point to choice. It follows that the rhetorical choices of our document are not haphazard but deliberate and point toward the presence of an authorship, that is, a plan.

We now may treat as an established fact the proposition that a set of highly restricted repertoires of formal possibilities confronted the writers of materials now collected in the diverse midrash-compilations. Set side by side, as I have laid matters out, each of the midrash-compilations may be distinguished from all the others, whether affines or utterly unrelated, on purely rhetorical (formal) grounds. So the highly formalized character of the rhetoric in any given document shows us a convention of authorship in the canon of the dual Torah, while the equally singular definition of the formal program paramount in any given document tells us that each authorship made its own choices. They chose some and neglected others; a long list of formal possibilities not utilized in Sifra but extensively employed in other documents could easily emerge from large-scale comparisons of the forms of diverse writings of the canon of the Judaism of the dual Torah.

We have now seen that quite specific rhetorical choices guided our authorship in its composition of sustained units of thought, involving two or more sentences. But what about the connections between one sentence and the next, that is, the logic of cogent discourse? Let us now proceed to the second such indication, namely, the evidence that a rather closely defined and highly restricted logical plan guided the authorship of Sifré to Deuteronomy not merely in joining rhetorically well-defined groups of sentences but also in connecting one sentence to the next.

Chapter Three

Logical Comparison

I. THE FOUR LOGICS OF COGENT DISCOURSE IN THE CANON OF JUDAISM IN THE FORMATIVE AGE

If the strict conventions of forms and literary structures make their mark on the very surface of documents, the inquiry into the logics of cogent discourse, a term explained immediately, carries us to the depths of the structures of thought of those same documents.[1] For the rhetoric dictates the material arrangement of words, while logic dictates the possibilities of thought: the ineffable determination of how thought arranged or set forth in one way makes sense, in another way, nonsense. And yet whether we explore the extrinsic traits of formal expression or the most profound layers of intelligible discourse and coherent thought that hold sentences together and form of them all propositions or presentations that can be understood, we produce a single result. It is that each document's authorship does make choices. Choosing modes of cogent discourse and coherent thought involves a repertoire that is exceedingly limited. Options in rhetoric by contrast prove quite diverse. But the work of comparison and contrast in both sorts of choices proves entirely feasible, since with regard to both rhetoric and logic we are required to compare fixed and external traits. There is no appeal to subjective taste and judgment.[2]

Now let me explain what is at issue when I speak of "logic." We begin from the beginning: what do I mean by "cogent discourse"? People wish not only to frame but also to communicate their ideas, and when they propose propositions for others' attention, they do so only by appeal to shared conventions of thought. To be understood by others, the one who

---

[1]Not only structures of thought, but structures of social order. In Chapter Five I shall argue that the social foundations of cogent discourse account for the centrality and also the long-term stability of the logics of intelligible thought in the description of the religious system at hand.

[2]Whether or not that also is the case when we move onward to the issue of topic and proposition remains to be seen in Chapter Four.

frames ideas has to compose thought in ways that others understand. That understanding requires in particular a shared conception of the connections between one thing and another, for instance, between one fact and another. When we know and can describe the character of those connections, which can be quite diverse, we point to what I designate the logics of intelligible discourse for a given group. Such logics serve where and how they serve, whether an entire culture or only two people who form a social entity of some sort – in our case, for our authorship. For that authorship presents statements, whether or not aimed at constituting propositions, to reach others and make sense to them – and that by definition. Such intelligible expression must evoke a shared logic, so that others make the same connections that, to the authorship, prove self-evident. It is that repertoire of logics that makes the thought of one person or our authorship intelligible to some other person(s).

In concrete terms, what this means is simple. One sentence – in modes of intelligible discourse familiar to us – not only stands beside, but generates another; a consequent statement follows from a prior one. We share a sense of connection, pertinence, relevance – the aptness of joining thought A to thought B to produce proposition 1. These (only by way of example) form intelligible discourses, turning facts into statements of meaning and consequence. To conduct intelligible discourse, therefore, people make two or more statements which, in the world in which they say their piece, are deemed self-evidently to hang together and form a proposition understood by someone else in that same world. It is the matter of self-evident cogency and intelligibility, in the document at hand, that now gains our attention.

Discourse shared by others begins when one sentence joins to a second one in framing a statement (whether or not presenting a proposition) in such a way that others understand *the connection* between the two sentences.[3] In studies of other documents of the canon of the Judaism of the dual Torah I have identified four different logics by which two or more sentences are deemed to cohere and to constitute a statement of consequence and intelligibility. One is familiar to us as philosophical logic, the second is equally familiar as the logic of cogent discourse attained through narrative. These two, self-evidently, are logics of a propositional order, evoking a logic of a philosophical character. The third is not propositional, and, as a matter of fact, it also is not ordinarily familiar to us at all. It is a mode of joining two or more statements – sentences – not on the foundation of meaning or sense or proposition but

---

[3]My fundamental hypothesis, which is far from being ready for analysis and testing, may even now be stated. What is shared among many documents of the Judaism of the dual Torah is the mode of connection common among them all. The system reaches definition in the interstices between sentence and sentence.

on the foundation of a different order altogether. The fourth mode of coherent discourse, distinct from the prior three, establishing connections at the most abstract and profound level of thought, which is through highly methodical analysis of many things in a single way. That forms the single most commonplace building block of thought in our document. It is, as a matter of fact, stunning in its logical power. But like the third logic it also is not propositional, though it yields its encompassing truths of order, proportion, structure, and self-evidence.

We turn to the two familiar modes of turning two sentences into a coherent statement, one weight and meaning, which both connects the two sentences, forming them into a whole, and also presents a statement that in meaning and intelligible proposition transcends the sum of the parts. Then I shall point to the third and fourth logics before us.

1. The first logic, most familiar to us in the West, establishes propositions that rest upon philosophical bases, e.g., through the proposal of a thesis and the composition of a list of facts that prove the thesis. This – to us entirely familiar, Western – mode of scientific expression through the classification of data that, in a simple way, we may call the science of making lists (*Listenwissenschaft*), is best exemplified by the Mishnah, but it dominates, also, in such profoundly philosophical-syllogistic documents as Leviticus Rabbah as well. Within the idiom of the canonial writings of the dual Torah, those documents bring us closest to the modes of thought with which we are generally familiar. A broad range of philosophical modes of stating and then proving or establishing propositions also characterizes Sifré to Deuteronomy. No philosopher in antiquity will have found unintelligible these types of units of thought.

This philosophical logic of cogent discourse works in a familiar way. Its issue is one of connection, not of fact but of the relationship between one fact and another. The two or more facts, that is, sentences, are connected through or in a conclusion. The conclusion or proposition is different from the established facts. When we set up as a sequence two or more facts and claim out of that sequence to propose a proposition different from, transcending, the facts at hand, we join the two sentences or facts in the philosophical logic of cogent discourse that is most common in our own setting. We may call this the logic of propositional discourse. We demonstrate propositions in a variety of ways, appealing to both a repertoire of probative facts and also a set of accepted modes of argument. In this way we engage in a kind of discourse that gains its logic from what, in general, we may call philosophy: the rigorous analysis and testing of propositions against the canons of an accepted reason. Philosophy accomplishes the miracle of making the whole more – or less – than the sum of the parts, that is, in the simple language I have used up to now, showing the connections between fact 1 and fact 2, in such wise as to yield proposition A. We begin with the irrefutable fact; our issue is not how facts gain their facticity, rather, how, from givens, people construct propositions or make statements that are deemed sense and nonsense or gibberish. So the problem is to explain the connections between and among facts, so accounting for the conclusions people draw, on the one side, or the acceptable associations people tolerate, on the other, in the exchange of language and thought.

Propositional logic also may be syllogistic, e.g., a variant on a famous syllogistic argument:

1.   All Greeks are philosophers.
2.   Demosthenes is a Greek.
3.   Therefore Demosthenes is a philosopher.

At issue is not mere facticity, rather, broadly speaking, the *connections* between facts. The problem subject to analysis here then is how one thing follows from something else, or how one thing generates something else, thus, as I said, connection. In that context, then, the sentences, 1, 2, and 3, standing entirely by themselves convey not a proposition but merely statements of a fact, which may or may not be true, and which may or may not bear sense and meaning beyond itself. Sentence 1 and sentence 2 by themselves state facts but announce no proposition. But the logic of syllogistic discourse joins the two into No. 3, which indeed does constitute a proposition and also (by the way) shows the linkage between sentence 1 and sentence 2. But there are more ways for setting forth propositions, making points, and thus for undertaking intelligible discourse, besides the philosophical, and syllogistic one with which we are familiar in the West. We know a variety of other modes of philosophical-propositional discourse, that is to say, presenting, testing, and demonstrating a proposition through appeal to fact and argument.

No less familiar to us is yet another way of carrying on cogent discourse through propositional logic. It is to offer a proposition, lay out the axioms, present the proofs, test the proposition against contrary argument, and the like. The demonstration of propositions we know, in general, as *Listenwissenschaft*, that is, a way to classify and so establish a set of probative facts, compels us to reach a given conclusion based on evidence and argument. These probative facts adduced in evidence for a proposition may derive from the classification of data, all of which point in one direction and not in another. A catalogue of facts, for example, may be so composed that, through the regularities and indicative traits of the entries, the catalogue yields a proposition. A list of parallel items all together point to a simple conclusion; the conclusion may or may not be given at the end of the catalogue, but the catalogue – by definition – is pointed. All of the catalogued facts are taken to bear self-evident connections to one another, established by those pertinent shared traits implicit in the composition of the list, therefore also bearing meaning and pointing through the weight of evidence to an inescapable conclusion. The discrete facts then join together because of some trait common to them all. This is a mode of classification of facts to lead to an identification of what the facts have in common and an explanation of their meaning. These and other modes of philosophical argument are entirely familiar to us all. In calling all of them "philosophical," I mean only to distinguish them from the other three logics we shall presently examine.

2. This brings us to the second, equally familiar logic of cogent, therefore intelligible discourse, which is narrative or, as I shall explain, teleological in character. A proposition emerges not only through philosophical argument and analysis, e.g., spelling out in so many words a general and encompassing proposition, and further constructing in proof of that explicit generalization a syllogism and demonstration. We may state and demonstrate a proposition in a second way, which resorts to narrative (itself subject to a taxonomy of its own) both to establish and to explain connections between naked facts. Let me spell out this second logic, which derives from narrative and evokes a teleology to connect one sentence, fact, or thought, to another. A proposition (whether or not it is stated explicitly) may be set forth and demonstrated by showing through the telling of a tale (of a variety of kinds, e.g., historical, fictional, parabolic, and the like) that a sequence of events, real or imagined, shows the ineluctable truth of a given proposition. The logic of connection demonstrated through narrative, rather than philosophy, is simply stated. It is connection attained and explained by invoking some mode of narrative in which a sequence of events, first this, then that, is understood to yield a proposition, first this, then that *because of this*. That sequence both states and establishes a proposition in a way different from the philosophical and argumentative mode of propositional discourse. Whether or not the generalization is stated in so many words rarely matters, because the power of well-crafted narrative is to make unnecessary explicit drawing of the moral.

That is why I argue that this second logic, besides the logic of philosophy and syllogistic argument, is one of that narrative, that sees cogency in the purpose, the necessary order of events seen as causative. That is then a logic or intelligiblity of connection that is attained through teleology: the claim of purpose, therefore cause, in the garb of a story of what happened because it had to happen. Narrative conveys a proposition through the setting forth of happenings in a framework of inevitability, in a sequence that makes a point, e.g., establishes not merely the facts of what happens, but the teleology that explains those facts. Then we speak not only of events – our naked facts – but of their relationship. We claim to account for that relationship teleologically, in the purposive sequence and necessary order of happenings. In due course we shall see how various kinds of narratives serve to convey highly intelligible and persuasive propositions.

3. We come, third, to the one genuinely odd, mode of discourse in our document,[4] one which, in our intellectual world and culture, is unfamiliar though not unknown. I call it the logic of fixed association, in which distinct facts or sentences or thoughts are held together without actually joining into sequential and coherent propositions of any kind. It is so alien to our Western modes of thought that I shall begin with an illustrative case that derives from Sifra. Then I shall generalize. What we have in the example is a sequence of absolutely unrelated sentences, made up in each instance of a clause of a verse, followed by a phrase of amplification. Nothing links one sentence (completed thought) to the ones fore or aft. Yet the compositors have presented us with what they represent side by side with sentences that do form large compositions, that is, that are linked one to the next by connections that we can readily discern. That seems to me to indicate that our authorship conceives one mode of connecting sentences to form a counterpart to another. Here is an example of what I mean by the logic of fixed association:

101. *Parashat Shemini Pereq 1*

CI:II

1.   A.   "Take the cereal-offering":

       B.   [Since on the day on which the altar was dedicated, which coincided with the eighth day of the consecration of the priests, the princes began to make their presentation, and that on the first day was Nachshon, so Num. 7:12, including basins "full of fine flour mixed with oil for a cereal-offering,"] this refers to the meal-offering brought by Nachshon.

       C.   "that remains":

       D.   this is the meal-offering of the eighth day.

       E.   "of the offerings by fire to the Lord": the priests have their claim to the residue only after the rest has been offered up by fire.

2.   A.   "and eat it unleavened":

       B.   What is the point of Scripture here?

       C.   Since it was for the occasion at hand that the meal-offering of the community was offered, a meal-offering of unleavened cakes, and an

---

[4]And of many other documents in the canon of the Judaism of the dual Torah. But I shall presently demonstrate that this is not the paramount logic of our document, as it is for others. And I presently shall explain the correlation of rhetoric and logic with the propositional program of our authorship.

equivalent offering is not presented in the coming generations, [there was no clear rule on how to consume it, and] therefore Scripture says, "and eat it unleavened."

3. A. "beside the altar":
   B. not in the holy place [outside of the Holy of Holies], nor on the altar.]
   C. I know only that the rule applies to the case at hand. How do I know that it encompasses all food in the status of Most Holy Things?
   D. Scripture says, "for it is most holy."

4. A. The language "it" in the nominative and accusative serves as exclusionary,
   B. thus omitting from the rule the thanksgiving-offering and the bread that accompanies it, the ram brought by the Nazirite and the bread that accompanies it, and the ram of consecration and the bread that accompanies it.

5. A. "You shall eat it in a holy place":
   B. What is the purpose of Scripture?
   C. Since Scripture says, "beside the altar," I know only that one may eat the food near the altar itself.
   D. How do I know that as to the rooms that are built on unconsecrated ground but open into holy ground, [one may eat the food there as well]?
   E. Scripture says, "You shall eat it in a holy place."

6. A. "because it is your due and your sons' due":
   B. It is the due of the sons, and it is not the due of the daughters.

7. A. "from the offerings by fire to the Lord":
   B. You have a right to the food only after the sacrificial portions have been placed on the altar fires.

8. A. "for so I am commanded":
   B. Just as I have been commanded, so the Lord has commanded.

9. A. "for so I am commanded":
   B. "to tell you that at the time even that one has suffered a bereavement [as with Nadab and Abihu] and not yet buried his dead, the priest may eat it."

10. A. "for so I am commanded":
    B. at the time of the event itself.

11. A. "as the Lord has commanded":
    B. "And it is not on my own authority that I speak to you."

12. A. "But the breast": this refers to the breast.
    B. "that is waved: this refers to the waving of the basket.
    C. "and the thigh: this refers to the thigh.
    D. "that is offered": this refers to the offering of the thanksgiving-offering.

13. A. "you shall eat in any clean place":
    B. Said R. Nehemiah, "Now were the items mentioned earlier not to be eaten in a clean place?
    C. "But this refers to a kind of cleanness that is not subject to uncleanness, that is, that does not have to be rendered clean of the uncleanness of the one afflicted by the skin ailment.
    D. "The point is that the items under discussion now may be eaten anywhere in Jerusalem [where those afflicted by the skin disease are not permitted to enter] "

14. A.   "you and your sons and your daughters with you":

B.   "you and your sons": by a properly conducted division [i.e., through the chance division of lots, not through human intervention].

C.   "your daughters with you": through a division by gift [from the father, that is, through human intervention].

D.   Or might one suppose that "you and your sons and your daughters with you" means that all should be done by a properly conducted division?

E.   When Scripture says, "and it shall be yours and your sons' with you, as a due for ever," it excludes a due for the daughters [and hence the procedure for dividing the food will differ for the daughters and not conform to the priestly rite of division].

F.   How then am I to interpret the phrase, "you and your sons and your daughters with you""

G.   "you and your sons": by a properly conducted division.

H.   "your daughters with you": through a division by gift.

15. A.   "for they are given...from the sacrifices of the peace-offerings of the people of Israel":

B.   this serves to encompass the sacrifices of peace-offerings of the community at large,

C.   indicating that on that day they should be there as well.

D.   For it is said, "He killed the ox also and the ram, the sacrifice of peace-offerings for the people" (Lev. 9:18).

16. A.   "The thigh that is offered and the breast that is waved they shall bring with the offerings by fire of the fat to wave for a wave-offering before the Lord":

B.   This teaches that the sacrificial fat is placed below [when the whole is waved.

The phrase-by-phrase amplification follows the program of the verses at hand and, so far as I can see, draws little from some other intellectual plan than that of the verses under discussion. It is an excellent example of the power of the logic of fixed association to join together utterly discrete sentences into what is, to our authorship and its readers, a perfectly cogent composition. The third logic therefore rests upon this premise:

> *an established sequence of words joins whatever is attached to those words into a set of cogent statements, even though it does not form of those statements propositions of any kind, implicit or explicit.*

The established sequence of words may be made up of names always associated with one another. It may be made up of a received text, with deep meanings of its own, e.g., a verse or a clause of Scripture. It may be made up of the sequence of holy days or synagogue lections, which are assumed to be known by everyone and so to connect on their own. The fixed association of these words, whether names, whether formula such as verses of Scripture, whether lists of facts, serves to link otherwise unrelated statements to one another and to form of them all not a proposition but, nonetheless, *an entirely intelligible sequence of connected or related sentences.*

How then does the logic of cogent discourse supplied by fixed association accomplish its goal? In the sample we have examined, we find side by side a sequence of sentences that bear no relationship or connection at all between one another. These discrete sentences have come before us in "commentary-form," for instance:

> "Clause 1": "this means A."
>
> "Clause 2": "this refers to Q."

Nothing joins A and Q. Indeed, had I used symbols out of different classifications altogether, e.g., A, a letter of an alphabet, and #, which stands for something else than a sound of an alphabet, the picture would have proved still clearer. Nothing joins A to Q or A to # except that clause 2 follows clause 1. The upshot is that no proposition links A to Q or A to # and so far as there is a connection between A and Q or A and # it is not propositional. Then is there a connection at all? I think the authorship of the document that set forth matters as they did assumes that there is such a connection. For there clearly is – at the very least – an order, that is, "clause 1" is prior to "clause 2," in the text that out of clauses 1 and 2 does form an intelligible statement, that is, two connected, not merely adjacent, sentences.

This third way in which two or more sentences are deemed, in the canonical literature of Judaism, to constitute a more than random, episodic sequence of unrelated allegations, A, X, Q, C, and so on, on its own, out of context, yields gibberish – no proposition, no sense, no joining between two sentences, no implicit connection accessible without considerable labor of access. But this third way can see cogent discourse even where there is no proposition at all, and even where the relationship between sentence A and sentence X does not derive from the interplay among the propositions at hand. It is hard for us even to imagine non-propositional, yet intelligible discourse, outside the realm of feeling or inchoate attitude, and yet, as we shall see, before us is a principle of intelligible discourse that is entirely routine, clearly assumed to be comprehensible, and utterly accessible. This third logic rests on a premise of education – that is, of prior discourse attained through processes of learning a logic not accessible, as are the logics of philosophy and narrative, but through another means.[5]

---

[5] I may refer also to negative traits of the logic of fixed association. The first negative trait of this mode of discourse is that it is not made cogent by addressing, or relating to, a given, shared proposition, hence, I underline, while fully exposed in words and not restricted to feeling or attitude or emotion, nonetheless it is a

The third logic rests upon the premise that an established sequence of words, joins whatever is attached to those words into a set of cogent statements, even though it does not form of those statements propositions of any kind, implicit or explicit. The established sequence of words may be made up of names always associated with one another. It may be made up of a received text, with deep meanings of its own, e.g., a verse or a clause of Scripture. It may be made up of the sequence of holy days or synagogue lections, which are assumed to be known by everyone and so to connect on their own. The fixed association of these words, whether names, whether formula such as verses of Scripture, whether lists of facts, serves to link otherwise unrelated statements to one another and to form of them all not a proposition but, nonetheless, *an entirely intelligible sequence of connected or related sentences.* Even though these negative definitions intersect and in a measure cover the same ground, each requires its own specification – but I shall ask only a mite more of the reader's indulgence.

To state matters affirmatively, the third logic is one of *fixed association.* That is, there is, in the document before us as in many other rabbinic writings, a logic that joins one sentence to another not because of what is said or the proposition at stake in what is said, but because of a fixed association among traits or formulas common to sequential

---

logic that is *non-propositional.* And yet, I would maintain, it is in its context deemed cogent and consecutive, as much as philosophical and narrative ways of presenting and proving propositions are received as cogent, and as much as sentences in philosophical and narrative discourse are understood as consecutive. A second also essentially negative trait of the logic under discussion is that the burden of establishing meaning rests not upon what is said but upon some other principle of cogency entirely. A set of associations will join what is otherwise discrete. In propositional discourse, what is said by Rabbi X relates because of the substance of the matter to what is said by Rabbi Y. We have seen, in our catalogue of forms, a propositional form of this kind. Thus the point of intersection of two or more sentences lies not with attributive, Rabbi X says, but with the proposition, *what* the rabbi maintains. If we for the moment call the attributive clause the protasis and what is attributed the apodosis, then propositional discourse centers upon the apodosis and non-propositional discourse upon the protasis. That is, two or more sentences link to a common point but not to one another, which is another way of calling this mode of discourse non-propositional. A third negative trait of these sequences of discrete facts, or sentences deserves explication on its own. It is that the sentences do not form a proposition even though they are deemed cogent with one another. "The dog stands on the corner. Chile bombed Peru." These two facts or sentences in no way connect. And yet, facts of a similarly unrelated character, sentences as wildly incongruous as these, can stand quite comfortably side by side in what is clearly proposed as a cogent unit of thought and intelligible discourse in our document. Our authorship clearly means to appeal to a source of cogency deriving from a principle of connection other than the propositional kind.

sentences but external to them all. That association is always fixed and extrinsic to the passage(s) at hand. I state for the document before us, there is not a single instance in which two or more facts, that is, discrete sentences, are set side by side on a principle of the intrinsic link of the one to the next (apart from a propositional link of course), which would be appropriately called free association: "there is this, and, by the way, this reminds me of that," when neither this nor that join to form a proposition. To take the case I gave earlier, free association would permit someone to present as a set of connected facts, lacking all proposition, something like the following: *The dog stands on the corner." [That reminds me:] "Chile [which I think is shaped like a dog's tail] bombed Peru."* A well-known example of how connection makes sense of otherwise unrelated facts is this simple statement: I can make sense of the Providence telephone book simply by adding the word "begat" between each entry.

The upshot is that a statement that relies for intelligibility upon the premise of fixed association, e.g., an established text (whether a list of names, whether a passage of Scripture, whether the known sequence of events, as in the Pesher-writings, whether the well-known sequence of events in the life of a holy man) differs in its fundamental logic of cogency from one that relies for intelligibility upon either narrative, on the one side, or philosophical and syllogistic thought, on the other. What holds the whole together? It is knowledge shared among those to whom this writing is addressed, hence the "fixed" part of "fixed association," as distinct from (mere) free association. Cogency therefore is social, therefore not ever the product of private, free association, any more than form ever permits individual manner of expressing ideas. Connection here rests on the premise of education or what we may call the system and structure of a textual community (using the phrase in no technical sense). That premise derives from prior discourse attained through processes of learning; it is not a logic readily accessible, as are the logics of philosophy and narrative, but one that comes only through the training of the mind, e.g., the learning of the terms that are fixed in their association with one another. Our authorship assumes that the discrete sentences will form an intelligible statement (even with an unarticulated proposition, though that need not detain us), in which sentence A joins sentence B to say something important, even though that statement is not conveyed by what A says and what B says. For these sentences to form connected statements, we have then to know that these names bear meaning, in their facticity (of course), but also in the order in which they occur, in the conglomerates which they comprise.

4. The fourth logic of intelligible discourse is discourse in which one analytical method applies to many sentences, with the result that many, discrete and diverse sentences are shown to constitute a single intellectual structure. A variety of explanations and amplifications, topically and propositionally unrelated, will be joined in a methodical way so as to produce a broadly applicable conclusion that many things really conform to a single pattern or structure. Such methodologically coherent analysis imposes upon a variety of data a structure that is external to all of the data, yet that imposes connection between and among facts or sentences. The connection consists in the recurrent order and repeated balance and replicated meaning of them all, seen in the aggregate. This is commonly done by asking the same question to many things and producing a single result many times. Unity of thought and discourse therefore derives not only from what is said, or even from a set of fixed associations.

Methodical analysis may be conducted by addressing a set of fixed questions, imposing a sequence of stable procedures, to a vast variety of data. That will yield not a proposition, nor even a sequence of facts formerly unconnected but now connected, but a different mode of cogency, one that derives from showing that many things follow a single rule or may be interpreted in a single way. It is the intelligible proposition that is general and not particular, that imposes upon the whole a sense of understanding and comprehension, even though the parts of the whole do not join together. What happens, in this mode of discourse, is that we turn the particular into the general, the case into a rule, and if I had to point to one purpose of our authorship overall, it is to turn the cases of the book of Deuteronomy into rules that conform, overall, to the way in which the Mishnah presents its rules: logically, topically, a set of philosophically defensible generalizations. We shall now examine instances in Sifra of methodical analysis.

II. THE LOGICS OF COGENT DISCOURSE OF SIFRA:
1. AN INITIAL STATEMENT

There are two paramount logics of cogent discourse in our document, first, methodical analysis, second, fixed associative logic. Methodical analysis repeatedly asks a single question of a vast range of diverse material. The net effect is to impart to a diverse text, covering many topics, a coherent character. Asking the same question of many things and producing answers of the same sort, utilizing rhetoric of a single pattern, thus turns discrete sentences into a cogent whole, even while not appealing to a common sense or a common proposition for that purpose. There are two paramount, recurrent modes of methodical analysis. The first I call "inclusionary/exclusionary," in that we repeatedly ask whether the law encompasses case X, and, if so, does it also encompass case Y? Or, the language of the case at hand excludes case X, and also case Y. What is at stake in this methodical analysis is the transformation of a case into an encompassing rule, and that is accomplished by generalizing on the case and so discovering, on the basis of the language of Scripture, both its extent and also its limits. The second is the demonstration that the taxonomic system of the Mishnah, which appeals solely to the indicative traits of things and not to Scripture's classification, is insufficient to establish rules.[6]

Let me give a single instance of both the former methodical analytical pattern, the inclusionary/exclusionary exercise, and also the latter, the insufficiency of logic unaffected by scriptural principles of category-formation or taxonomy, and the reader will in other examples given elsewhere in this book find its counterparts, sometimes formally, always intellectually and logic, everywhere. The operative rhetoric here is "I know only this...how about that....?"

CLXIV:I

1. A. "And whoever sits on anything on which he who has the discharge has sat will be unclean [shall wash his clothes and bathe himself in water and be unclean until the evening]" (Lev. 15:6).

   B. I know only that this is the case if he sits on it and [actually] touches it. [That is to say, if the Zab is in direct contact with the chair, then he imparts uncleanness to it.]

   C. How do I know that [if the Zab sits on] ten chairs, one on the other, and even [if he sits] on top of a heavy stone, [what is underneath is clean]? [If the chair bears the weight of the Zab, even though the Zab is not touching the chair, the chair is made unclean.]

   D. Scripture says, "And he who sits on the utensil on which the Zab has sat will be unclean" –

   E. In any place in which the Zab sits and imparts uncleanness, the clean person sits and becomes unclean.

   F. I know only that when the Zab sits on it, and the Zab is there [that it is unclean]. How do I know that I should treat the empty as the full one?

   G. Scripture says, "Utensil" – to treat the empty like the full.

   H. I know only that this [rule concerning transmission of the Zab's uncleanness merely through applying the burden of his weight, even without his actually being in contact with the object] applies to the chair. How do I know that it applies to the saddle?

Now we shift to the critique of classification based on hierarchical logic of taxonomy as is evidenced in the Mishnah:[7]

---

[6]I have explained this matter at great length in *Uniting the Dual Torah*.

[7]But when the critique is set forth, it is never in Sifra addressed to the framing of a passage found in the Mishnah but always to a theoretical problem beyond the range of a Mishnah-rule. When in Sifra a Mishnah-rule is cited verbatim, it is never subjected to the critique of applied reason that forms the centerpiece of Sifra's authorship's program of thought. In this way our authorship takes up a mediating position, criticizing method but never proposition; the propositions of the Oral

I.   And it is logical:

J.   If we have found that Scripture does not distinguish between the one
      who carries and the one who is carried in respect to sitting, so we
      should not distinguish between the one who is carried and the one
      who carries with respect to the saddle.

K.   But what difference does it make to me that Scripture did not
      distinguish between carrying and being carried in respect to the chair?

L.   For it did not distinguish touching it and carrying it.

M.   Should we not distinguish between carrying and being carried with
      reference to the saddle,

N.   for lo, it has indeed distinguished touching it from carrying it?

O.   Scripture [accordingly is required] to state, "A utensil" – to encompass
      even the saddle.

Here is a fine example of a mode of logic that establishes its fixed and
formal character through repetition. When we see enough cases of what
we have in hand, we realize that the logic of methodical analysis, asking
the same question many times, does serve in Sifra as in Sifré to
Deuteronomy to establish a profound sense of cogency and coherence
among topically diverse discourses. The inclusionary method will utilize
diverse rhetoric, but it always is characterized by the intent to encompass
within a single law a variety of cases.

The intent is the same as that of the Mishnah, therefore, namely, to
show the rule governing diverse cases. The contrary exercise, the one that
excludes examples from a rule, is to be stipulated. That, of course, is also
what the framers of the Mishnah propose through their making of lists of
like and unlike things and determination of the rule that governs them all.
So when the framers of the Mishnah appeal to the making of lists, they do
no more, and no less, than is accomplished by our authorship in its
exegetical exercises of exclusion and inclusion. Here our authorship
therefore demonstrates the possibility of doing through rewriting the
Written Torah precisely what the Oral Torah is meant to do. The
judgment on modes of cogent discourse operative in the Mishnah is
tacitly negative; we do things this way because this is the way to do them,
that is to say, through appeal to, and amplification of, the Written Torah –
not through appeal to, and ordering of, traits of things sorted out
independently of the Written Torah.

A single example will suffice to show the principles of cogency on
which our authorship depends. For that purpose, we turn to a sizable
sample chapter. I present the chapter complete, then ask how sentences
are joined into sense-units, and, more important, each unit is set into
place side by side with others.

Torah stand firm, but require restatement within the framework of the Written
Torah. That is, again, the thesis of *Uniting the Dual Torah*.

10. Parashat Vayyiqra Dibura Denedabah Parashah 5

X:I

1. A. "If [his offering for a burnt-offering is from the flock, of sheep or of goats, he shall make his offering a male without blemish. It shall be slaughtered before the Lord on the north side of the altar, and Aaron's sons, the priests, shall dash its blood against all sides of the altar. When it has been cut up into sections, the priest shall lay them out, with the head and the suet, on the wood that is on the fire upon the altar. The entrails and the legs shall be washed with water; the priest shall offer up and turn the whole into smoke on the altar. It is a burnt-offering, an offering by fire, of pleasing odor to the Lord" (Lev. 1:10-13)]:

B. Lo, this matter adds to the earlier one. [That is to say, rules governing the burnt-offering made of an animal from the herd apply to the burnt-offering made of an animal from the flock and vice versa.]

C. Then what purpose was there in setting forth free-standing statements [such as those that commence without reference to speaking or saying]?

D. It was so as to give Moses a pause to collect his thoughts between the statement of one passage and the next, between the presentation of one topic and the next.

E. And lo, that yields an argument *a fortiori:*

F. If one who was listening to words from the mouth of the Holy One, and who was speaking by the inspiration of the Holy Spirit, nonetheless had to pause to collect his thoughts between one passage and the next, between one topic and the next,

G. all the more so an ordinary person in discourse with other common folk [must speak with all due deliberation].

The same question raised earlier recurs, underlining the methodical inquiry that is imposed throughout.

X:II

1. A. "[If his offering for a burnt-offering is] from the flock, of sheep or of goats":

B. These specifications ["of sheep, or of goats" after "of the flock"] serve as exclusionary statements, omitting from the list of acceptable types of animal-offering a beast that is superannuated, sick, or filthy.

2. A. "...his offering...":

B. the reference to the personal pronoun excludes the possibility of using a stolen beast.

3. A. "of sheep or of goats":

B. this excludes hybrids.

4. A. "Now you maintain that these several exclusionary specifications serve solely for the stated purpose.

B. "But perhaps the intent is solely to exclude those beasts that have been the medium for committing a transgression, or that have threshed with an ox and an ass together while they were consecrated, or produce that has grown as mixed seeds in a vineyard, or produce of the seventh year, or produce that has been worked on the intermediate days of the festival, the Day of Atonement, the Sabbath, [and the like]?

C.   "[After specifying 'flock,' which encompasses both sheep and goats,] Scripture says, '...sheep...for a burnt-offering..., or goats...for a burnt-offering.'

D.   "This [additional specification serves as a generalizing rule, thus] encompassing all these cases [and not solely the ones listed above[," the words of R. Judah.

Nos. 1-3 go over several exclusions implicit in the specifications. Then, at No. 4, Judah wishes to extend the catalogue of prohibited classifications, and this he does by an exegetical device that treats the specified items as exemplary of a general rule. The rest follows. The fixed association is imposed by the base-verse; no proposition joins one unit to the next. Methodical analysis directs the presentation of a fixed program of questions. In our document these commonly concern the exclusion or inclusion of items not covered. The exclusionary, then inclusionary inquiry dominates above. It is certainly the most common methodical analysis available to our authorship. When one covers a fair part of Sifra as a whole, that recurrent set of questions joins discrete parts to one another and imparts to the whole a fine sense of composition and order.

X:III

1. A.   R. Simeon says, "Scripture says, "...sheep...for a burnt-offering..., or goats...for a burnt-offering.'

    B.   "This serves to encompass within the rule a beast that has been substituted for a burnt-offering [which, in accord with Lev. 27:10, takes on the status of the animal that was originally consecrated, so that both of them then have to be offered]."

    C.   But is this proposition not to be proven merely on the basis of logic?

    D.   If animals designated as substitutes for those in the status of peace-offerings, for which purpose fowl cannot be designated, themselves nonetheless are suitable to be offered up, the substitute designated in place of an animal consecrated as a burnt-offering, for which purpose a fowl may be designated, surely should be validly consecrated [which is the proposition of B].

    E.   [But the two types of sacrificial protocol, peace-offerings and whole-offerings, are not comparable, so the argument of D is null, for] if you have stated the rule for peace-offerings, which may validly derive from either female or male beasts, will you apply the same rule to animals designated for burnt-offerings, which may derive only from male but not from female beasts. Since a burnt-offering may not derive from a female but only from a male beast, [there should be other pertinent restrictions as well, with the consequence] that a beast that has been designated as its substitute should not be deemed valid for offering.

    F.   That is why it was necessary for Scripture to make this point:

    G.   Scripture says, "...sheep...for a burnt-offering..., or goats...for a burnt-offering."

H.   This serves to encompass within the rule a beast that has been substituted for a burnt-offering [which, in accord with Lev. 27:10, takes on the status of the animal that was originally consecrated, so that both of them then have to be offered]."

We find ourselves on the familiar turf of proving that Scripture serves as the sole source of appropriate rules, because exercises of comparison and contrast prove invariably flawed. Here we have two methodical inquiries, first, B, the inclusionary question, second, C, the recurrent and paramount issue of the source of correct classification for purposes of hierarchical logic.

X:IV

1. A.   R. Eleazar says, "Why does Scripture say, '...sheep...for a burnt-offering..., or goats...for a burnt-offering'?

   B.   "One might have reasoned as follows:

   C.   "I know only that a beast should be offered up as a burnt-offering if it is purchased from the excess of funds contributed to begin with for the provision of beasts for the burnt-offering.

   D.   "How do I know that the excess of funds contributed for the purchase of animals for use as sin-offerings, the excess of funds contributed for purchase of animals used as guilt-offerings, for the purchase of the tenth-ephah of fine flour, for the purchase of birds for use in the purification rites of Zab-males and Zab-females and women after childbirth, the excess of funds contributed for the purchase of offerings for the rites of the Nazir and the leper to be purified,

   E.   "[and further:] one who consecrates his possessions, among which were things that were suitable for use on the altar, for example, wine, oil, and fowl –

   F.   "how do we know that they are to be sold for the purposes of that same species [e.g., to pilgrims who require wine or oil or fowl for an offering], and with the proceeds animals to be designated for us as burnt-offerings are to be purchased?

   G.   "Scripture says, '...sheep...for a burnt-offering..., or goats...for a burnt-offering,'

   H.   "which serves to encompass all these cases."

   I.   And sages say, "Let the proceeds fall to a fund for the purpose of purchasing freewill-offerings."

   J.   But is it not the fact that beasts that are offered as freewill-offerings fall into the classification of burnt-offerings? So what is at issue between R. Eleazar and sages?

   K.   The difference is this: when a burnt-offering is brought in fulfillment of an obligation, the person who brings it relies upon the beast for that purpose in carrying out his obligation, brings in its regard drink-offerings, and the drink-offerings are paid for by the one who benefits from the offering, and if he was a priest, the right of preparing the beast and the hide belong to him.

   L.   But when a burnt-offering is brought as a freewill-offering, the one who brings it may not rely upon it in fulfillment of an obligation, and he does not bring the drink-offerings in its connection, and the cost of the drink-offerings derives from communal funds, and even though the donor may be a priest, the right of preparing the beast and the hide go not to him in particular but to the members of the priestly watch of that particular week.

The exercise has no bearing upon any other passage in our context, and it concerns issues entirely abstracted from the details at hand. The purpose is to distinguish the burnt-offering brought as a freewill-offering, which is the subject of the scriptural passage at hand, and the burnt-offering brought in fulfillment of an individual's obligation, which is the next major subject. We stand too far from the unit beyond to propose that we deal with a transitional exercise. The reason for including the passage here, then, is solely the fact that Eleazar appeals to our text to prove his point. Otherwise the passage hardly fits. But the key-language is the question of D, which introduces the inclusionary issue and generates the remaining discussion. Once more we see that the whole holds together through process of thought, rather than through proposition.

X:V

1. A. "It shall be slaughtered [before the Lord on the north side of the altar]":
    B. That particular offering is slaughtered at the north side of the altar, but fowl brought as a burnt-offering are not slaughtered at the north side of the altar.

We come now to another example of the case against taxonomy beyond the frame of scriptural categories: hierarchical classification and its fallacy.

    C. But is the opposite of that proposition not a matter of logic?
    D. If a beast deriving from the flock, for which a priest in particular is not assigned the task, the location of the rite at the north of the altar is established as a requirement, a fowl, for which a priest in particular is assigned the task of slaughter, surely should be assigned a place at the north of the altar as well?
    E. Because of the possibility of reaching that false conclusion, it was necessary for] Scripture to state explicitly, "*It* shall be slaughtered [before the Lord on the north side of the altar]" –
    F. That particular offering is slaughtered at the north side of the altar, but fowl brought as a burnt-offering are not slaughtered at the north side of the altar.
2. A. R. Eliezer b. Jacob says, "'*It* shall be slaughtered [before the Lord on the north side of the altar]' – that particular offering is slaughtered at the north side of the altar, but a beast that is designated a Passover offering is not slaughtered at the north side of the altar."
    B. But is the contrary not logical? If a burnt-offering, which is not assigned a particular time for its slaughter, is assigned a particular place of slaughter,

C. a beast designated as a Passover offering, which is assigned a particular time for its slaughter, surely should be assigned a particular place for slaughter.

D. Because of the possibility of reaching that false conclusion, it was necessary for] Scripture to state explicitly, "*It* shall be slaughtered [before the Lord on the north side of the altar]" –

E. That particular offering is slaughtered at the north side of the altar, but fowl brought as a burnt-offering are not slaughtered at the north side of the altar.

3. A. R. Hiyya says, "'*It* shall be slaughtered [before the Lord] on the north side of the altar,' but the one who does the slaughtering does not have to be standing at the north side of the altar.

B. "Now we know as fact that the one who receives the blood does have to be standing at the north side of the altar and does have to receive the blood at the north side of the altar. If he stood at the south side of the alrtar and received the blood at the north side of the altar, he has invalidated the offering.

C. "Might one think that the same rule applies to the one who slaughters the beast?

D. "Scripture says, '*It* [shall be slaughtered [before the Lord] on the north side of the altar,' but the one who does the slaughtering does not have to be standing at the north side of the altar.

No. 1 explains in a negative way why the proof from Scripture is required for the proposition at hand. No. 2 goes over the same exercise, with the result that the differentiating indicators among the diverse types of offerings are laid forth. The implicit proposition hardly requires specification. No. 3 entertains yet another false proposition, this time classifying two actions as one and then showing that the single classification does not fit – because of Scripture's own decree. It is the counterpart to the argument of Nos. 1, 2. Here is another methodical inquiry, of the sort that will occupy us again in Chapters Seven and Eight. Its formal character as a recurrent pattern of thought, and the function of the form in holding the document together and giving it that uniformity that a mere formal joining of discrete bits and pieces of exegesis, should not be missed.

X:VI

1. A. "[It shall be slaughtered before the Lord] on the north side of the altar":

B. For the actual side of the altar stands at the northern limits of the altar. [The altar is not bisected, with half assigned to the south, the other half to the north, but the northern side of the altar is at the very dividing point between north and south vis-à-vis the altar itself.]

C. And where is the face of the altar? It is at the south. Thus we learn that the ramp is at the southern side of the altar.

D. R. Judah says, "'And the ramp shall face east' (Ezek. 43:17), so that the person who goes up on it turns to his right, which is eastward. Lo, we learn therefore that the ramp is at the southern side of the altar."

2. A. "[It shall be slaughtered before the Lord] on the north side of the altar":

B.   "**For the whole altar is deemed north, [T. Zeb. 7:1A]**, so that if one has slaughtered Most Holy Things at the head of it, they are deemed valid," **the words of R. Yosê.**

C.   **R. Yose b. R. Judah says, "From the midway point of the altar and to the north is deemed north, and from the midway point and outward is deemed south" [M. Zeb. 6:1C].**

We have at B-C and D two proofs for the same proposition. It seems to me the passage is included only because of the intersection with the detail referring to the north side of the altar. No. 2 is tacked on for obvious reasons. Here we cannot point to elements of thought or expression or inquiry that join the passage to what has gone before.

What holds one sentence together with another, or one set of sentences together with another set? To state the simple fact, we have two principles of cogent discourse in play here.[8] First, within each unit of thought bearing an Arabic numeral, the (to us) normal philosophical principle governs. What that means is that propositions are proven, syllogistic argument undertaken, and, in all, we have a well-crafted argument leading to a desired conclusion, and that is what holds the whole together. No. 1 adduces the fact at hand to prove the proposition of the argument *a fortiori* at **1.F-G**: people should speak with deliberation. A deeper logic is at hand, of course, since the methodical inquiry (not set forth here) into connections between one passage and another recurs throughout. We recall in this context the opening question of the lection for Behar: what has this to do with that? The workings of a methodical-analytical logic are more difficult to discern; and they affect the formation of the document at a more encompassing level of discourse. We cannot miss them.

When we come to No. 1, we see a sequence of sentences that do not form a paragraph, that is, No. 1 has nothing to do with No. 2, No. 2 with No. 3, and so on. For the whole to form some sort of sense-unit, we have therefore to appeal to the logic of fixed association, here represented by the base-verse: "If his offering for a burnt-offering is] from the flock, of sheep or of goats." That is what links sentence to sentence, each sentence represented by an Arabic numeral. Then there is that further link, which we call the methodical analytical one. That occurs at No. 4 and holds the whole together in yet another way. The one thing we do not find is the sort of propositional cogency to which, in normal discourse, we are used.

---

[8]The same is the fact for the two Talmuds, as I show in my *The Formation of the Jewish Intellect* (in press). I do not claim that the mixed logics of cogent discourse mark Sifra apart from all other documents; that is not the case. But the resort to two logics that are uncommon in the Mishnah and dominant in Sifra is a definitive indicator of difference between choices made by one authorship and those selected by another.

That is not here. **X:III** proves a point and also carries on a sustained methodical analysis, as we shall see in the next chapter. The point or proposition occurs at **X:III.1B.** The methodical analysis is at **Cff.**, where we show that logic unsustained by Scripture (for reasons I shall clarify in Chapter Seven) will not serve. The same cogency holds together the lettered components of **X:IV** as well as **X:V.** **X:VI** brings us back to a sequence of unrelated and episodic, miscellaneous thoughts. What holds the whole together is only the constant reference to the base-verse. So much for the cogency of the parts. But what holds the whole together? One thing, and one thing alone: the sequence of clauses of the verses of Scripture that are under discussion.

The chapter of Sifra just now reviewed represents a large part of the whole of Sifra. Whatever the inner cogency of a given paragraph – a completed unit of thought – the sequence, order, and cogency of paragraphs depend wholly upon the base-verses of the book of Leviticus, one after another. We could set in a different sequence altogether, that is, reorder, any set of paragraphs of Sifra with no loss – or gain! – of meaning, since the paragraphs hold together as poorly or as well in any order. Only Scripture holds them together in their present position. That is why the logic of fixed association, and that alone, accounts for the cogency of the document as a whole. The contrast to the Mishnah hardly needs to be drawn. The Mishnah is cogent not only in the order and sequence of its sentences, whether episodic and miscellaneous or sustained and protracted in proposition and discourse. The Mishnah-tractates are cogent, beginning, middle, and end, from one sentence to the next, and that is because the cogency derives, whole and not only in part, from the exposition of the topic at hand, – that and one other thing: from the proposition concerning that topic that the framers of the Mishnah wish to lay forth. It is the simple fact that Sifra's authorship resorted to diverse logics for the joining of one sentence to another, one paragraph to another. The Mishnah's authorship appealed to only a single logic of cogent discourse, and that was the same logic that served for the presentation and demonstration of propositions: it was philosophical logic of a syllogistic character.

III. THE LOGICS OF COGENT DISCOURSE OF SIFRA:
2. CATALOGUE OF THE LOGIC OF COGENT DISCOURSE OF SIFRA

For this illustrative survey of the types and proportions of forms in Sifra I catalogue the exempla of Chapters 21-40, 56-65, 101-105, 121-125, 160-173, 202-206, 226-230, and 251-255, that is, 69 out of 277 chapters of Sifra or in excess of 25% of the whole. Since my translation has shown the uniform and formally coherent character of the document, that sample is very sizable indeed. Not only so, but I have taken my sample from different parts of the document. Furthermore, since most of the selections are only parts of *parashiyyot* we examine all of *Parashat Zabim,* as before. Examining a complete *parashah* gives us a different kind of sample, namely, one of the thirteen whole *parashiyyot* into which the document is divided. This survey of a complete *parashah* moreover permits us to determine whether or not there is a fixed order in the types of logics that are used. Hence these illustrations cover the range of materials in Sifra to test whether there is a limited and fixed pattern of formal preferences characteristic of the document as a whole. This purposive sample quite adequately serves the purpose of the present study.

1. Propositional Logic

XXI:I [Classification of two species into a single genus.]

XXI:II [Verse + "this teaches that" + Tosefta-citation.]

XXI:V [Verse + citation of Mishnah-passage. The Mishnah is represented as a secondary amplification of Scripture. The passage proceeds to another clause followed by "this teaches," another propositional statement.

XXIV:II ["Might one suppose" + "Scripture says" + Mishnah-citation. The pericope clearly is propositional in its inner cogency.]

XXVI:I-II [Seeing the two pericopes as Finkelstein maintains, we have nothing other than a dispute on a proposition, Mishnah-style.]

XXVI:IV [Citation of clause + "this teaches" + Mishnah-pericope.]

XXVII:I [The language is clarified in a sustained and propositional way, that is, "what is the correct way to...."]

XXVII:III [Dispute of Aqiba and Simeon is highly propositional.]

XXX:III.1-4 [Sequence of citations of Mishnah-sentences tacked on to phrases of the base-verse.]

XXXI:I [Since traits pertain to this which do not pertain to that and verse, Scripture had to specify.... This is a highly-propositional discourse and holds together well.]

XXXI:IV [Cogent statement of how Scripture on its own opposes a proposition, yielding another proposition.]

XXXII:II.1 [There is a sequence of propositional statements that yield a dispute.]

XXXIV:II [Why does Scripture rule...there are rules that apply here but not there.... This presents not only much information but also a splendid taxonomic proposition.]

XXXV:II.1-4 [Protracted citation of the Mishnah's propositions concerning classification of things.]

XXXVI:II [Just as...so...: proposition, pure and simple.]

XXXVII:II [Verse + "this teaches that" + Mishnah-pericope.]

XXXVIII:I [Verse + might one suppose + proof + Mishnah-passage.]

XL:I [Propositions on a theme.]

LVII:I.1-3 ["How so" + Mishnah-passages interspersed with proofs from Scripture for the propositions of the Mishnah, e.g., "how do we know that...." This same composition then ignores the Mishnah and asks perhaps..."how do we know that"...."Scripture says"..., the whole highly repetitive. But the Mishnah supplies the issues. Then we proceed beyond: how do we know that..., in a sustained and systematic inquiry. This entire composition seems to me both propositional and also, and especially, methodical-analytical. Hence I list it in both lists.]

LVIII:I [Just as above.]

LIX:I: This is the governing principle + proposition.

LIX:II: R. Aqiba says + propositions.

LX:I.1-3 [Verse of Scripture plus how do we know that..., repeated inquiry followed by arguments of a propositional character.]

LX:I.10 [How do you know that + citation of Mishnah.]

LXI:I.1 [Verse plus Mishnah-ruling.]

LXI:I.4 [As above + secondary proof.]

LXI:II.13-14: [Sequence of propositions not bound to brief amplifications of clauses of a verse.]

LXII:I.1: [Judah says, Eliezer says, etc.]

LXIII:I.3 [Verse + Mishnah-passage.]

LXIV:I.3 [Mishnah-citation + proofs.]

LXIV:II.10 -Mishnah-citation + proof.]

LXV:I.1-2 [Protracted citation of Mishnah-statements + proofs of Scripture.]

LXV:II.1-7 [Sequence of propositions of named authorities, leading to citation of Mishnah.]

CI:I.1, 2 [There are two distinct questions answered here in separate propositional statements.]

CIV:I.5 [Mishnah-passage cited at great length.]

CXXI:II.8: Sustained exposition of traits that apply to fowl and domesticated beasts.

CXXII:V.1-2: Scripture compares...just as...so....

CXXIII:I.6-11 [Proof of Mishnah-propositions.]

CXXIV:II.1 [Sustained discourse involving Aqiba.]

CXXIV:II.5 [Verse + Mishnah-citation.]

CXXV:I.3 [Mishnah-citation standing essentially on its own.]

CXXV:III [Sequence of propositions.]

CLXI:II [Citation of a Mishnah-passage.]

CLXIII:II [Simple proposition.]

CLXIII:III [Citation of Mishnah-passage.]

CLXIV:III [If these rules are stated...why are they also stated...the reason is that there are rules pertaining... which do not pertain.... Clear mishnaic proposition, pure and simple, based on comparison and contrast.]

CLXVII:II [Citation of clause of verse + on this basis + citation of Mishnah-passage.]

CLXVII:IV [What we have here is a sustained dialogue based on mishnaic logic of comparison and contrast.]

CLXVIII:III.6 [Proposition based on comparison of A to B: what is like follows the same rule.]

CLXIX:IV.1 [The appeal here is to comparison and contrast: just as ...so...then might one suppose?... Then appeal to Scripture. This is overall a formulation we should expect in the Mishnah, since the argument is based on comparison and contrast.]

CLXIX:IV.2 [Proof + Mishnah-citation.]

CLXX:I.7-8 [You turn out to rule as follows + propositions based on comparison and contrast.]

CLXXI:I.3-4 [Mishnah-citation.]

CCII:I.3, 5, 7, 8 [In this connection sages have said + Mishnah-citation.]

CCII:II [As above.]

CCIII:III.4 [Mishnah-citation joined by "this teaches that," a standard prologue for a propositional statement.]

CCIII:IV [How do we know that + Mishnah-citations + proofs from Scripture.]

CCIV:I.4 [Sustained discourse, presenting sizable propositions.]

CCIV:I.7 [What is the form of reverence + Mishnah-pericope.]

CCIV:II.1 [Citation of verse + Mishnah-pericope.]

CCV:I.5 [Proposition based on Scripture + Mishnah-citation.]

CCV:II.5 [Pericope of the Mishnah simply parachuted down, whole and complete, without clear pertinence.]

CCVI:I.1 [There is a clear proposition here, which draws upon a variety of verses to prove the point at hand. This is a fine example of a propositional statement, assembling facts in support of a generalization.]

CCXXVI:I.3-8 [Here we have a fine example of the insertion, whole, of a sizable Mishnah-passage within the framework of verses of the book of Leviticus. The whole is highly propositional in focus and purpose.]

CCXXVIII:I.1-6 [Here we have a sequence of propositional demonstrations: "how do we know that...."]

CCXXVIII:II.1 ["What has the Sabbath to do with the appointed seasons...and how do we know that...."]

CCXXIX:I.1-7 [As above.]

CCLI:I.1-2 [Introduction for, and then statement of, a Tosefta-passage.]

CCLII:I-12 [The entire program here derives from Mishnah or Tosefta, and the sustained discourse is propositional throughout.]

CCLIII:I.1-15 [As above, without variation.]

CCLIV:I.1-2 [As above.]

CCLIV:I.11-13 [Propositions deriving from Mishnah or Tosefta.]

CCLV:I.6 [Paragraph of the Mishnah, parachuted down.]

2. Teleological Logic

I cannot point to a great many units of sustained and completed thought in which an author(ship) appeals for cogency of discourse to teleological logic. True, we find occasional allusions to stories. But only one passage in our sample consists of a story with a beginning, middle, and end, and only in that passage does a story bear the burden of a message fundamental to the structure of discourse.

CCXXVII:I.5 [Proposition then illustrated by a sustained and coherent story. This shows us what can have been done, were an interest in making points through cogency attained by narrative or teleological logic to have guided our authorship.]

3. Fixed Associative Logic

XXI:III [Clauses of verse, no sustained proposition. Leads to a citation of Mishnah's rule, but the point of the Mishnah falls outside the frame of reference of the cited and amplified clauses.]

XXIII:IV [Ad hoc amplification of a single verse/rule.]

XXV:II.5-8: Clause plus amplification, several times, without a proposition joining the several clauses. This is pure commentary of an ad hoc and episodic character.

XXVI:V [Sequence of ad hoc exegeses. At this point we note no clear order of logics, rather a mix of this and that, depending on the program of the compilers.]

XXVII:II [Episodic amplification.]

XXIX:I.1-4 [Sequence of clauses and their amplifications.]

XXX:I [Episodic amplification of clauses, each in a few words + on this basis sages have stated + Mishnah-paragraph, utterly out of line with the foregoing. This is jerry-built, hence an example of pure fixed-associative logic.

XXX:III.5-8 [Clauses and amplifications.]

XXXII:I [=XXX:I]

XXXIII:II [Sequence of ad hoc amplifications.]

XXXIV:I.1-2 [The sequence of units of this composite are joined only by the base-verse. Some of them, however, do set forth propositions, e.g., No. 1.]

XXXIX:III.7-22 [A massive sequence of brief amplifications of brief citations of the base-verse.]

LX:I.6-8: [Citations of clauses of a verse and then brief amplification.

LXI:I.2: Random proposition.]

LXI:II.1-8, 10 [Here is a fine example of a sequence of random amplifications of clauses, which all together do not yield a single proposition.]

LXII:I.2-7, 11-14: [Sequence of episodic citations and amplifications of verses.]

LXIV:II:1-6,M 11-14 [Episodic proofs of unrelated propositions.]

LXV:II.8-12 [Episodic and brief amplifications of phrases of a base-verse.]

CI:II. [Long sequence of ad hoc comments on this and that. While some of the comments take up a methodical analytical program, the net effect of the composition is to create a set of clauses associated only through the fixed association defined by the base-verse. So what we have is nothing other than phrase by phrase amplification.]

CII:I.1-22 [Sequence of phrase by phrase amplifications clarify the story at hand. The materials do not hold together except as implicit contributions to a prevailing thesis.]

CIII:I.1 [As above.]

CXXI:II.9-13 [These episodic amplifications do not coalesce and leave the impression of forming a random set of statements rather than a sustained methodical-analytical exercise. But the classification is surely open to challenge.]

CXXIII:I.1-5 [This sequence of completed statements seems to me random and not pointed and propositional.]

CXXV:I.1-3 [Sequence of episodic observations, yielding a citation of Mishnah.]

CXXV:II.1, 3 [As above.]

CLXVII:I.1-2 [Two discrete items.]

CLXVII:V [Sustained sequence of episodic observations on this and that. Nothing holds the whole set of sentences/propositions together except for the base-verse.]

CLXVIII:II [As above.]

CLXXI:I.1-2 [Discrete exegeses.]

CLXXIII:II [This is a random program of items held together only by the base-verse. I see no sustained application of the principles of methodical analysis.]

CCIII:I [All I see here are discrete propositions, sentences that do not form a whole and cogent statement. The presence of "how do we know" does not turn the passage as a whole

into a propositional unit; there is no program, and the points made do not relate to one another.]

CCIII:II [Episodic glosses.]

CCIII:III.1-3 [As above.]

CCIV:I.1-3 [Episodic observations and clarifications. This is not the same as an exercise in inclusion or exclusion. Compare CCIV:I.5-6.]

CCIV:II.2-3 [Episodic remarks.]

CCV:I.1-4 [These sentences do not form a sustained proposition.]

CCV:II.1-4 [As above.]

CCV:II.6-8 [As above.]

CCVI:I.6-7 [Random observations.]

CCVI:II.1-16 [While the same word precipitates the same comment again and again, viewed as a whole, this sequence of sentences bears no common proposition and also does not set forth a model of a methodical-analytical exercise of proportion and substance. Hence it forms a fine instance of the power of fixed-associative logic to hold together discrete and episodic statements.]

CCXXVII:I.2-4, 6-8 [Episodic remarks. It is the case that these remarks respond in a conventional way to conventional words, but we have no methodical-analytical program in place here.]

CCLI:II.1-21 [Episodic, miscellaneous collection, without a cogent conception or a sustained proposition or even a protracted discussion. This is another fine example of the fixed associative logic at work.]

CCLV:I.1-5, 7-11 [Sequence of random propositions, not connected to one another. The sequence includes some propositions, e.g., in this connection sages have said, but the whole is not sustained but only ad hoc and episodic.]

4. Methodical-Analytical Logic

We note that these items also present propositions, but the presentation is based not on an argument of classification, such as the Mishnah's and Tosefta's authorships present, but rather on the application of a fixed mode of analysis, methodically applied. That is why we list these items separately; they are propositional, as are the items on the first of the four lists, but the proposition rests on a different kind of cogency from the kind that applies, over all, to the items on List No. 1.

XXI:IV [How come you encompass... after Scripture has used inclusionary language, it has then made an exclusion....]

XXII:I [Proposition + how do I know...I might propose...how do I know...it is a matter of logic.]

XXII:II-XXIII:I [Simeon says + proposition. But this entire matter yields "is that proposition not a matter of logic."]

XXIII:II [As above.]

XXIII:III [As above: Why encompass but exclude...after Scripture has used inclusionary language, it has further used exclusionary language....]

XXIV:I [I know that...how do I know that...Scripture says....]

XXIV:III [I know only...how do I know that...Scripture says....]

XXIV:IV [As above, This is a sustained and enormous discussion.]

XXV:I [Since it is said...might one suppose...? Scripture specifies... therefore excluding.... This proceeds to an exercise in criticism of taxonomy without Scripture's classification. Very fine example of methodical analysis, viewing in a single way a variety of topics.]

XXV:II [As above. + Mishnah-citation.]

XXVI:III [This refers to...might one suppose...plus argument from taxonomy + it is a matter of logic.]

XXVII:IV [Is it not a matter of logic?]

XXVII:V [As above.]

XXVIII:I.1 [The law encompasses this...how do I know that....]

XXVIII:I.2 [Citation + Mishnah-proposition + sustained proposition on the same theme. But the familiar methodical-analytical inquiry is I know only...how do I know that the same rule encompasses....]

XXVIII:II [How come you include X and exclude Y?]

XXVIII:III [Is not the contrary proposition a matter of mere logic?]

XXVIII:IV.1, 2, 3, 4 [As above. Several discrete instances.]

XXIX:I.5 [I shall exclude those but I shall not exclude ...for it is a matter of logic....]

XXIX:II [Is not the opposite of that proposition not a matter of logic? Several cases in a row.]

XXIX:III [What is the sense of Scripture here? Since it is said...I infer...I know only...how do I know...I encompass, but how do I know...Might one maintain...I know only...how do I know...I encompass....]

XXIX:IV [The contrary to that position surely is a matter of logic.]

XXX:II [Why does Scripture say so? Since it is said...might one suppose... then I shall eliminate...might one suppose....]

XXXI:II [Is it not a matter of logic?]

XXXI:III.1 [Why...to validate...Scripture further adds...for one might have argued as follows....]

XXXII:II.2 [Clause + might one suppose + Scripture says + Since Scripture says, might one suppose....]

XXXII:III [It is a matter of logic....]

XXXIII:I [Why does Scripture repeat... one might have reasoned...and that is a matter of logic....]

XXXIV:I.3 [Sustained argument *a fortiori* yielding Scripture's required proof.]

XXXIV:III [Sequence of inclusionary and exclusionary proofs resting on primacy of Scripture as always.]

XXXIV:IV [As above.]

XXXIV:V [When Scripture says, what is included...I add to that list.., just as above. This is a large and sustained sequence of fixed methodical proofs.]

XXXV:I [Inclusionary/exclusionary exercise.]

XXXV:II [Verse + might one suppose...Scripture says....]

XXXVI:I.1, 2 [Is that proposition not a matter of logic?]

XXXVI:III [Inclusionary/exclusionary exercise.]

XXXVII:I [Is that proposition not a matter of logic?]

XXXVII:II.2 [Might one suppose...and it is a matter of logic....]

XXXIX:I [Is this not a matter of logic?]

XXXIX:II [As above.]

XXXIX:III.1-6 [I know only...how about...Scripture says...if in the end we encompass...why does Scripture say...it is to indicate....]

XXXIX:IV [Is not the opposite a matter of mere logic?]

XL:II [Is not the opposite not a matter of logic?]

LVI:I [How do we know...Scripture says...might one suppose... Scripture says... (repeated inquiry in perfect balance and order).]

LVII:I.1-3 [How so + Mishnah-passages interspersed with proofs from Scripture for the propositions of the Mishnah, e.g., "how do we know that...." This same composition then ignores the Mishnah and asks perhaps...how do we know that...Scripture says..., the whole highly repetitive. But the Mishnah supplies the issues. Then we proceed beyond: how do we know that..., in a sustained and systematic inquiry. This entire composition seems to me both propositional and also, and especially, methodical-analytical. Hence I list it in both lists.]

LVIII:I [Just as above.]

LIX:II. [Aqiba's propositions are inclusionary and exclusionary in a systematic way.]

LX:I.9 [Argument against taxonomy without Scripture.]

LXI:I.3: [Is the opposite not a matter of logic?]

LXI:II.9 [Is not the opposite not a matter of logic?]

LXI:II.11-12 [Exclusionary/inclusionary exercise.]

LXII:I.8-10. 15-16: [Inclusion/exclusion.]

LXIII:I.1, 2 [Exclusion/inclusion.]

LXIII:I.3-5 [Just as...so when...or might one maintain...how do I know... Scripture says...or might one suppose...how do I know...]

LXIII:II [Citation + excluding + is that not to be proven merely by logic?]

LXIV:I.1-2 [Citation + excluding...how do I know that the law encompasses...I shall encompass...but as to...Scripture says..., etc.]

LXIV:II.77ff. [The point is...he must...how do we know that...for one might have suppos-

ed...Scripture says...that serves to encompass....and how do we know....]

LXV:I.3 [Proof of limitations of logic.]

CIII:II [Inclusionary/exclusionary exercise, e.g., I know only...how about...might one suppose....]

CIII:III [As above.]

CIV:I [This serves to encompass...might one suppose....I know only...how do I know....I know that...it is to be shown through a logical argument....]

CV:I [How do we know that the prohibition extends to..., repeated inclusionary proof. Then: how do we know that....it is a matter of logic....]

CV:II [Exclusion/inclusion; proof that logic does not serve. We note that these two fixed methodical-analytical approaches occur together as often as they appear on their own.]

CXXI:I.1-7 [Inclusionary statement.]

CXXI:II [Inclusionary/exclusionary.]

CXXII:I.1-7 [I know only that...are covered by the law...how do I know that....]

CXXII:II.1-2 [What is the point of Scripture? Because it is said..., I might infer....]

CXXII:III [Might I think that...might I think that...and is the opposite not logical.... A sequence of exclusions and inclusions and a test of logic unaffected by Scripture.]

CXXII:IV [Is not the proposition a matter of logic?]

CXXII:V.3-4 [Inclusionary.]

CXXIII:I.13-14 [Might one suppose... Scripture says...: exclusionary; logical argument of a systematic order.]

CXXIV:I [I know only that...how do I know that it encompasses....]

CXXIV:II.2, 3-4 [Logical argument concerning appropriate analogy, other systematic questions.]

CXXV:II.2 [Is not the contrary proposition not a matter of logic?]

CXXV:II.4 [Inclusionary argument.]

CLX:I [Inclusionary study of who is subject to the law: I know only...how do I know that I should encompass...]

CLX:II [Logic.]

CLX:III [As above.]

CLX:IV [As above.]

CLXI:I [As above.]

CLXI:II [Inclusionary exercise.]

CLXI:III [Is this not a matter of logic?]

CLXI:IV [As above.]

CLXII:I [Exclusionary problem: I shall eliminate but not...I know that...how do I know that the law covers...might I then encompass... Or might I exclude....]

CLXII:II [As above.]

CLXII:III [As above.]

CLXII:IV [Is not the contrary logical?]

CLXIII:I.1-2 [As above.]

CLXIII:I.3-6 [Exclusionary/inclusionary study.]

CLXIII:III [As above.]

CLXIV:I [I know that...how do I know that....]

CLXIV :II [Same plan as above. + Is it not an argument *a fortiori*?]

CLXIV:IV [Exclusionary.]

CLXIV:V [As above.]

CLXV:I [Test of logic on its own.]

CLXV:II [As above.]

CLXV:III [As above.]

CLXV:IV [Exclusionary exercise.]

CLXVI:I [I know only...how do I know...might one suppose...the contrary proposition is a matter of logical proof....]

CLXVI:II [As above.]

CLXVII:I.3 [As above, mixture of methodical analyses.]

CLXVII:III [Might one suppose.... Exclusionary exercise, then: is it not a matter of logic?]

CLXVIII:I [Exclusion/inclusion.]

CLVIII:III [Exclusion/inclusion.]

CLXIX:I [I know only...how do I know...; sequence of inclusionary and exclusionary exercises.]

CLXIX:II [Is not the opposite logical?]

CLXIX:III [Just as above.]

CLXX:I.1-6 [Exclusion, inclusion.]

CLXX:II [Is that proposition not merely a matter of logic?]

CLXX:III [I know only...how do I know...?]

CLXXI:II [Inclusionary/exclusionary definitions.]

CLXXII:I [As above.]

CLXXII:II [As above.]

CLXXIII:I [This sequence is essentially the exposition of a methodical program, just as at Chapter 170.]

CCII:I.1-2 [Exclusionary/inclusionary. At each point the upshot is a Mishnah-citation, cited at List No. 1.]

CCII:II [As above.]

CCIV:I.5-6 [Might one suppose... Scripture says..., repeated exclusions.]

CCIV:III [Systematic exclusions.]

CCVI:I.2-5 [Inclusionary/exclusionary.]

CCXXVI:I.1-2 [Inclusionary/exclusionary.]

CCXVII:I.1 [Inclusionary work of discipline and strict order.]

CCXXX:I.1-4 [Here we have a sequence of methodical-analytical inquiries. The first is inclusionary; the second concerns the role of logic; the third is "what is the point of this verse of Scripture," and the fourth is inclusionary. I cannot find a better example of how a fixed methodical-analytical program guides the response to verses of Scripture and their themes. If there were a recurrent order in which the methods were applied, we should see some evidence of it here. I see none.]

CCLIV:I.3-11 [Sequence of methodical-analytical items, partly inclusionary; partly "what is the point of Scripture here?"]

5. Proportions of the Use of Logics of Cogent Discourse in Sifra

A simple logical program, consisting of three logics of cogent discourse, served for every statement in the illustrative material I have now surveyed. An author of a pericope could make use of one or more of three logics to join one sentence or fact to another sentence or fact. We may state with finality that our authorship made choices about how cogent and coherent statements would be made to hold together in its document. Counting each entry as a single item presents a gross and simple picture of the proportions of the types of logics we have catalogued. Since numerous entries in each of the catalogues encompass more than a single item, the understatement of the numbers of examples in any one catalogue will be balanced by understatements of the numbers of examples in the other catalogues. Overall, my count is as follows:

Form	Number of entries	Percentage of the whole
Commentary	121	55%
Dialectical	57	26%
Citation	42	19%
	220	100%

Type of Logic	Number of entries	Percentage of the whole
Propositional	73	30.4%
Teleological	1	0.4%
Fixed Associative	43	17.9%
Methodical-Analytical	123	51.0%
	240	99.7%

The operative logics are mainly propositional, approximately 82%, inclusive of propositional, teleological, and methodical-analytical compositions. Whether these propositional statements constitute expressions of a topical program is a topic to address in Chapter Four. An authorship intending what we now call a commentary will have found paramount use for the logic of fixed association. That logic clearly served only a modest purpose in the context of the document as a whole. Our authorship developed a tripartite program. It wished to demonstrate the limitations of the logic of hierarchical classification, such as predominates in the Mishnah; that forms a constant theme of the methodical analytical logic. It proposed, second, to restate the Mishnah within the context of Scripture, that is, to rewrite the Written Torah to make a place for the Oral Torah. This is worked out in the logic of propositional discourse. And, finally, it wished in this rewriting to re-present the whole Torah as a cogent and unified document. Through the logic of fixed association it in fact did re-present the Torah. The three logics correspond, in their setting within the inner structure of cogent discourse, to the three paramount purposes to which our authorship devoted Sifra. This is precisely the same result we attained in Chapter Two. There we noted that the forms of the document admirably expressed the polemical purpose of the authorship at hand. What they wished to prove was that a taxonomy resting on the traits of things without reference to Scripture's classifications cannot serve. They further wished to restate the Oral Torah in the setting of the Written Torah. And, finally, they wished to accomplish the whole by rewriting the Written Torah. The dialectical form accomplished the first purpose, the citation-form the second, and the commentary-form the third. We have now produced the same result twice. I have now to demonstrate that, as to the logic of cogent discourse, our authorship made choices particular to itself and distinctive to the accomplishment of its own purpose. To accomplish that purpose we now compare their program of the logic of cogent discourse with the program paramount in the Mishnah and the Tosefta.

IV. THE LOGICS OF COGENT DISCOURSE OF THE MISHNAH AND OF THE TOSEFTA

To appreciate what is fresh and interesting in Sifra's enormous interest in cogency achieved through methodical-analytical discourse, let us turn to writing that is equally coherent and intelligible, but in no way comparable in its principle of logical discourse. Our authorship makes things appear to hold together by asking the same kind of questions of very diverse evidence. The method is therefore the constant, and not the proposition. There are two quite different, but equally coherent, writings to consider, the Mishnah and the Pentateuch. The Mishnah's logic of cogent discourse establishes propositions that rest upon philosophical bases, e.g., through the proposal of a thesis and the composition of a list of facts that (e.g., through shared traits of a taxonomic order) prove the thesis. The Mishnah presents rules and treats stories (inclusive of history) as incidental and of merely taxonomic interest. Its logic is propositional, and its intellect does its work through a vast labor of classification, comparison, and contrast generating governing rules and generalizations. The Pentateuch by contrast provides an account of how things were in order to explain how things are and set forth how they should be, with the tabernacle in the wilderness the model for (and modeled after) the temple in the Jerusalem abuilding. The Mishnah speaks in a continuing present tense, saying only how things are, indifferent to the *were* and the *will-be*. The Pentateuch focuses upon self-conscious "Israel," saying who they were and what they must become to overcome how they now are. The Mishnah understands by "Israel" as much the individual as the nation and identifies as its principal actors, the heroes of its narrative, not the family become a nation, but the priest and the householder, the woman and the slave, the adult and the child, and other castes and categories of person within an inward-looking, established, fully landed community. Given the Mishnah's authorship's interest in classifications and categories, therefore in systematic hierarchization of an orderly world, one can hardly find odd that (re)definition of the subject-matter and problematic of the systemic social entity.

Let us dwell on this matter of difference in the prevailing logic, because the contrast allows us to see how one document will appeal to one logic, another to a different logic. While the Pentateuch appeals to the logic of teleology to draw together and make sense of facts, so making connections by appeal to the end and drawing conclusions concerning the purpose of things, the Mishnah's authorship knows only the philosophical logic of syllogism, the rule-making logic of lists. The Pentateuchal logic reached concrete expression in narrative, which served to point to the direction and goal of matters, hence, in the nature of things, of history. Accordingly, those authors, when putting together diverse materials, so shaped everything as to form of it all as continuous a narrative as they could construct, and through that "history" that they made up, they delivered their message and also portrayed that message as cogent and compelling. If the Pentateuchal writers were theologians of history, the Mishnah's aimed at composing a natural philosophy for supernatural, holy Israel. Like good Aristotelians, they would uncover the components of the rules by comparison and contrast, showing the rule for one thing by finding out how it compared with like things and contrasted with the unlike.[9] Then, in their view, the unknown would become known, conforming to the rule of the like thing, also to the opposite of the rule governing the unlike thing.

That purpose is accomplished, in particular, though list-making, which places on display the data of the like and the unlike and implicitly (ordinarily, not explicitly) then conveys the role. That is why, in exposing the interior logic of its authorship's intellect, the Mishnah had to be a book of lists, with the implicit order, the nomothetic traits, dictating the ordinarily unstated general and encompassing rule. And all this why? It is in order to make a single statement, endless times over, and to repeat in a mass of tangled detail precisely the same fundamental judgment. The Mishnah in its way is as blatantly repetitious in its fundamental statement as is the Pentateuch. But the power of the Pentateuchal authorship, denied to that of the Mishnah, lies in their capacity always to be heard, to create sound by resonance of the surfaces of things. The Pentateuch is a fundamentally popular and accessible piece of writing. By contrast, the Mishnah's writers spoke into the depths, anticipating a more acute hearing than they ever would receive. So the repetitions of Scripture reenforce the message, while the endlessly

---

[9]Compare G. E. R. Lloyd, *Polarity and Analogy. Two Types of Argumentation in Early Greek Thought* (Cambridge, 1966: Cambridge University Press). But the core-logic of *Listenwissenschaft* extends back to Sumerian times.

repeated paradigm of the Mishnah sits too deep in the structure of the system to gain hearing from the ear that lacks acuity or to attain visibility to the untutored eye. So much for the logic. What of the systemic message? Given the subtlety of intellect of the Mishnah's authorship, we cannot find surprising that the message speaks not only in what is said, but in what is omitted.

The framers of the Mishnah appeal solely to the traits of things. The authorship of Sifra by contrast insists that by themselves, the traits of things do not settle anything.[10] Only Scripture designates classifications that serve. When we understand the logical basis of *Listenwissenschaft*, we shall understand the issue in a clear way. *Listenwissenschaft* defines a way of aproving propositions through classification, so establishing a set of shared traits that form a rule which compels us to reach a given conclusion. Probative facts derive from the classification of data, all of which point in one direction and not in another. A catalogue of facts, for example, may be so composed that, through the regularities and indicative traits of the entries, the catalogue yields a proposition. A list of parallel items all together point to a simple conclusion; the conclusion may or may not be given at the end of the catalogue, but the catalogue – by definition – is pointed. All of the catalogued facts are taken to bear self-evident connections to one another, established by those pertinent shared traits implicit in the composition of the list, therefore also bearing meaning and pointing through the weight of evidence to an inescapable conclusion. The discrete facts then join together because of some trait common to them all. This is a mode of classification of facts to lead to an identification of what the facts have in common and – it goes without saying, an explanation of their meaning. These and other modes of philosophical argument are entirely familiar to us all. In calling all of them "philosophical," I mean only to distinguish them from the other three logics we shall presently examine. Now we see how fundamental to thought was Sifra's authorship's insistence that Scripture, not things viewed on their own, dictates the classification of things.

The diverse topical program of the Mishnah, time and again making the same points on the centrality of order, works itself out in a single logic of cogent discourse, one which seeks the rule that governs diverse cases. And, as we now see, that logic states within its interior structure the fundamental point of the document as a whole. The correspondence of logic to system here, as in the Pentateuch viewed overall, hardly presents surprises. Seeing how the logic does its work within the document therefore need not detain us for very long. Two pericopes of the Mishnah

---

[10]I have spelled out this matter in *Uniting the Dual Torah: Sifra and the Problem of the Mishnah* (Atlanta, 1988: Scholars Press for Brown Judaic Studies).

show us the logic that joins fact to fact, sentence to sentence, in a cogent proposition, that is, in our terms, a paragraph that makes a statement. To see how this intellect does its work we turn first to Mishnah-tractate Berakhot, Chapter Eight, to see list-making in its simplest form, and then to Mishnah-tractate Sanhedrin, Chapter Two, to see the more subtle way in which list-making yields a powerfully-argued philosophical theorem. In the first of our two abstracts we have a list, carefully formulated, in which the announcement at the outset tells us what is catalogued, and in which careful mnemonic devices so arrange matters that we may readily remember the conflicting opinions. So in formal terms, we have a list that means to facilitate memorization. But in substantive terms, the purpose of the list and its message(s) are not set forth, and only ample exegesis will succeed in spelling out what is at stake. Here is an instance of a Mishnah-passage which demands an exegesis not supplied by the Mishnah's authorship.

Mishnah-tractate Berakhot Chapter Eight

8

1.   A.   These are the things which are between the House of Shammai and the House of Hillel in [regard to] the meal:

[1]   B.   The House of Shammai say, "One blesses over the day, and afterward one blesses over the wine."

        And the House of Hillel say, "One blesses over the wine, and afterward one blesses over the day."

[2] 8.2. A.   The House of Shammai say, "They wash the hands and afterward mix the cup."

        And the House of Hillel say, "They mix the cup and afterward wash the hands."

[3] 8:3. A.   The House of Shammai say, "He dries his hands on the cloth and lays it on the table."

        And the House of Hillel say, "On the pillow."

[4] 8:4. A.   The House of Shammai say, "They clean the house, and afterward they wash the hands."

        And the House of Hillel say, "They wash the hands, and afterward they clean the house."

[5] 8:5. A.   The House of Shammai say, "Light, and food, and spices, and *Havdalah.*"

        And the House of Hillel say, "'Light, and spices, and food, and *Havdalah.*"

[6]   B.   The House of Shammai say, "'Who created the light of the fire.'"

        And the House of Hillel say, "'Who creates the lights of the fire.'"

The mnemonic serving the list does its work by the simple reversal of items. If authority A has the order 1, 2, then authority be will give 2, 1. Only entry [3] breaks that pattern. What is at stake in the making of the list is hardly transparent, and why day/wine vs. wine/day, with a parallel, e.g., clean/wash vs. wash/clean, yields a general principle the authorship does not indicate. All we know at this point, therefore, is that we deal with list-makers. But how lists work to communicate principles awaits exemplification.

The next abstract allows us much more explicitly to identify the *and* and the *equal* of Mishnaic discourse, showing us through the making of connections and the drawing of conclusions the propositional and essentially philosophical mind that animates the Mishnah. In the following passage, drawn from Mishnah-tractate Sanhedrin Chapter Two, the authorship wishes to say that Israel has two heads, one of state, the other of cult, the king and the high priest, respectively, and that these two offices are nearly wholly congruent with one another, with a few differences based on the particular traits of each. Broadly speaking, therefore, our exercise is one of setting forth the genus and the species. The genus is head of holy Israel. The species are king and high priest. Here are the traits in common and those not shared, and the exercise is fully exposed for what it is, an inquiry into the rules that govern, the points of regularity and order, in this minor matter, of political structure. My outline, imposed in bold-face type, makes the point important in this setting.

Mishnah-tractate Sanhedrin   Chapter Two

1. The rules of the high priest: subject to the law, marital rites, conduct in bereavement

2:1.

A.   A high priest judges, and [others] judge him;

B.   gives testimony, and [others] give testimony about him;

C.   performs the rite of removing the shoe [Deut. 25:7-9], and [others] perform the rite of removing the shoe with his wife.

D.   [Others] enter levirate marriage with his wife, but he does not enter into levirate marriage,

E.   because he is prohibited to marry a widow.

F.   [If] he suffers a death [in his family], he does not follow the bier.

G.   "But when [the bearers of the bier] are not visible, he is visible; when they are visible, he is not.

H.   "And he goes with them to the city gate," the words of R. Meir.

I.   R. Judah says, "He never leaves the sanctuary,

J.   "since it says, *'Nor shall he go out of the sanctuary'* (Lev. 21:12)."

K.   And when he gives comfort to others,

L.   the accepted practice is for all the people to pass one after another, and the appointed [prefect of the priests] stands between him and the people.

M.   And when he receives consolation from others,

N.   all the people say to him, "Let us be your atonement."

O.   And he says to them, "May you be blessed by Heaven."

P.   And when they provide him with the funeral meal,

Q.   all the people sit on the ground, while he sits on a stool.

2. The rules of the king: not subject to the law, marital rites, conduct in bereavement

2:2.

A.   The king does not judge, and [others] do not judge him;

B.   does not give testimony, and [others] do not give testimony about him;

C.   does not perform the rite of removing the shoe, and others do not perform the rite of removing the shoe with his wife;

D.   does not enter into levirate marriage, nor [do his brother] enter levirate marriage with his wife.

E.   R. Judah says, "If he wanted to perform the rite of removing the shoe or to enter into levirate marriage, his memory is a blessing."

F.   They said to him, "They pay no attention to him [if he expressed the wish to do so]."

G.   [Others] do not marry his widow.

H.   R. Judah says, "A king may marry the widow of a king.

I.   "For so we find in the case of David, that he married the widow of Saul,

J.   "For it is said, *'And I gave you your master's house and your master's wives into your embrace'* (II Sam. 12:8)."

2:3

A.   [If] [the king] suffers a death in his family, he does not leave the gate of his palace.

B.   R. Judah says, "If he wants to go out after the bier, he goes out,

C.   "for thus we find in the case of David, that he went out after the bier of Abner,

D.   "since it is said, *'And King David followed the bier'* (2 Sam. 3:31)."

E.   They said to him, "This action was only to appease the people."

F.   And when they provide him with the funeral meal, all the people sit on the ground, while he sits on a couch.

3. Special rules pertinent to the king because of his calling

2:4

A.   [The king] calls out [the army to wage] a war fought by choice on the instructions of a court of seventy-one.

B.   He [may exercise the right to] open a road for himself, and [others] may not stop him.

C.   The royal road has no required measure.

D.   All the people plunder and lay before him [what they have grabbed], and he takes the first portion.

E.   *"He should not multiply wives to himself"* (Deut. 17:17) – only eighteen.

F.   R Judah says, "He may have as many as he wants, so long as they *do not entice him* [to abandon the Lord (Deut. 7:4)]."

G.   R. Simeon says, "Even if there is only one who entices him [to abandon the Lord] – lo, this one should not marry her."

H.   If so, why is it said, "He should not multiply wives to himself"?

I.   Even though they should be like Abigail (1 Sam. 25:3).

J.   *"He should not multiply horses to himself"* (Deut. 17:16) – only enough for his chariot.

K.   *"Neither shall he greatly multiply to himself silver and gold"* (Deut. 17:16) – only enough to pay his army.

L.   *"And he writes out a scroll of the Torah for himself"* (Deut. 17:17).

M.   When he goes to war, he takes it out with him; when he comes back, he brings it back with him; when he is in session in court, it is with him; when he is reclining, it is before him,

N.   as it is said, *"And it shall be with him, and he shall read in it all the days of his life"* (Deut. 17:19).

2:5

A.   [Others may] not ride on his horse, sit on his throne, handle his sceptre.

B.   And [others may] not watch him while he is getting a haircut, or while he is nude, or in the bath-house,

C.   since it is said, *"You shall surely set him as king over you"* (Deut. 17:15) – that reverence for him will be upon you.

The subordination of Scripture to the classification-scheme is self-evident. Scripture supplies facts. The traits of things – kings, high priests – dictate classification-categories on their own, without Scripture's dictate.

The philosophical cast of mind is amply revealed in this essay, which in concrete terms effects a taxonomy, a study of the genus, national leader, and its two species, [1] king, [2] high priest: how are they alike, how are they not alike, and what accounts for the differences. The premise is that national leaders are alike and follow the same rule, except where they differ and follow the opposite rule from one another. But that premise also is subject to the proof effected by the survey of the data consisting of concrete rules, those systemically inert facts that here come to life for the purposes of establishing a proposition. By itself, the fact that, e.g., others may not ride on his horse, bears the burden of no systemic proposition. In the context of an argument constructed for nomothetic, taxonomic purposes, the same fact is active and weighty. The whole depends upon three premises: [1] the importance of comparison and contrast, with the supposition that [2] like follows the like, and the unlike follows the opposite, rule; and [3] when we classify, we also hierarchize, which yields the argument from hierarchical classification: if this, which is the lesser, follows rule X, then that, which is the greater, surely should follow rule X. And that is the whole sum and substance of the logic of *Listenwissenschaft* as the Mishnah applies that logic in a practical way.

No natural historian can find the discourse and mode of thought at hand unfamiliar; it forms the foundation of all disposition of data in quest of meaning. For if I had to specify a single mode of thought that established connections between one fact and another, it is in the search for points in common and therefore also points of contrast. We seek connection between fact and fact, sentence and sentence in the subtle and balanced rhetoric of the Mishnah, by comparing and contrasting two things that are like and not alike. At the logical level, too, the Mishnah falls into the category of familiar philosophical thought. Once we seek regularities, we propose rules. What is like another thing falls under its rule, and what is not like the other falls under the opposite rule. Accordingly, as to the species of the genus, so far as they are alike, they share the same rule. So far as they are not alike, each follows a rule contrary to that governing the other.

So the work of analysis is what produces connection, and therefore the drawing of conclusions derives from comparison and contrast: the *and,* the *equal.* The proposition then that forms the conclusion concerns the essential likeness of the two offices, except where they are different, but the subterranean premise is that we can explain both likeness and difference by appeal to a principle of fundamental order and unity. To make these observations concrete, we turn to the case at hand. The important contrast comes at the outset. The high priest and king fall into a single genus, but speciation, based on traits particular to the king, then distinguishes the one from the other. All of this exercise is conducted essentially independently of Scripture; the classifications derive from the system, are viewed as autonomous constructs; traits of things define classifications and dictate what is like and what is unlike. Let us now see how the authorship of Sifra judges that mode of category-formation.

V. THE LOGICS OF COGENT DISCOURSE OF SIFRÉ TO DEUTERONOMY

The four logics catalogued for Sifra originated in my study of Sifré to Deuteronomy.[11] The logic that links one sentence to the next by focusing on a proposition to be proved appeals for connection to the principles of philosophical syllogism. I included in this catalogue the passages that wish to turn a detail of a case into a general rule, in which the generalization is not of a methodical character but important for a

---

[11]As I said earlier, since I have not systematically analyzed the logics of any prior document, I cannot conduct any comparisons here except for the one between Sifra and Sifré to Deuteronomy. The result, however, demonstrates that there are significant differences between the two texts and shows that analysis and comparison of the logics operative in other documents should prove interesting. My sense is that the logics that are utilized serve the larger proposition and polemic of a document, just as do the types of rhetoric that are found paramount, as we saw in Chapter Two. Hence there is a correspondence between the programmatic intent of an authorship and its rhetorical and logical media for expressing its message. The conception that the medium corresponds with the message hardly begins in this obscure corner of humanistic learning.

particular detail of law. In Sifré to Deuteronomy I count 690 individual units of thought in which two or more sentences are joined together by a connection defined through a proposition. There may be more than that number, but I do not believe any count will yield less.

I find remarkably slight resort to narratives in legal contexts. But that is only a general impression. I count 61 narratives of various kinds, or, more accurately, units of discourse that find cogency in narrative rather than in proposition. My best sense is that it was not through narrative that the bulk of the units of completed thought, resting on making connections between two or more sentences, was composed. Narrative logic of connection is treated as null in some writings, such as The Fathers, while it does predominate in other compositions, e.g., The Fathers According to Rabbi Nathan.

Fixed-associative discourse in Sifré to Deuteronomy yields 159 entries in this catalogue. Compared to the whole, it is not a sizable proportion. Most documents establish connections between two sentences or among three or more sentences not through appeal to fixed-associative cogency, but through resort to propositional logic of one kind or another (inclusive of methodical analysis).[12] Cogent discourse attained through fixed analytical method in Sifré to Deuteronomy produces 232 entries. But that understates the proportion, to the whole, of major units of discourse that hold together through methodical analytical logic. The prevailing logic of Sifré to Deuteronomy is not exegetical but propositional. Most units of cogent discourse in Sifré to Deuteronomy appeal for cogency to propositions, not to fixed associations, such as characterize commentaries and other compilations of exegeses of verses of Scripture. Let us begin with a rough statistical summary comparing Sifra's to Sifré to Deuteronomy's choices among the four logics at hand.

---

[12]That matter of methodical analysis covers both Talmuds' reading of the Mishnah, which is so remarkably disciplined as to serve as the finest example of the matter that we have. Any notion that Mishnah-exegesis in the Talmuds is free association is based on impressions formed merely in episodic reading of this and that, skipping from here to there in search of thematically pertinent items, such as characterizes yeshiva-study in this country, or (merely) the guesswork of the romantic and the wildly uninformed literary critics of the day. Anyone who has studied either Yerushalmi or Bavli Mishnah-exegesis knows how a fixed and rigorous program imposes its agenda everywhere.

Sifra:

Type of Logic	Number of entries	Percentage of the whole
Propositional	73	30.4%
Teleological	1	0.4%
Fixed Associative	43	17.9%
Methodical-Analytical	123	51.0%
	240	99.7%

Sifré to Deuteronomy:

Type of Logic	Number of entries	Percentage of the whole
Fixed-Associative	159	13.9%
Propositional	690	60.4%
Narrative	61	5.3%
Methodical-Analytical	232	20.3%
	1142	99.9%

In Sifré to Deuteronomy, of the propositional units of cogent discourse, 60.4% in fact constitute propositional discourse, 5.3% find cogency in narrative, and 20.3% in the methodical-analytical mode. Since that mode presents not one but two propositions, we find ourselves on firm ground in maintaining that the logic of Sifré to Deuteronomy is a logic not of exegesis but of sustained proposition of one kind of another. Our document's authorship links one sentence to another by appeal to connections of proposition, not mere theme, and only occasionally asks the structure of a verse or sequence of verses to sustain the intelligible joining of two or more sentences into a coherent and meaningful statement.

The differences between Sifra and Sifré to Deuteronomy are these:

1. Propositional logic: Sifré to Deuteronomy contains two times the proportion of propositional compositions. We shall see in Chapter Four that Sifré to Deuteronomy is a highly propositional compilation, while Sifra is not.

2. Teleological logic: Sifré to Deuteronomy contains thirteen times the proportion of narrative compositions than does Sifra. Since teleological logic is propositional in its foundation, that disproportion is readily understood.

3. Fixed associative logic: the two documents make use of approximately the same proportions of this mode of stringing sentences or facts together, 17.9% against 13.9%, a differential of 1.2 times the proportion in Sifra over Sifré to Numbers. That does not seem to me a significant difference, given the rough-and-ready mode of classification employed at this stage in the work.

4. Methodical-analytical logic: Sifra's authorship presents *two and a half* times the proportion of completed units of thought held together by the logic of systematic methodical analysis than does that of Sifré to Deuteronomy. The message of Sifra depends upon repetition of a single highly abstract proposition expressed in concrete terms. Hence the repetition of the same inquiry over a sizable number of diverse entries makes the point Sifra's authorship wishes to make. Sifré to Deuteronomy makes its points as propositions, not as repeated demonstrations of fundamental attributes of thought, such as is the paramount medium of thought and expression of Sifra.

The striking difference therefore comes at the end. The authorship of Sifra has a very clear notion of precisely the questions it wishes persistently to address and it follows that program through the majority of the pericopes of its document. These questions then form the distinctive trait of mind of Sifra in comparison to Sifré to Deuteronomy. The resort to teleological logic in both documents is negligible in proportion to the whole; the utilization of fixed associative logic is pretty much in equal proportions; and Sifré to Deuteronomy is characterized by an interest in propositional discourse, while in Sifra that mode of discourse is subsumed under the logic of fixed analysis. This underlines what is particular, in this context, to our authorship: it knows precisely what it wishes to ask to a majority of passages of the book of Leviticus, and that concerns not proposition but the correct mode of thought and analysis.

VI. THE COMPARISON: ALIKE AND NOT ALIKE

Do the rhetoric and logic of the two documents derive from the (supposed) purpose of the authorship of forming a commentary? Not at all. To the contrary, in general, the logic of Sifra and of Sifré to Deuteronomy is sustained, propositional, mostly philosophical, and not that of commentary. What holds things together for our authorships only a fifth of the time relies upon the verses at hand to impose order and cogency upon discourse. Both authorships ordinarily appeal to propositions to hold two or more sentences together. If, by definition, a commentary appeals for cogency to the text that the commentators propose to illuminate, then ours are documents that in no essential way fall into the classification of a commentary. The logic is not that of a commentary, and the formal repertoire shows strong preference for other than commentary-form.

Like Sifré to Deuteronomy, Sifra is, in fact, a highly argumentative, profoundly well-crafted and cogent set of propositions. We may indeed speak of a message, a topical program, such as, in general, a commentary that in form appeals to a clause of a verse and a phrase of a sentence, and in logic holds things together through fixed associations, is not apt to set forth. A commentary makes statements about meanings of verses, but it does not make a set of cogent statements of its own. I have now shown that in rhetoric and in logic Sifra like Sifré to Deuteronomy takes shape in such a way as to yield a statement, or a set of cogent statements. Such a document as ours indicates that an authorship has found a need for propositions to attain cogency or impart connections to two or more sentences, calls upon narrative, demands recurrent methodical analyses. The text that is subjected to commentary only occasionally is asked to join sentence to sentence. Yet, turning to Sifra in particular, we have now to find out whether the remarkably cogent and propositional discourse paramount in our document is meant to present a detailed program of doctrines, such as is the case in some other midrash-compilations. Now that we have explored the deep structures of thought, finding out how positions were reached and cogently set forth, we turn to the result of the workings of rhetoric and logic. What we now want to know is what our authorship proposed to say: the topical agenda, the propositional program.

Part Two

COMPARISONS OF TOPIC AND PROPOSITION AMONG SPECIES OF MIDRASH-COMPILATIONS

SPECIES: THE ADDRESS TO THE BOOK OF LEVITICUS

Chapter Four

Topical Comparison

I. TOPIC, PROPOSITION, AND THE DIALOGUE WITH SCRIPTURE

At issue in the description and analysis of the topical program of a document is a deceptively simple question. We ask what subject an authorship has chosen to discuss, and, further, what the propositions concerning that subject an authorship sets forth. When we describe a document's topic and the problematic of the topic – the thing the authorship wants to know and say about that topic – I further propose to correlate the topical program with the rhetorical and logical traits of a piece of writing. Now that we know how our authorship has chosen among a repertoire of modes of expression and thought a distinctive manner of patterning language and a singular means of conducting cogent and intelligible discourse, the logical next question confronts us. I want to ask in particular about the correspondence between medium of expression and of thought and the message conveyed in one way and not in some other.

All parties share the same ground, that outlined by Scripture, and that fact legitimates comparison of the topical programs of the several midrash-compilations. But it also misleads if we assume that, because everyone reads the same revelation, therefore any party to public discourse will set forth a message congruent with that of any other party to the same discourse. The first consideration in defining the program of discourse calls attention to the centrality of Scripture. Can we not simply list the verses discussed by an authorship to determine the topical program of that authorship? All examples of the classification of writing under consideration sustain a dialogue with Scripture, so, on the face of matters, the topic of each document ought to derive from revelation.[1] But knowing that all authorships in common address Scripture, viewed as God's revelation to Israel, does not allow us to predict the topical program of any particular writing. Proof of that proposition derives from our

---

[1]We here review points covered in Chapter One.

document and its companion. For, as we shall see in a moment, two authorships read the book of Leviticus, the one producing Leviticus Rabbah, the other, Sifra, and the topical programs of those two authorships bear no interesting resemblances. Indeed they scarcely intersect. The authorship of Sifra pursued the topical program of Scripture verse by verse, beginning to end.[2] The counterpart compilers of Leviticus Rabbah discuss thirty-seven verses of Leviticus and set forth thirty-seven propositions. So knowing that Scripture defines a program of subjects and may even set forth propositions for inquiry enlightens not at all. That is why the comparison and contrast of topical programs and specific propositions as set forth by diverse authorships proves illuminating. Alas, when we come to Sifra, we identify only with great difficulty the topical program of our authorship so far as that program transcends the successive verses of the book of Leviticus; no sustained polemic particular to the comments on the verses presents itself. We shall see a clear and sustained message, but one that is implicit throughout; the conception of a topical program will prove awry to Sifra.

The reason that the question of the topic of a document is not a simple one is best set forth through our pertinent example, the two compilations of midrash-exegesis organized around the book of Leviticus. When in the case of a midrash-compilation addressed to the book of Leviticus, we ask about the components of a topical program, we should like to know whether an authorship has focused upon the topics of that book or upon some other list of topics altogether. Specifically, the book of Leviticus concerns sacrifice and the cult, the sanctity of Israel and in particular its priestly caste, the distributive economics of Temple effected through the disposition of crops and land, and the like. Are these the principal foci of discussion? In addressing these topics, an author can introduce a wholly different program, e.g., allegorically reading one thing in terms of something else. Then the exposition of the topics of the book of Leviticus will enjoy only slight attention. A different topical program will attach itself to the book of Leviticus, from the range of subjects that that book covers. In the case of the book of Leviticus, a set of historical questions of a salvific character can take the place of the inquiry into cultic questions concerning sanctification with which the priestly writers originally dealt. That example may now be restated in terms pertinent to a variety of documents. In more general terms an authorship may follow the topical

---

[2]The authorship of Sifré to Deuteronomy as we have their work omit reference to sizable tracts of that document, but I cannot point to three successive verses of the book of Leviticus on which our authorship does not comment in some way or other. The situation with Sifré to Numbers will become clear when the translation is complete. The Rabbah-authorships in general, including Genesis Rabbah, do not take as their responsibility verse-by-verse commentaries.

program of the biblical writing on which it chooses to comment, or it may well treat that program as a pretext for discourse on entirely other matters. Therein lies one complexity of topical analysis.

But, as I have already hinted, there is yet another source of puzzlement. An authorship may treat a topic but present no propositions that we can identify. That is to say, the authorship may simply paraphrase, clarify, generate some secondary considerations, without expressing any systematic interest in saying more than the text says in its own terms and language. In commenting on words and phrases, for instance, no important propositions may emerge. The topical program of a document may prove not even an expansion or disquisition upon themes of Leviticus but simply a repetition and paraphrase of the topical program of that book.

There is yet another possibility, one that, we already realize, will take pride of place in our study of Sifra. An authorship may address a variety of topics in a single way. Then, while it has no topical program distinctive to itself, it does convey the particular message that it has chosen to set forth. When an authorship repeatedly asks a single question in the confrontation with diverse data, it does so in such a way as to treat no identified subject-matter at all. Rather the authorship aims to prove various encompassing principles that are not particular to any theme but generative of modes of thought as these apply to every theme. In that context we find it difficult to claim that a given document follows a topical program at all. Yet the document does set forth a message and may be shown to intend to demonstrate a clear-cut proposition. That is to say, the authorship presents propositions *illustrated by its treatment of a variety of subjects*, all of them incidental to what is really at stake in the discourse and its sustained argument.

Yet what of "Judaism" overall? I refer to a topical program that will be implicit in any inquiry conducted by any authorship. For theoretical purposes, let me now rapidly lay matters out in the most abstract and encompassing way that I can. Speaking only very generally, I see three principal topics on which authorships of midrash-compilations may present propositions. These correspond to the three relationships into which, in sages' world, that is, the sages' conception of their social entity, their "Israel," entered: [1] with heaven, [2] on earth, and [3] within. These relationships yield, for our rubrics, systematic statements that concern relationships [1] between Israel and God, with special reference to the covenant, the Torah, and the land; [2] Israel and the nations, with interest in Israel's history, past, present, and future; [3] Israel on its own terms, with focus upon Israel's distinctive leadership. So much for a theoretical program. Do these theoretical categories of topics with their propositions serve? Alas, these capacious rubrics, which in theory may well serve diverse midrash-compilations, each with its own distinctive viewpoint and intellectual method, tell us little about the topical program of the several documents at hand. And were we to employ them in organizing the episodic sayings and opinions found in Sifra, we should find a mass of materials pertinent to a theme but not cogent with one another in any interesting way. The three categories would constitute the intellectual counterpart to the logic of fixed association. For knowing the three potential categories of topics, we cannot predict the actual program of Sifra – or of any document. Indeed, a survey of the principal readings of the book of Leviticus, those of Leviticus Rabbah and of Sifra, will show us how complex and diverse are the topical responses to the same book of Scripture. Then we shall compare the topical programs of Sifra and Leviticus Rabbah to the topical programs of the two other taxa into which each of these documents fit, the two Sifrés for Sifra, Genesis Rabbah and Pesiqta deRab Kahana for Leviticus Rabbah.

We therefore move from what is theoretically possible to what is practically feasible: the address, to various documents, of a program of questions pertinent to each. To make matters more concrete, I define the two broad questions with which we now deal.

[1]   Does the document at hand deliver a particular message and viewpoint or does it merely serve as a repository for diverse, received materials?

[2]   Does the authorship deliver its message, its choices as to form and meaning, or merely transmit someone else's?

To broaden the question let me unpack secondary questions. First, do we have a cogent statement or a mere scrapbook? Comparing one compilation to another yields the correct way of finding the answer. A document may serve solely as a convenient repository of prior sayings and stories, available materials that will have served equally well (or poorly) wherever they took up their final location. A composition may exhibit a viewpoint, a purpose of authorship distinctive to its framers or collectors and arrangers. Such a characteristic literary purpose would be so powerfully particular to one authorship that nearly everything at hand can be shown to have been (re)shaped for the ultimate purpose of the authorship at hand. These then are collectors and arrangers who demand the title of authors. Context and circumstance then form the prior condition of inquiry, the result, in exegetical terms, the contingent one.

Now to explain how we shall deal with the case at hand. The particular problem of Sifra requires us to demonstrate, first of all, that a document can set forth a sequence of cogent propositions. For even at the outset of our analysis, I find it difficult to frame a hypothesis that Sifra follows any sort of topical program independent of that of the book of Leviticus, and, more important, that our authorship wishes to set forth any propositions particular to the themes or subject-matter of the book of Leviticus. Our comparison therefore must begin not with Sifra but with those documents that do treat topical programs distinctive to their authorship and that – I have already demonstrated in the books listed in the preface – do make points or argue propositions particular to those programs. Only then, with the topical programs and programmatic traits of other midrash-compilations in hand, will the true character of Sifra, viewed in the present perspective, become clear.

II. THE TOPICAL PROGRAM OF LEVITICUS RABBAH: PROPOSITIONS

As I noted just now, the framers of Leviticus Rabbah to begin with treat topics, not particular verses. That formal difference from Sifra underlines a more substantive one. The authorship of Leviticus Rabbah makes generalizations that are freestanding and demonstrated through sustained presentation of appropriate evidence and even implicit argument. The writers or compilers express cogent propositions through extended compositions, rather than (at best) emoting episodic ideas. By contrast, in Sifra (as in Genesis Rabbah), things people wished to say were attached to predefined statements based on an existing text, constructed in accord with an organizing logic independent of the systematic expression of a single, well-framed idea. That is to say, the sequence of verses of Leviticus, for Sifra, and Genesis, for Genesis Rabbah, and their contents played a massive role in the larger-scale organization of each of the midrash-compilations and expression of its propositions. But in each of its thirty-seven chapters or *parashiyyot,* the authorship of Leviticus Rabbah so collected and arranged its materials as to present an abstract proposition. That proposition is not expressed only or mainly through episodic restatements, assigned, as I said, to an order established by a base text (whether Genesis or Leviticus or a Mishnah-tractate for that matter). Rather it emerges through a logic of its own. What is noteworthy[3] in Leviticus Rabbah is the move from an essentially exegetical mode of logical discourse to a fundamentally philosophical one. It is the shift from discourse framed around an established (hence old) text to syllogistic argument organized around a proposed (hence new) theorem or proposition. What changes, therefore, is the way in which cogent thought takes place, as people moved from discourse contingent on some prior principle of organization to discourse autonomous of a ready-made program inherited from an earlier paradigm.

---

[3]I think it is also new and unprecedented in the unfolding of the canon, assuming a date for Leviticus Rabbah of ca. 450, and, for Genesis Rabbah, of ca. 400. But no proposition in this book depends upon a particular date for a given document.

Reading one thing in terms of something else, the builders of Leviticus Rabbah systematically adopted for themselves and adapted to their own circumstance the reality of the Scripture, its history and doctrines. Specifically, they transformed that history from a sequence of one-time events, leading from one place to some other, into the fixtures of enduring tableau of an ever-present mythic world. Persons who lived once now operate forever; events take on that circularity that allows them to happen again and again, every day. No longer was there one Moses, one David, one set of happenings of a distinctive and never-to-be-repeated character. Now whatever happens, of which the thinkers propose to take account, must enter and be absorbed into that established and ubiquitous pattern and structure founded in Scripture. One-time history is therefore transformed into all-time social structure. It is not that biblical history repeats itself. Rather, biblical history no longer constitutes history as a story of things that happened once, long ago, and pointed to some one moment in the future. Rather it becomes an account of things that happen every day – hence, an ever-present mythic world, or, in anachronistic terms, history is turned into social science.

That mode of thought explains why, in Leviticus Rabbah, Scripture as a whole does not dictate the order of discourse, let alone its character. In this document they chose in Leviticus itself a verse here, a phrase there. These then presented the pretext for propositional discourse commonly quite out of phase with the cited passage.[4] The verses that are quoted ordinarily shift from the meanings they convey to the implications they contain, speaking about something, anything, other than what they seem to be saying. So the as-if frame of mind brought to Scripture brings renewal to Scripture, so as to require seeing everything with fresh eyes. The result of the new vision was a reimagining of the social world envisioned by the authorship of the document, that is, the everyday world of Israel in its Land in that difficult time. For what the sages now proposed was a reconstruction of existence along the lines of the ancient design of Scripture as they read it. What that meant was that, from a sequence of one-time and linear events, everything that happened was turned into a repetition of known and already experienced paradigms, hence, once more, a mythic being. The source and core of the myth, of course, derive from Scripture – Scripture reread, renewed, reconstructed along with the society that revered Scripture.

The mode of thought that dictated the issues and the logic of the document instructed the thinkers to see one thing in terms of something

---

[4]A principal exercise of exegetes therefore has been to explain why a given base-verse yields the lesson that is attached to it. The subtlety of the explanations underlines the simple fact that in this context the verse does not generate the proposition and is not meant to.

else. Thinking as they did, the framers of the document saw Scripture in a new way, just as they saw their own circumstance afresh, rejecting their world in favor of Scripture's, reliving Scripture's world in their own terms. That, incidentally, is why their topical program did not encompass history, an account of what was happening and what it meant. It was not that they did not recognize or appreciate important changes and trends reshaping their nation's life. They could not deny that reality. In their apocalyptic reading of the dietary and leprosy laws, for instance, they made explicit their close encounter with the history of the world as they knew it. But they had another mode of responding to history. It was to treat history as if it were already known and readily understood: history as social science. Whatever happened had already happened. Scripture dictated the contents of history, laying forth the structures of time, the rules that prevailed and were made known in events. Self-evidently, these same thinkers projected into Scripture's day the realities of their own, turning Moses and David into rabbis, for example. But that is how people think in that mythic, enchanted world in which, to begin with, reality blends with dream, and hope projects onto future and past alike how people want things to be.

Let us turn, now, from these somewhat abstract observations to a concrete account of what happened, in particular, when the thinkers at hand undertook to reimagine reality – both their own and Scripture's. Exactly how did they think about one thing in terms of another, and what did they choose, in particular, to recognize in this rather complex process of juggling unpalatable present and unattainable myth? When they read the rules of sanctification of the priesthood, they heard the message of the salvation of all Israel. Leviticus became the story of how Israel, purified from social sin and sanctified, would be saved. Let us turn to the classifications of rules that sages located in the social laws of Leviticus. The first, and single paramount, category takes shape within the themes associated with the national life of Israel.

The principal lines of structure flow along the fringes: Israel's relationships with others. These are horizontal, with the nations, and vertical, with God. But, from the viewpoint of the framers of the document, the relationships form a single, seamless web, for Israel's vertical relationships dictate the horizontals as well; when God wishes to punish Israel, the nations come to do the work. The relationships that define Israel, moreover, prove dynamic, not static, in that they respond to the movement of the Torah through Israel's history. When the Torah governs, then the vertical relationship is stable and felicitous, the horizontal one secure, and, when not, God obeys the rules and the nations obey God. So the first and paramount, category takes shape within the themes associated with the national life of Israel. The principal lines of structure flow along the fringe, Israel's relationships with others. The relationships form a single, seamless web, for Israel's vertical relationships dictate the horizontals as well; when God wishes to punish Israel, the nations come to do the work. The relationships that define Israel, moreover, prove dynamic, not static, in that they respond to the movement of the Torah through Israel's history. When the Torah governs, then the vertical relationship is stable and felicitous, the horizontal one secure, and, when not, God obeys the rules and the nations obey God.

The topical program yields a set of propositions as follows: God loves Israel, so gave them the Torah, which defines their life and governs their welfare. Israel is alone in its category (*sui generis*), so what is a virtue to Israel is a vice to the nation, life-giving to Israel, poison to the gentiles. True, Israel sins, but God forgives that sin, having punished the nation on account of it. Such a process has yet to come to an end, but it will culminate in Israel's complete regeneration. Meanwhile, Israel's assurance of God's love lies in the many expressions of special concern, for even the humblest and most ordinary aspects of the national life: the food the nation eats, the sexual practices by which it procreates. These life-sustaining, life-transmitting activities draw God's special interest, as a mark of his general love for Israel. Israel then is supposed to achieve its life in conformity with the marks of God's love. These indications moreover signify also the character of Israel's difficulty, namely, subordination to the nations in general, but to the fourth kingdom, Rome, in particular. Both food laws and skin diseases stand for the nations. There is yet another category of sin, also collective and generative of collective punishment, and that is social. The moral character of Israel's life, the treatment of people by one another, the practice of gossip and small-scale thuggery – these too draw down divine penalty. The nation's fate therefore corresponds to its moral condition. The moral condition, however, emerges not only from the current generation. Israel's richest hope lies in the merit of the ancestors, thus in the Scriptural record of the merits attained by the founders of the nation, those who originally brought it into being and gave it life.

The world to come is so portrayed as to restate these same propositions. Merit overcomes sin, and doing religious duties or supererogatory acts of kindness will win merit for the nation that does them. Israel will be saved at the end of time, and the age, or world, to follow will be exactly the opposite of this one. Much that we find in the account of Israel's national life, worked out through the definition of the liminal relationships, recurs in slightly altered form in the picture of the world to come. The world to come will right all presently unbalanced relationships. What is good will go forward, what is bad will come to an end. The simple message is that the things people revere, the cult and its majestic course through the year, will go on; Jerusalem will come back, so too the Temple, in all their glory. Israel will be saved through the merit of the ancestors, atonement, study of Torah, practice of religious duties. The prevalence of the eschatological dimension at the formal structures, with its messianic and other expressions, here finds its counterpart in the repetition of the same few symbols in the expression of doctrine. The theme of the moral life of Israel produces propositions concerning not only the individual but, more important, the social virtues that the community as a whole must exhibit.

This brings us to the laws of society for Israel's holy community as the authorship of Leviticus Rabbah sets forth those laws. The message to the individual constitutes a revision, for this context, of the address to the nation: humility as against arrogance, obedience as against sin, constant concern not to follow one's natural inclination to do evil or to overcome the natural limitations of the human condition. Israel must accept its fate, obey and rely on the merits accrued through the ages and God's special love. The individual must conform, in ordinary affairs, to this same paradigm of patience and submission. Great men and women, that is, individual heroes within the established paradigm, conform to that same pattern, exemplifying the national virtues. Among these, of course, Moses stands out; he has no equal. The special position of the humble Moses is complemented by the patriarchs and by David, all of whom knew how to please God and left as an inheritance to Israel the merit they had thereby attained.

If we now ask about further recurring themes or topics, there is one so commonplace that we should have to list the majority of paragraphs of discourse in order to provide a complete list. It is the list of events in Israel's history, meaning, in this context, Israel's history solely in scriptural times, down through the return to Zion. The one-time events of the generation of the flood, Sodom and Gomorrah, the patriarchs and the sojourn in Egypt, the exodus, the revelation of the Torah at Sinai, the golden calf, the Davidic monarchy and the building of the Temple, Sennacherib, Hezekiah, and the destruction of northern Israel, Nebuchadnezzar and the destruction of the Temple in 586 B. C., the life of Israel in Babylonian captivity, Daniel and his associates, Mordecai and Haman – these events occur over and over again. They turn out to serve as paradigms of sin and atonement, steadfastness and divine intervention, and equivalent lessons. We find, in fact, a fairly standard repertoire of scriptural heroes or villains, on the one side, and conventional lists of Israel's enemies and their actions and downfall, on the other. The boastful, for instance, include the generation of the flood, Sodom and Gomorrah, Pharaoh, Sisera, Sennacherib, Nebuchadnezzar, the wicked empire (Rome) – contrasted to Israel, "despised and humble in this world." The four kingdoms recur again and again, always ending, of course, with Rome, with the repeated message that after Rome will come Israel. But Israel has to make this happen through its faith and submission to God's will. Lists of enemies ring the changes on Cain, the Sodomites, Pharaoh, Sennacherib, Nebuchadnezzar, Haman.

Accordingly, the mode of thought brought to bear upon the theme of history remains exactly the same as before: list making, with data exhibiting similar taxonomic traits drawn together into lists based on common monothetic traits or definitions. These lists then through the power of repetition make a single enormous point. They prove a social law of history. The catalogues of exemplary heroes and historical events serve a further purpose. They provide a model of how contemporary events are to be absorbed into the biblical paradigm. Since biblical events exemplify recurrent happenings, sin and redemption, forgiveness and atonement, they lose their one-time character. At the same time and in the same way, current events find a place within the ancient, but eternally present, paradigmatic scheme. So no new historical events, other than exemplary episodes in lives of heroes, demand narration because, through what is said about the past, what was happening in the times of the framers of Leviticus Rabbah would also come under consideration. This mode of dealing with biblical history and contemporary events produces two reciprocal effects. The first is the mythicization of biblical stories, their removal from the framework of ongoing, unique patterns of history and sequences of events and their transformation into accounts of things that happen all the time. The second is that contemporary events too lose all of their specificity and enter the paradigmatic framework of established mythic existence. So (1) the Scripture's myth happens every day, and (2) every day produces reenactment of the Scripture's myth.

In seeking the substance of the mythic being invoked by the exegetes at hand, who read the text as if it spoke about something else and the world as if it lived out the text, we uncover a simple fact. At the center of the pretense, that is, the as-if mentality of Leviticus Rabbah and its framers, we find a simple proposition. Israel is God's special love. That love is shown in a simple way. Israel's present condition of subordination derives from its own deeds. It follows that God cares, so Israel may look forward to redemption on God's part in response to Israel's own regeneration through repentance. When the exegetes proceeded to open the scroll of Leviticus, they found numerous occasions to state that proposition in concrete terms and specific contexts. The sinner brings on his own sickness. But God heals through that very ailment. The nations of the world govern in heavy succession, but Israel's lack of faith guaranteed their rule and its moment of renewal will end it. Israel's leaders – priests, prophets, kings – fall into an entirely different category from those of the nations, as much as does Israel. In these and other concrete allegations, the same classical message comes forth. Accordingly, at the foundations of the pretense lies the long-standing biblical-Jewish insistence that Israel's sorry condition in no way testifies to Israel's true worth – the grandest pretense of all. All of the little evasions of the primary sense in favor of some other testify to this, the great denial that what is, is what counts. Leviticus Rabbah makes that statement with art and imagination. But it is never subtle about saying so.

Salvation and sanctification join together in Leviticus Rabbah. The laws of the book of Leviticus, focused as they are on the sanctification of the nation through its cult, in Leviticus Rabbah indicate the rules of salvation as well. The message of Leviticus Rabbah attaches itself to the book of Leviticus, as if that book had come from prophecy and addressed the issue of the meaning of history and Israel's salvation. But the book of Leviticus came from the priesthood and spoke of sanctification. The paradoxical syllogism – the as-if reading, the opposite of how things seem – of the composers of Leviticus Rabbah therefore reaches simple formulation. In the very setting of sanctification we find the promise of salvation. In the topics of the cult and the priesthood we uncover the national and social issues of the moral life and redemptive hope of Israel. The repeated comparison and contrast of priesthood and prophecy, sanctification and salvation, turn out to produce a complement, which comes to most perfect union in the text at hand.

The focus of Leviticus Rabbah and its laws of history is upon the society of Israel, its national fate and moral condition. Indeed, nearly all of the *parashiyyot* of Leviticus Rabbah turn out to deal with the national, social condition of Israel, and this in three contexts: (1) Israel's setting in the history of the nations, (2) the sanctified character of the inner life of Israel itself, (3) the future, salvific history of Israel. So the biblical book that deals with the holy Temple now is shown to address the holy people. Leviticus really discusses not the consecration of the cult but the sanctification of the nation – its conformity to God's will laid forth in the Torah, and God's rules. So when we review the document as a whole and ask what is that something else that the base-text is supposed to address, it turns out that the sanctification of the cult stands for the salvation of the nation. So the nation now is like the cult then, the ordinary Israelite now like the priest then. The holy way of life lived now, through acts to which merit accrues, corresponds to the holy rites then. The process of metamorphosis is full, rich, complete. When everything stands for something else, the something else repeatedly turns out to be the nation. This is what Leviticus Rabbah spells out in exquisite detail, yet never missing the main point. It is in the context of that highly cogent message that we shall ask whether Sifra sets forth any propositions, let alone a cogent and stunning judgment so powerfully laid out in Leviticus Rabbah. But first we shall have to make certain that the treatment of the book of Leviticus by the authorship of Leviticus Rabbah is particular and significant, not simply a repetition of generally prevailing propositions in a singular context.

III. THE TOPICAL PROGRAM OF LEVITICUS RABBAH COMPARED WITH THAT OF GENESIS RABBAH

The mode of thought paramount in Leviticus Rabbah proves entirely congruent with the manner of reflection characteristic of Genesis Rabbah, and the propositions concerning history and the social laws of Israel are the same. But there are sufficient differences to show that each document is meant to bear its distinctive message. Where the two authorships differ is in detail; the main points are identical. We see that fact in a simple survey of the propositions of Genesis Rabbah. For, as in Leviticus Rabbah, so here, if I had to point to the single most important proposition of Genesis Rabbah, it is that, in the story of the beginnings of creation, humanity, and Israel, we find the message of the meaning and end of the life of the Jewish people. This appeal to not history but rule-making precedent runs parallel to the equivalent interest in regularities in Leviticus Rabbah. Where the authorship of Genesis Rabbah differs is the choice of the paradigm, which is now the age of beginnings; but that choice leads to quite distinctive propositions, which, to be sure, prove quite congruent to those important in Leviticus Rabbah.

As the rules of Leviticus set forth the social laws of Israel's history in Leviticus Rabbah, so the particular tales of Genesis are turned into paradigms of social laws in Genesis Rabbah.[5] The deeds of the founders

---

[5]The parallel mode of thought in Sifré to Deuteronomy and in Sifra is the exercise of inclusion and exclusion, which turns a case or an example into a law with clear-cut application or exclusion. That mode of generalizing law forms the counterpart to the interest in generalizing laws from incidents or anecdotes that is characteristic of Genesis Rabbah. In both cases we observe the move from an essentially ad hoc and episodic mode of thinking to a philosophical and scientific one. The profound interest in generalization, rather than merely precedent or ad hoc observation, characteristic of the authorships of Sifra and Sifré to Deuteronomy, for law, and of Leviticus Rabbah and Genesis Rabbah, for history, seems to me one of the deepest and most indicative traits of mind of the Judaism of the Dual Torah in its intellectual origin and marks that Judaism as deeply philosophical. No student of the writings of the Church fathers can find that fact surprising, even though the idiom of the formative intellects of the Judaism of the Dual Torah is less accessible, within the philosophical mode, than that of the formative intellects of Christianity, particularly Catholic (not Gnostic) Christianity.

supply signals for the children about what is going to come in the future. So the biography of Abraham, Isaac, and Jacob also constitutes the paradigm by which to interpret the history of Israel later on. If the sages could announce a single syllogism and argue it systematically, that is the proposition on which they would insist. The sages understood that stories about the progenitors, presented in the book of Genesis, define the human condition and proper conduct for their children, Israel in time to come. Accordingly, they systematically asked Scripture to tell them how they were supposed to conduct themselves at the critical turnings of life. In a few words let me restate the conviction of the framers of Genesis Rabbah about the message and meaning of the book of Genesis:

> We now know what will be in the future. How do we know it? Just as Jacob had told his sons what would happen in time to come, just as Moses told the tribes their future, so we may understand the laws of history if we study the Torah. And in the Torah, we turn to beginnings: the rules as they were laid out at the very start of human history. These we find in the book of Genesis, the story of the origins of the world and of Israel.

> The Torah tells us not only what happened but why. The Torah permits us to discover the laws of history. Once we know those laws, we may also peer into the future and come to an assessment of what is going to happen to us – and, especially, of how we shall be saved from our present existence. Because everything exists under the aspect of a timeless will, God's will, and all things express one thing, God's program and plan, in the Torah we uncover the workings of God's will. Our task as Israel is to accept, endure, submit, and celebrate.

I cannot see any difference, in principle, between this view of the meaning and uses of the Torah and the view expressed in Leviticus Rabbah. The point of difference is in topic, not proposition, let alone problematic. In Genesis Rabbah the entire narrative of Genesis is so formed as to point toward the sacred history of Israel, the Jewish people: its slavery and redemption; its coming Temple in Jerusalem; its exile and salvation at the end of time. The powerful message of Genesis in Genesis Rabbah proclaims that the world's creation commenced a single, straight line of events, leading in the end to the salvation of Israel and through Israel all humanity. Israel's history constitutes the counterpart of creation, and the laws of Israel's salvation form the foundation of creation. Therefore a given story out of Genesis, about creation, events from Adam to Noah and Noah to Abraham, the domestic affairs of the patriarchs, or Joseph, will bear a deeper message about what it means to be Israel, on the one side, and what in the end of days will happen to Israel, on the other.

So the persistent theological program requires sages to search in Scripture for meaning for their own circumstance and for the condition of their people. If, therefore, In the story of the beginnings of creation, humanity, and Israel, we find the message of the meaning and end of the life of the Jewish people. The deeds of the founders supply signals for the children about what is going to come in the future. The biography of Abraham, Isaac, and Jacob also constitutes a protracted account of the history of Israel later on. If the sages could announce a single syllogism and argue it systematically, that is the proposition upon which they would insist. Sages read the book of Genesis as if it portrayed the history of Israel and Rome. Why Rome in the form it takes in Genesis Rabbah? And how come the obsessive character of sages disposition of the theme of Rome? Were their picture merely of Rome as tyrant and destroyer of the Temple, we should have no reason to link the text to the problems of the age of redaction and closure. But now it is Rome as Israel's brother, counterpart, and nemesis, Rome as the one thing standing in the way of Israel's, and the world's, ultimate salvation. So the stakes are different, and much higher. It is not a political Rome but a Christian and messianic Rome that is at issue: Rome as surrogate for Israel, Rome as obstacle to Israel. Why? It is because Rome now confronts Israel with a crisis, and, I argue, the program of Genesis Rabbah constitutes a response to that crisis. Rome in the fourth century became Christian. Sages respond by facing that fact quite squarely and saying, "Indeed, it is as you say, a kind of Israel, an heir of Abraham as your texts explicitly claim. But we remain the sole legitimate Israel, the bearer of the birthright – we and not you. So you are our brother: Esau, Ishmael, Edom." And the rest follows.

By rereading the story of the beginnings, sages discovered the answer and the secret of the end. Rome claimed to be Israel, and, indeed, sages conceded, Rome shared the patrimony of Israel. That claim took the form of the Christians' appropriate of the Torah as "the Old Testament," so sages acknowledged a simple fact in acceding to the notion that, in some way, Rome too formed part of Israel. But it was the rejected part, the Ishmael, the Esau, not the Isaac, not the Jacob. The advent of Christian Rome precipitated the sustained, polemical, and, I think, rigorous and well-argued rereading of beginnings in light of the end. Rome then marked the conclusion of human history as Israel had known it. Beyond? The coming of the true Messiah, the redemption of Israel, the salvation of the world, the end of time. So the issues were not inconsiderable, and when the sages spoke of Esau/Rome, as they did so often, they confronted the life-or-death decision of the day.

The authorship of Genesis Rabbah focuses its discourse on the proposition that the book of Genesis speaks to the life and historical condition of Israel, the Jewish people. The entire narrative of Genesis is so formed as to point toward the sacred history of Israel, the Jewish people: its slavery and redemption; its coming Temple in Jerusalem; its exile and salvation at the end of time. The powerful message of Genesis in the pages of Genesis Rabbah proclaims that the world's creation commenced a single, straight line of events, leading in the end to the salvation of Israel and through Israel all humanity. Therefore a given story will bear a deeper message about what it means to be Israel, on the one side, and what in the end of days will happen to Israel, on the other. And that is precisely the proposition endlessly represented by the authorship of Leviticus Rabbah. The subjects change, the point remains the same. And that fact will strike us as the result of considered choice when we turn to Sifra and the two Sifrés, which make other points and exhibit other concerns.

IV. THE TOPICAL PROGRAM OF LEVITICUS RABBAH COMPARED WITH THAT OF PESIQTA DERAB KAHANA

Closely related to Leviticus Rabbah in that its authorship has borrowed five *parashiyyot* from the earlier writing, Pesiqta deRab Kahana moves beyond the appeal to scriptural history (as in Genesis Rabbah) or to scriptural case-law (as in Leviticus Rabbah). Rather they set forth propositions entirely independent of the received Scripture and so produced the most sustainedly theological compilation, worked out in the modes of argument of philosophy and in the idiom of scriptural exegesis, of midrash-exegeses that derives from late antiquity. In Pesiqta deRab Kahana I see three independently argued propositions.

The first is that God loves Israel, that love is unconditional, and Israel's response to God must be obedience to the religious duties that God has assigned, which will produce merit. Much of the argument for this proposition draws upon the proof of history as laid out in Scripture and appeals to history transformed into paradigm. Israel's obedience to God is what will save Israel. That means doing the religious duties as required by the Torah, which is the mark of God's love for – and regeneration of – Israel. The tabernacle symbolizes the union of Israel and God. When Israel does what God asks above, Israel will prosper down below. If Israel remembers Amalek down below, God will remember Amalek up above and will wipe him out. A mark of Israel's loyalty to God is remembering Amalek. God does not require the animals that are sacrificed, since man could never match God's appetite, if that were the issue, but the savor pleases God [as a mark of Israel's loyalty and obedience]. The first sheaf returns to God God's fair share of the gifts that God bestows on Israel, and those who give it benefit, while those who hold it back suffer. The first sheaf returns to God God's fair share of the gifts that God bestows on Israel, and those who give it benefit, while those who hold it back suffer. Observing religious duties, typified by the rites of The Festival, brings a great reward of that merit that ultimately leads to redemption. God's ways are just, righteous and merciful, as shown by God's concern that the offspring remain with the mother for seven days. God's love for Israel is so intense that he wants to hold them back for an extra day after The Festival in order to spend more time with them, because, unlike the nations of the world, Israel knows how to please God. This is a mark of God's love for Israel.

The second proposition moves us from the ontology to the history of that *sui generis*-social entity that is Israel. It is that God is reasonable and when Israel has been punished, it is in accord with God's rules. God forgives penitent Israel and is abundant in mercy. The good and the wicked die in exactly the same circumstance or condition. Laughter is vain because it is mixed with grief. A wise person will not expect too much joy. But when people suffer, there ordinarily is a good reason for it. That is only one sign that God is reasonable and God never did anything lawless and wrong to Israel or made unreasonable demands, and there was, therefore, no reason for Israel to lose confidence in God or to abandon him. God punished Israel to be sure. But this was done with reason. Nothing happened to Israel of which God did not give fair warning in advance, and Israel's failure to heed the prophets brought about her fall. And God will forgive a faithful Israel. Even though the Israelites sinned by making the golden calf, God forgave them and raised them up. On the New Year, God executes justice, but the justice is tempered with mercy. The rites of the New Year bring about divine judgment and also forgiveness because of the merit of the fathers. Israel must repent and return to the Lord, who is merciful and will forgive them for their sins. The penitential season of the New Year and Day of Atonement is the right time for confession and penitence, and God is sure to accept penitence. By exercising his power of mercy, the already-merciful God grows still stronger in mercy.

The third proposition is that God will save Israel personally at a time and circumstance of his own choosing. While I take for granted that the hope for future redemption animates the other compilations, we look in vain in some of them, Sifra for a prime example, for an equivalent obsession with messianic questions. Israel may know what the future redemption will be like, because of the redemption from Egypt. The paradox of the red cow, that what imparts uncleanness, namely touching the ashes of the red cow, produces cleanness is part of God's ineffable wisdom, which man cannot fathom. Only God can know the precise moment of Israel's redemption. That is something man cannot find out on his own. But God will certainly fulfill the predictions of the prophets about Israel's coming redemption. The Exodus from Egypt is the paradigm of the coming redemption. Israel has lost Eden – but can come home, and, with God's help, will. God's unique power is shown through Israel's unique suffering. In God's own time, he will redeem Israel. The lunar calendar, particular to Israel, marks Israel as favored by God, for the new moon signals the coming of Israel's redemption, and the particular new moon that will mark the actual event is that of Nisan. When God chooses to redeem Israel, Israel's enemies will have no power to stop him, because God will force Israel's enemies to serve Israel, because of Israel's purity and loyalty to God. Israel's enemies are punished, and what they propose to do to Israel, God does to them. Both directly and through the prophets, God is the source of true comfort, which he will bring to Israel. Israel thinks that God has forsaken them. But it is Israel who forsook God, God's love has never failed, and will never fail. Even though he has been angry, his mercy still is near and God has the power and will to save Israel. God has designated the godly for himself and has already promised to redeem them. He will assuredly do so. God personally is the one who will comfort Israel. While Israel says there is no comfort, in fact, God will comfort Israel. Zion/Israel is like a barren woman, but Zion will bring forth children, and Israel will be comforted. Both God and Israel will bring light to Zion, which will give light to the world. The rebuilding of Zion will be a source of joy for the entire world, not for Israel alone. God will rejoice in Israel, Israel in God, like bride and groom.

There is a profoundly cogent statement made through the composition of this document, and this is the message of Pesiqta deRab Kahana: God loves Israel, that love is unconditional, and Israel's response to God must be obedience to the religious duties that God has assigned, which will produce merit. God is reasonable and when Israel has been punished, it is in accord with God's rules. God forgives penitent Israel and is abundant in mercy. God will save Israel personally at a time and circumstance of his own choosing. Israel may know what the future redemption will be like, because of the redemption from Egypt. Pesiqta deRab Kahana therefore has been so assembled as to exhibit a viewpoint, a purpose of its particular authorship, one quite distinctive, in its own context (if not in a single one of its propositions!) to its framers or collectors and arrangers. Why the authorship of Leviticus Rabbah will not have concurred in a general way I cannot say. But I also cannot find these propositions in Leviticus Rabbah, which presents its own points.[6] And when these particular propositions do make an appearance in Leviticus Rabbah or in Genesis Rabbah, they do not receive that emphasis that characterizes Pesiqta deRab Kahana's authorships presentation of them.

---

[6]I immediately qualify that there are chapters of Pesiqta deRab Kahana which originate in Leviticus Rabbah. In form and in polemic, in plan and in program, the materials assembled in Pesiqta deRab Kahana cohere, to such a degree that on the basis of traits of cogency we can differentiate materials in Pesiqta deRab Kahana that are original to Leviticus Rabbah from those distinctive to Pesiqta deRab Kahana.

Both documents address issues of salvation, but I find Pesiqta deRab Kahana's message of salvation couched in explicitly messianic terms, which is not the case in Leviticus Rabbah. And, as we move toward Sifré to Deuteronomy, Sifré to Numbers, and Sifra, we shall find noteworthy the centrality in the Rabbah-compilations of historical-salvific issues, for, in the other family of midrash-compilations, people focus upon other matters entirely.

V. THE TOPICAL PROGRAM OF SIFRÉ TO DEUTERONOMY

Let me lay out what I conceive to be the topical and propositional programs of Sifre to Deuteronomy. In that document we do find a highly propositional statement, well within the range of the type of discourse we have noted in other midrash-compilations. To set forth what I conceive to be the propositions paramount in this compilation, I begin with what seem to me primary, and that is, the matter of Israel's relationship with God and the responsibilites of a covenanted relationship. These encompass, first of all, the theme of Israel and God and the implications of the covenant. The basic proposition, spelled out in detail, is that Israel stands in a special relationship with God, and that relationship is defined by the contract, or covenant, that God made with Israel. The covenant comes to particular expression, in Sifré to Deuteronomy, in two matters, first, the land, second, the Torah. Each marks Israel as different from all other nations, on the one side, and as selected by God, on the other. In these propositions, sages situate Israel in the realm of heaven, finding on earth the stigmata of covenanted election and concomitant requirement of loyalty and obedience to the covenant. These propositions find a place in the foreground of Sifré to Deuteronomy, while, so far as I can see, they do not form the centerpiece of interest and discourse in the Rabbah-compilations.

First comes the definition of those traits of God that our authorship finds pertinent. God sits in judgment upon the world, and his judgment is true and righteous. God punishes faithlessness. But God's fundamental and definitive trait is mercy. The way of God is to be merciful and gracious. The basic relationship of Israel to God is one of God's grace for Israel. God's loyalty to Israel endures, even when Israel sins. When Israel forgets God, God is pained. Israel's leaders, whatever their excellence, plead with God only for grace, not for their own merit. Correct attitudes in prayer derive from the need for grace, Israel having slight merit on its own account. Israel should follow only God, carrying out religious deeds as the covenant requires, in accord with the instructions of prophets. Israel should show mercy to others, in the model of God's merciful character.

Second, the contract, or covenant, produces the result that God has acquired Israel, which God created. The reason is that only Israel accepted the Torah, among all the nations, and that is why God made the covenant with Israel in particular. Why is the covenant made only with Israel? The gentiles did not accept the Torah, Israel did, and that has made all the difference. Israel recognized God forthwith; the very peace of the world and of nature depends upon God's giving the Torah to Israel. That is why Israel is the sole nation worthy of dwelling in the palace of God and that is the basis for the covenant too. The covenant secures for Israel an enduring relationship of grace with God. The covenant cannot be revoked and endures forever. The covenant, terms of which are specified in the Torah, has duplicate terms: if you do well, you will bear a blessing, and if not, you will bear a curse. That is the singular mark of the covenant between God and Israel. A mark of the covenant is the liberation from Egypt, and that sufficed to impose upon Israel God's claim for their obedience. An important sign of the covenant is the possession of the land. Part of the covenant is the recognition of merit of the ancestors. God promised, in making the covenant, recognition for the children of the meritorious deeds of the ancestors. The conquest of the land and inheriting it are marks of the covenant, which Israel will find easy because of God's favor. The inheritance of the land is a mark of merit, inherited from the ancestors. The land is higher than all others and more choice. All religious duties are important, those that seem trivial as much as those held to be weightier.

God always loves Israel. That is why Israel should carry out the religious duties of the Torah with full assent. All religious duties are equally precious. Israel must be whole-hearted in its relationship with God. If it is, then its share is with God, and if not, then not. But Israel may hate God. The right attitude toward God is love, and Israel should love God with a whole heart. The reason that Israel rebels against God is prosperity. Then people become arrogant and believe that their prosperity derives from their own efforts. But that is not so, and God punishes people who rebel to show them that they depend upon God. When Israel practices idolatry, God punishes them, e.g., through exile, through famine, through drought, and the like. Whether or not Israel knows or likes the fact, it is the fact that Israel therefore has no choice but to accept God's will and fulfill the covenant.

The heaven and the earth respond to the condition of Israel and therefore carry out the stipulations of the covenant. If Israel does not carry out religious duties concerning heaven, then heaven bears witness against them. That centers of course on the land of Israel in particular. Possession of the land is conditional, not absolute. It begins with grace, not merit. It is defined by the stipulation that Israel observe the covenant, in which case Israel will retain the land. If Israel violates the covenant, Israel will lose the land. When Israel inherits the land, in obedience to the covenant and as an act of grace bestowed by God, it will build the temple, where Israel's sins will find atonement. The conquest of the land itself is subject to stipulations, just as possession of the land, as an act of God's grace, is marked by religious obligations. If Israel rebels or rejects the Torah, it will lose the land, just as the Canaanites did for their idolatry.

The land is not the only, or the most important, mark of the covenant. It is the fact that Israel has the Torah which shows that Israel stands in a special relationship to God. The Torah is the source of life for Israel. It belongs to everyone, not only the aristocracy. Children should start studying the Torah at the earliest age possible. The study of the Torah is part of the fulfillment of the covenant. Even the most arid details of the Torah contain lessons, and if one studies the Torah, the reward comes both in this world and in the world to come. The possession of the Torah imposes a particular requirement, involving an action. The most important task of every male Israelite is to study the Torah, which involves memorizing, and not forgetting, each lesson. This must go on every day and all the time. Study of the Torah should be one's main obligation, prior to all others. The correct motive is not for the sake of gain, but for the love of God and the desire for knowledge of God's will. People must direct heart, eyes, ears, to teachings of the Torah. Study of the Torah transforms human relationships, so that strangers become the children of the master of the Torah whom they serve as disciples. However unimportant the teaching or the teacher, all is as if on the authority of Moses at Sinai. When a person departs from the Torah, that person becomes an idolator. Study of the Torah prevents idolatry. The Torah's verses may be read in such a way that different voices speak discrete clauses of a single verse. One of these will be the Holy Spirit, another, Israel, and so on.

This brings us to the relationship between Israel and the nations, hence to the meaning of history. The covenant, through the Torah of Sinai, governs not only the ongoing life of Israel but also the state of human affairs universally. The history of Israel forms a single, continuous, cycle, in that what happened in the beginning prefigures what will happen at the end of time. Events of Genesis are reenacted both in middle history, between the beginning and the end, and also at the end of times. So the traits of the tribal founders dictated the history of their families to both the here and now and also the eschatological age. Moses was shown the whole of Israel's history, past, present, future. The times of the patriarchs are reenacted in the messianic day. That shows how Israel's history runs in cycles, so that events of ancient times prefigure events now. The prophets, beginning with Moses, describe those cycles. What happens bears close ties to what is going to happen. The prophetic promises too were realized in temple times, and will be realized at the end of time.

The periods in the history of Israel, marked by the exodus and wandering, the inheritance of the land and the building of the Temple, the destruction, are all part of a divine plan. In this age Rome rules, but in the age to come, marked by the study of the Torah and the offering of sacrifices in the temple cult, Israel will be in charge. That is the fundamental pattern and meaning of history. The Holy Spirit makes possible actions that bear consequences only much later in time. The prefiguring of history forms the dominant motif in Israel's contemporary life, and the reenacting of what has already been forms a constant. Israel therefore should believe, if not in what is coming, then in what has already been. The very names of places in the land attest to the continuity of Israel's history, which follows rules that do not change. The main point is that while Israel will be punished in the worst possible way, Israel will not be wiped out.

But the cyclical character of Israel's history should not mislead. Events follow a pattern, but knowledge of that pattern, which is provided by the Torah, permits Israel both to understand and also to affect its own destiny. Specifically, Israel controls its own destiny through its conduct with God. Israel's history is the working out of the effects of Israel's conduct, moderated by the merit of the ancestors. Abraham effected a change in God's relationship to the world. But merit, which makes history, is attained by one's own deeds as well. The effect of merit, in the nation's standing among the other nations, is simple. When Israel enjoys merit, it gives testimony against itself, but when not, then the most despised nation testifies against it. But God is with Israel in time of trouble. When Israel sins, it suffers. When it repents and is forgiven, it is redeemed. For example, Israel's wandering in the wilderness took place because of the failure of Israel to attain merit. Sin is what causes the wandering in the wilderness. People rebel because they are prosperous. The merit of the ancestors works in history to Israel's benefit. What Israel does not merit on its own, at a given time, the merit of the ancestors may secure in any event. The best way to deal with Israel's powerlessness is through Torah-study; the vigor of engagement with Torah-study compensates for weakness.

It goes without saying that Israel's history follows a set time, e.g., at the fulfillment of a set period of time, an awaited event will take place. The prophets prophesy concerning the coming of the day of the Lord. Accordingly, nothing is haphazard, and all things happen in accord with a plan. That plan encompasses this world, the time of the Messiah, and the world to come, in that order. God will personally exact vengeance at the end of time. God also will raise the dead. Israel has overcome difficult times and can continue to do so. The task ahead is easier than the tasks already accomplished. Israel's punishment is only once, while the punishment coming upon the nations is unremitting. Peace is worthwhile and everyone needs it. Israel's history ends in the world to come or in the days of the Messiah. The righteous inherit the Garden of Eden. The righteous in the age to come will be joyful. God acts in history and does so publicly, in full light of day. That is to show the nations who is in charge. The Torah is what distinguishes Israel from the nations. All the nations had every opportunity to understand and accept the Torah, and all declined it; that is why Israel was selected. And that demonstrates the importance of both covenant and the Torah, the medium of the covenant. The nations even had a prophet, comparable to Moses. The nations have no important role in history, except as God assigns them a role in relationship to Israel's conduct. The nations are estranged from God by idolatry. That is what prevents goodness from coming into the world. The name of God rests upon Israel in greatest measure. Idolators do not control heaven. The greatest sin an Israelite can commit is idolatry, and those who entice Israel to idolatry are deprived the ordinary protections of the law. God is violently angry at the nations because of idolatry. As to the nations' relationships with Israel, they are guided by Israel's condition. When Israel is weak, the nations take advantage, when strong, they are sycophantic. God did not apportion love to the nations of the world as he did to Israel.

What about Israel at home, the community and its governance? A mark of God's favor is that Israel has (or, has had and will have) a government of its own. Part of the covenantal relationship requires Israel to follow leaders whom God has chosen and instructed, such as Moses and the prophets. Accordingly, Israel is to establish a government and follow sound public policy. Its leaders are chosen by God. Israel's leaders, e.g., prophets, are God's servants, and that is a mark of the praise that is owing to them. They are to be in the model of Moses, humble, choice, select, well-known. Moses was the right one to bestow a blessing, Israel were the right ones to receive the blessing. Yet all leaders are mortal, even Moses died. The saints are leaders ready to give their lives for Israel. The greatest of them enjoy exceptionally long life. But the sins of the people are blamed on their leaders. The leaders depend on the people to keep the Torah, and Moses thanked them in advance for keeping the Torah after he died. The leaders were to be patient, honest, give a full hearing to all sides, make just decisions, in a broad range of matters. To stand before the judge is to stand before God. God makes sure that Israel does not lack for leadership. The basic task of the leader is both to rebuke and also to console the people. The rulers of Israel are servants of God. The prophets exemplify these leaders, in the model of Moses, and Israel's rulers act only on the instruction of prophets. Their authority rests solely on God's favor and grace. At the instance of God, the leaders of Israel speak, in particular, words of admonition. These are delivered before death, when the whole picture is clear, so that people can draw the necessary conclusions. These words, when Moses spoke them, covered the entire history of the community of Israel. The leaders of Israel address admonition to the entire community at once. No one is excepted. But the Israelites can deal with the admonition. They draw the correct conclusions. Repentance overcomes sin, as at the sin of the golden calf. The Israelites were contentious, nitpickers, litigious, and, in general, gave Moses a difficult time. Their descendants should learn not to do so. Israel should remain united and obedient to its leaders. The task of the community is to remain united. When the Israelites are of one opinion below, God's name is glorified above. This survey of the propositions set forth in Sifré to Deuteronomy shows us that, were we to have to point to a single document for the representation of the Judaism of the Dual Torah, it would have to be this one. And that then sets the standard for measuring the propositional character of other writings and shows us, by contrast, the ad hoc and episodic character of such propositions, independent of mere textual paraphrase, as may make their way into the pages of Sifra.

Sifré to Deuteronomy also presents an account of the structure of the intellect. The explicit propositional program of our document is joined by a set of implicit ones. These comprise repeated demonstration of a point never fully stated. The implicit propositions have to do with the modes of correct analysis and inquiry that pertain to the Torah. Let me give a minor example. One may utilize reason in discovering the meaning and the rules of Scripture. Analogy for example provides adequate ground for extending a rule. There are many instances in which that same mode of reasoning is placed on display. The upshot is that while not made explicit, the systematic and orderly character of Scripture is repeatedly demonstrated, with the result that out of numerous instances, we may on our own reach the correct conclusion. Two implicit propositions predominate. The first, familiar from Sifré to Numbers as well as Sifra, is that pure reason does not suffice to produce reliable results. Only through linking our conclusions to verses of Scripture may we come to final and fixed conclusions. The implicit proposition, demonstrated many times, may therefore be stated very simply. The Torah (written) is the sole source of reliable information. Reason undisciplined by the Torah yields unreliable results. These items may occur, also, within the rubrics of the specific propositions that they contain. Some of them moreover overlap with the later catalogue, but, if so, are not listed twice. Our authorship will have found itself entirely at home in this corner of Sifré to Deuteronomy. And in the following, it will have claimed for itself the position of role-model for the other authorship, for Sifra's authorship did sustainedly and brilliantly what seemed important, also to that of Sifré to Deuteronomy.

The second of the two recurrent modes of thought is the more important. It is the demonstration that many things conform to a single structure and pattern. We can show this uniformity of the law by addressing the same questions to disparate cases and, in so doing, composing general laws that transcend cases and form a cogent system. What is striking, then, is the power of a single set of questions to reshape and reorganize diverse data into a single cogent set of questions and answers, all things fitting together into a single, remarkably well-composed structure. Not only so, but when we review the numerous passages at which we find what, in the logical repertoire I called methodical-analytical logic, we find a single program. It is an effort to ask whether a case of Scripture imposes a rule that limits or imparts a rule that augments the application of the law at hand. A systematic reading of Scripture permits us to restrict or to extend the applicability of the detail of a case into a rule that governs many cases. A standard repertoire of questions may be addressed to a variety of topics, to yield the picture of how a great many things make essentially a single statement. This seems to me the single most common topical inquiry in Sifré to Deuteronomy. It covers most of the laws of Deut. 12-26. The list of explicit statements of the proposition that the case at hand is subject to either restriction or augmentation, that the law prevailing throughout is limited to the facts at hand or exemplified by those facts, is considerable. The size, the repetitious quality, the obsessive interest in augmentation and restriction, generalization and limitation – these traits of logic and their concomitant propositional results form the centerpiece of the whole. And, I should maintain, that is not a merely subjective judgment, but a result that others can replicate with little difficulty. There can be no doubt that as to a highly propositional program Sifré to Deuteronomy falls into the same classification as Leviticus Rabbah, Genesis Rabbah, and Pesiqta deRab Kahana. The authorship proposed to explore not only modes of thought and argumentation but also profound propositions as to Israel's condition, context, and expectations.

VI. THE PROBLEM OF SIFRÉ TO NUMBERS

When we come to Sifré to Numbers, we enter a document in which we cannot present a similar topical plan. In this aspect, as we shall see presently, Sifra is more like Sifré to Numbers than any other midrash-compilation of late antiquity. Indeed, to find in Sifré to Numbers some programmatic coherence, we find that we have to resort solely to a reconstruction of the formal traits of the document, then to a translation of those traits into implicit propositions they seem to me to contain. For as to its sequence of topics, the topical program derives from the book of Numbers and consists in the paraphrase and gloss of what Scripture says, and, as to its distinctive propositions, I see none of that transcendent quality that so impresses us in Leviticus Rabbah, Genesis Rabbah, Pesiqta deRab Kahana, and Sifré to Numbers. In the 116 chapters of Sifré to Numbers that I translated, I could find any number of episodic propositions, but no sustained and coherent program such as I just now set forth on the foundations of the other Sifré. The kind of generalizing paragraphs that I offered in the characterization of not merely the topics but the problematics and propositions of the Rabbah-compilations I simply could not compose for this writing. Accordingly, we turn immediately to those things that do recur, formally and forcefully, in this Sifré: the formal patterning of language.

Let us now briefly characterize the formal traits of Sifré to Numbers as a commentary. These, readers will recall from Chapter Two, may be reduced to two classifications, based on the point of origin of the verses that are catalogued or subjected to exegesis: exegesis of a verse in the book of Numbers in terms of the theme or problems of that verse, hence, intrinsic exegesis; exegesis of a verse in Numbers in terms of a theme or polemic not particular to that verse, hence, extrinsic exegesis.

The forms of extrinsic exegesis: The implicit message of the external category proves simple to define, since the several extrinsic classifications turn out to form a cogent polemic. Let me state the recurrent polemic of external exegesis.

1. *The Syllogistic Composition:* Scripture supplies hard facts, which, properly classified, generate syllogisms. By collecting and classifying facts of Scripture, therefore, we may produce firm laws of history, society, and Israel's everyday life. The diverse compositions in which verses from various books of the Scriptures are compiled in a list of evidence for a given proposition – whatever the character or purpose of that proposition – make that one point. And given their power and cogency, they make the point stick. I see no proposition with which the Rabbah-authorships will not have unanimously concurred. But when we come to Sifra, we look in vain for this mode of argument. I can point to only a few syllogistic compositions in the document; most of the propositional compositions derive from the Mishnah or the Tosefta. In this respect, in the aggregate Sifra differs.

2. *The Fallibility of Reason Unguided by Scriptural Exegesis:* Scripture alone supplies reliable basis for speculation. Laws cannot be generated by reason or logic unguided by Scripture. Efforts at classification and contrastive-analogical exegesis, in which Scripture does not supply the solution to all problems, prove few and far between. Here, of course, we are entirely at home. Sifra's authorship sustainedly and brilliantly carries forward not only the critique of hierarchical classification and the logical arguments deriving from it, but also, as I shall show later in this chapter, also the rehabilitation, on proper foundations, of that some mode of thought.

In the context of Sifré to Numbers, this polemic forms the obverse of the point above. So when extrinsic issues intervene in the exegetical process, they coalesce to make a single point. Let me state that point with appropriate emphasis the recurrent and implicit message of the forms of external exegesis:

Scripture stands paramount, logic, reason, analytical processes of classification and differentiation, secondary. Reason not built on scriptural foundations yields uncertain results. The Mishnah itself demands scriptural bases.

What about the polemic present, however, in the *intrinsic* exegetical exercises? This clearly does not allow for ready characterization. As we saw, at least three intrinsic exegetical exercises focus on the use of logic, specifically, the logic of classification, comparison and contrast of species of a genus, in the explanation of the meaning of verses of the book of Numbers. The internal dialectical mode, moving from point to point as logic dictates, underlines the main point already stated: logic produces possibilities, Scripture chooses among them. Again, the question, why is this passage stated? commonly produces an answer generated by further verses of Scripture, e.g., this matter is stated here to clarify what otherwise would be confusion left in the wake of other verses. So Scripture produces problems of confusion and duplication, and Scripture – and not logic, not differentiation, not classification – solves those problems. To state matters simply: Scripture is complete, harmonious, perfect. Logic not only does not generate truth beyond the limits of Scripture but also plays no important role in the harmonization of difficulties yielded by what appear to be duplications or disharmonies. These forms of internal exegesis then make the same point that the extrinsic ones do.

In so stating, of course, we cover all but the single most profuse category of exegesis, which in both Sifra and in Sifré to Numbers I have treated as simple and undifferentiated: [1] verse of Scripture or a clause, followed by [2] a brief statement of the meaning at hand. That is the single paramount form in Sifé to Numbers, by contrast to Sifra occupying the central position in the repertoire of forms. Here, in the process of paraphrase and amplification of successive phrases of verses, I see no unifying polemic in favor of, or against, a given proposition. The most common form also proves the least pointed: X bears this meaning, Y bears that meaning, or, as we have seen, citation of verse X, followed by, [what this means is].... Whether simple or elaborate, the upshot is the same. What can be at issue when no polemic expressed in the formal traits of syntax and logic finds its way to the surface? What do I do when I merely clarify a phrase? Or, to frame the question more logically: what premises must validate my *intervention*, that is, my willingness to undertake to explain the meaning of a verse of Scripture? These seem to me propositions that must serve to justify the labor of intrinsic exegesis as we have seen its results here:

[1] My independent judgment bears weight and produces meaning. I – that is, my mind – therefore may join in the process.

[2] God's revelation to Moses at Sinai requires my intervention. I have the role, and the right, to say what that revelation means.

[3] What validates my entry into the process of revelation is the correspondence between the logic of my mind and the logic of the document.

Why do I think so? Only if I think in accord with the logic of the revealed Torah can my thought-processes join issue in clarifying what is at hand: the unfolding of God's will in the Torah.[7] To state matters more accessibly: if the Torah does not make statements in accord with a syntax and a grammar that I know, I cannot so understand the Torah as to explain its meaning. But if I can join in the discourse of the Torah, it is because I speak the same language of thought: syntax and grammar at the deepest levels of my intellect.

[4] Then affirmatively and finally to present what I conceive to be the generative proposition: Since a shared logic of syntax and grammar joins my mind to the mind of God as revealed in the Torah, I can say what a sentence of the Torah means. So I too can amplify, clarify, expand, revise, rework: that is to say, create a commentary. It follows that the intrinsic exegetical forms stand for a single proposition:

While Scripture stands paramount, logic, reason, analytical processes of classification and differentiation, secondary, nonetheless, man's mind joins God's mind when man receives and sets forth the Torah.

Beyond all concrete propositions, the document as a whole through its fixed and recurrent formal preferences or literary structures makes two complementary points.

---

[7] In reaching this conclusion in my study of Sifré to Numbers, I adumbrated the conclusion I would come to at the end of *Uniting the Dual Torah*.

[1]   *Reason unaided by Scripture produces uncertain propositions.*

[2]   *Reason operating within the limits of Scripture produces truth.*

It remains to observe that just as Genesis Rabbah bears formal and substantive affinity to Leviticus Rabbah; the plan and program of both documents present an essential congruity, so too in plan and in program alike Sifra and Sifré to Numbers form a community. The forms and polemic of Sifra and Sifré to Numbers cohere, with the forms so designed as to implicitly state and so to reenforce the substantive argument of both books. In topical traits we may classify Sifra, serving Leviticus, and Sifré to Numbers as inner-directed, facing within, toward issues of the interior life of the community vis-à-vis revelation and the sanctification of the life of the nation, and, intellectually, as centered on issues urgent to sages themselves. For to whom are the debates about the relationship between Torah and logic, reason and revelation, going to make a difference, if not to the intellectuals of the textual community at hand? Within the same classification-scheme, Genesis Rabbah and Leviticus Rabbah and Sifré to Deuteronomy appear outer-directed, addressing issues of history and salvation, taking up critical concerns of the public life of the nation vis-à-vis history and the world beyond. Sifra and Sifré to Numbers address sanctification, Sifré to Deuteronomy, Genesis Rabbah, and Leviticus Rabbah, salvation.

VII. DOES SIFRA SET FORTH PROPOSITIONS?
THE TOPICAL PROGRAM OF SIFRA

In representing the topical program and propositions of the Rabbah-compilations and Sifré to Deuteronomy, I simply restated in propositional form what I took to be the main point of successive paragraphs and chapters of those documents, then classified those statements and set them forth in logically coherent form. The equivalent process of paraphrase, classification, and organization of the materials of Sifra in my judgment can yield no equivalent representation of a topical program, let alone propositions. For a topical program Sifra takes the book of Leviticus. For propositions Sifra's authorship presents episodic and ad hoc sentences. If we ask how these sentences form propositions other than amplifications of points made in the book of Leviticus itself, and how we may restate those propositions in a coherent way, so far as I can see, nothing sustained and coherent emerges. Short of leading the reader through all two hundred seventy-seven chapters of Sifra, I have chosen as my illustrations of the proposition that Sifra does not constitute a propositional document transcending its precipitating text two sustained passages, one concerning Leviticus 25:1-17, the other, Leviticus 19:1-17. The former shows us that, in place of its own propositions (whatever they might have been), our authorship substitutes the Mishnah's. I show that we cannot have had Sifra without the Mishnah, for the passage at hand, and that proves, in my judgment, that our authorship has no proposition(s) of its own, and, further, that its topical program is simply the book on which it has chosen to work. The latter shows us how our authorship has treated the opportunity for generalization and propositional discourse presented by Leviticus 19:1ff., surely one of the great occasions for setting forth a sustained and coherent program of thought. We see essentially the same picture as before. That does not mean our authorship had nothing that it wished to say. It does mean that what our authorship wanted to set forth did not consist in a program of topics and propositions concerning those topics.

1. A Sample: Sifra to Leviticus 25:1-17 ▪ Sifra Parashat Behar Chapters 245 through 250

We consider a sample of Sifra, six chapters of the two hundred seventy-seven into which the document is divided. In this way, as I said, we shall consider the relationship between the topical program of Sifra and the verses of the book of Leviticus that are addressed by a sizable sample of the document. Let us begin by reviewing the verses of Scripture that form the structure and dictate the order of discourse in the passage of Sifra we take as our sample. Nothing in what follows is comprehensible without knowledge of the order, program, and propositions, of the scriptural passage at hand. That means that, when and where the Mishnah is cited, it will be solely in the context of Scripture's presentation of the topic. A detailed picture of what Sifra's authorship wishes to say concerning scriptural topics would demonstrate that the propositions and problematic concerning a given topic derive in the main from what is settled as law in the Mishnah. That makes all the more striking the form of discourse. We deal with Lev. 25:1-17, as follows:

> The Lord said to Moses on Mount Sinai, Say to the people of Israel, When you come into the land which I give you, the land shall keep a sabbath to the Lord. Six years you shall sow your field, and six years you shall prune your vineyard and gather in its fruits; but in the seventh year there shall be a sabbath of solemn rest for the land, a sabbath to the Lord; you shall not sow your field or prune your vineyard. What grows of itself in your harvest you shall not reap, and the grapes of your undressed vine you shall not gather; it shall be a year of solemn rest for the land. The sabbath of the land shall provide food for you, for yourself and for your male and female slaves and for your hired servant and the sojourner who lives with you; for your cattle also and for the beasts that are in your land all its yield shall be for food (Lev. 25:1-7).

> And you shall count for yourself seven weeks of years, seven times seven years, so that the time of the seven weeks of years shall be to you forty-nine years. Then you shall send abroad the ram's horn on the tenth

day of the seventh month; on the day of atonement you shall send abroad the trumpet throughout all your land. And you shall hallow the fiftieth year and proclaim liberty throughout the land to all its inhabitants; it shall be a jubilee for you, when each of you shall return to his property and each of you shall return to his family. A jubilee shall that fiftieth year be to you; in it you shall neither sow nor reap what grows of itself, nor gather the grapes from the undressed vines. For it is a jubilee; it shall be holy to you; you shall eat what it yields out of the field (Lev. 25:8-12).
In this year of jubilee each of you shall return to his property. And if you sell a property to your neighbor or buy from your neighbor, you shall not wrong [here: defraud by reason of overcharge] one another. According to the number of years after the jubilee, you shall buy from your neighbor, and according to the number of years for crops he shall sell to you. If the years are many you shall increase the price, and if the years are few you shall diminish the price, for it is the number of the crops that he is selling to you. You shall not wrong one another, but you shall fear your God: for I am the Lord your God (Lev. 25:13-17).

Now let us turn to the treatment of these verses in the passage at hand.

245. Parashat Behar Parashah 1

CCXLV:I

1. A.   "The Lord said to Moses on Mount Sinai":
   B.   What has the topic of the sabbatical year of the land to do in particular with Mount Sinai [that of all subjects, this is the one that is explicitly tied to revelation at Sinai]?
   C.   Is it not the fact that all religious duties were announced at Sinai?
   D.   The point is that just as in the case of the sabbatical year both the governing principles and the details were announced from Sinai,
   E.   so all of the other religious duties' governing principles and details were announced from Sinai.

The generalization is important to our authorship, linking to Sinai the revelation of all rules and details. But nothing in context follows up on this generalization, as we now see.

2. A.   "When you come [into the land which I give you, the land shall keep a sabbath to the Lord]":
   B.   Might one suppose that the sabbatical year was to take effect once they had reached Transjordan?
   C.   Scripture says, "into the land."
   D.   It is that particular land.
   E.   Might one suppose that the sabbatical year was to take effect once they had reached Ammon and Moab?
   F.   Scripture says, "which I give you,"
   G.   and not to Ammon and Moab.

This is the familiar exercise of exclusion, which goes forward in what follows.

H. And on what basis do you maintain that when they had conquered the land but not divided it, divided it among familiars but not among fathers' houses so that each individual does not yet recognize his share –

I. might one suppose that they should be responsible to observe the sabbatical year?

J. Scripture says, "[Six years you shall sow] your field,"

K. meaning, each one should recognize his own field.

L. "...your vineyard":

M. meaning, each one should recognize his own vineyard.

N. You turn out to rule:

O. **Once the Israelites had crossed the Jordan, they incurred liability to separate dough-offering and to observe the prohibition against eating the fruit of fruit trees for the first three years after planting and the prohibition against eating produce of the new growing season prior to the waving of the sheaf of new grain [that is, on the fifteenth of Nisan].**

P. **When the sixteenth of Nisan came, they incurred liability to wave the sheaf of new grain.**

Q. **With the passage of fifty days from then they incurred the liability to the offering of the Two Loaves.**

R. **At the fourteenth year they became liable for the separation of tithes.**

S. **They began to count the years of the sabbatical cycle, and in the twenty-first year after entry into the land, they observed the sabbatical year.**

T. **In the sixty-fourth year they observed the first Jubilee [T. Men. 6:20].**

3. A. "the land shall keep a sabbath to the Lord":

Now comes work at inclusion and exclusion once more.

B. might one suppose that the sabbath should involve not digging pits, ditches, and wells, not repairing immersion-pools?

C. Scripture says, "you shall not sow your field or prune your vineyard" –

D. I know that the prohibition extends only to sowing.

E. How do I know that it covers also sowing, pruning, ploughing, hoeing, weeding, clearing, and cutting down?

F. Scripture says, "your field you shall not...your vineyard...you shall not":

G. none of the work that is ordinarily done in your field and in your vineyard.

4. A. And how do we know that farmers may not fertilize, prune trees, smoke the leaves or cover over with powder for fertilizer?

B. Scripture says, "your field you shall not...."

5. A. And how do we know that farmers may not trim trees, nip off dry shoots, trim trees?

B. Scripture says, "your field you shall not...."

6. A. Since Scripture says, "you shall not sow your field or prune your vineyard,"

B. might one suppose that the farmer also may not hoe under the olive trees, fill in the holes under the olives trees, or dig between one tree and the next?

C. Scripture says, "you shall not sow your field or prune your vineyard" –

D. sowing and pruning were subject to the general prohibition of field labor. Why then were they singled out?

E. It was to build an analogy through them, as follows:

F. what is distinctive in sowing and pruning is that they are forms of labor carried on on the ground or on a tree.

G. So I know that subject to the prohibition are also other forms of labor that are carried on on the ground or on a tree, [excluding from the prohibition, therefore, the types of labor listed at B].

7. A. Might one suppose that the Jubilee year should count in the years of the sabbatical cycle?

B. Scripture says, "six years you shall sow your field or prune your vineyard" –

C. years of sowing count in the years of the sabbatical cycle, but the Jubilee year [in which the prohibitions of the seventh year are in force],

D. but the Jubilee year does not count in the years of the sabbatical cycle.

8. A. And how do we know that in **the case of rice, durra, millet, and sesame, which took root before the new year [of the seventh year], that the farmer may collect them in the seventh year [since they are not part of the crop of that year but of the prior year] [M. Shebiit 2:7A-D] (translation Louis Newman, *The Sanctity of the Seventh Year. A Study of Mishnah-Tractate Shebiit* [Chico, 1983: Scholars Press for Brown Judaic Studies] ad loc.)?**

B. Scripture says, "and gather in its fruits...in the seventh year."

C. Then might one suppose that even though in the sixth year they had not yet taken root [one may still harvest them in the seventh year]?

D. Scripture says, "Six years you shall sow your field, and six years you shall prune your vineyard and gather in its fruits" –

E. in the six years they sow and in the six years they gather,

F. but they do not sow in the sixth year and gather in the seventh.

9. A. R. Jonathan b. Joseph says, "How do we know that in the case of a crop that reached a third of its growth prior to the New Year, you may gather in the crop in the seventh year?

B. "Scripture says, 'and gather in its fruits,'"

C. "once it has reached a third of its full growth [prior to the advent of the seventh year."

The process of inclusion and exclusion accounts for nearly the entire exposition. The opening, redactional observation and the next, methodical one give way to a sustained and cogent inquiry: what forms of labor in the sabbatical year are permitted, what prohibited, in the fields and vineyards? No. 2 undertakes the exclusion of labor not dealing with the production of agricultural produce and the inclusion under the prohibition of labor that serves the interests of the crop, 2.B, E. Nos. 3, 4, 5 carry forward that same fundamental exercise. In the Mishnah, some sort of generalization or list (it is the same thing) is likely to have emerged;

here we are left with the governing analogy. No. 7 is intruded; it has no clear bearing; the redactors' reason for including it is clear. It rests on the same proof-text that is under discussion. Hence the framers have not allowed the principle they wish to lay out to dictate omissions of material relevant on account of the principles of aggregation and conglomeration that govern a different kind of composition altogether. No. 7 introduces yet another distinct principle, given its place in order for the same reason as the foregoing: its proof-text positions the principle here. The point is that while crops that have grown in the seventh year are prohibited, those of the sixth, spilling over into the seventh, are not. No. 8 makes that same point. The upshot is that the principle of composition is fundamentally exegetical, in that (whether made up or ready-made) set-piece compositions are laid out in accord with the sequence of the verses, and, for the piece at hand, there is no pretense at the presentation of a sustained and sequential program of principles, propositions, or even modes of argument. As to a topical program, it is that of Scripture. As to propositions, I see none subject to generalization, e.g., God loves Israel, the covenant affects Israel's destiny, holiness is what is to characterize the life of Israel, and the like. True, all of these principles can find in the discourse at hand suitable exemplification, and I am sure that our authorship will have concurred in precisely that point. But the road from the details before us to the kinds of generalizations generated by the Rabbah-compilations and Sifré to Deuteronomy is circuitous and unmapped; the best means of transport is by air.

246. Parashat Behar Pereq 1

CCXLVI:I

1. A. And how do we know that the thirty days prior to the New Year on which the seventh year commences are deemed equivalent to the sabbatical year [so that the prohibitions of the sabbatical year apply a month prior to the commencement of that year]?

   B. Scripture says, "but in the seventh year there shall be a sabbath of solemn rest for the land."

2. A. In this connection sages have said:

   B. **White figs which appear in the seventh year – the restrictions of the sabbatical year apply to them in the second year of the new sabbatical cycle, rather than in the seventh year itself, because they take three years to ripen fully.**

   C. **R. Judah says, "Persian figs which appear in the seventh year – the restrictions of the sabbatical year apply to them in the year following the sabbatical year, that is, in the first year of the new sabbatical cycle rather than in the seventh year itself, because they take two years to ripen fully."**

   D. **Sages said to him, "They ruled concerning white figs alone" (translation Louis Newman, *The Sanctity of the Seventh Year. A**

Study of Mishnah-Tractate Shebiit [Chico, 1983: Scholars Press for Brown Judaic Studies] ad loc.).

3.   A.   "a sabbath of solemn rest for the land, [a sabbath to the Lord]":

     B.   Just as is said with reference to the Sabbath that celebrates creation, "a sabbath of solemn rest for the Lord," so in reference to the seventh year, "a sabbath to the Lord."

4.   A.   "you shall not sow your field or prune your vineyard":

     B.   all kinds of labor that pertain to your field,

     C.   all kinds of labor that pertain to your vineyard.

5.   A.   "What grows of itself in your harvest you shall not reap":

     B.   On the foundation of this statement sages founded the rule that what grows of itself is forbidden in the seventh year.

6.   A.   "and the grapes of your undressed vine you shall not gather":

     B.   From what is cultivated in the land you shall not cut grapes, but you may cut grapes from what is left as ownerless property. [Once a crop is declared ownerless, anyone may come and make use of it.]

7.   A.   "...you shall not gather":

     B.   You may not gather in the way in which people usually gather.

     C.   In this connection sages have said:

     D.   **Figs of the Sabbatical year – they do not dry them in the ordinary drying place, but one does dry them in a deserted place [where one does not ordinarily process figs]. They do not trample grapes of the sabbatical year in a vat, but one does trample them in a trough. And they do not prepare olives of the sabbatical year in an olive-press or with an olive-crusher, but one does crush them and place them in a small press.**

     E.   **R. Simeon says, "One even grinds them in an olive press and places them in a small press in order to complete the processing of the olives" [M. Shebiit 8:6A-H (translation Louis Newman, *The Sanctity of the Seventh Year. A Study of Mishnah-Tractate Shebiit* [Chico, 1983: Scholars Press for Brown Judaic Studies] ad loc.).**

8.   A.   "a sabbath of solemn rest":

     B.   Once the seventh year has come to an end, even though the produce of that year continue under the rule of release of that year, one may nonetheless undertake work on the fruit tree itself,

     C.   even though the produce remains prohibited until the fifth day of the month of Shebat.

9.   A.   "The sabbath of the land shall provide food for you":

     B.   what derives from the rest-period of the land you may eat.

     C.   But you may not consume what has been kept in preserve.

     D.   In this connection sages have said,"

     E.   **As regards a field that was improved during the sabbatical year –**

     F.   **the House of Shammai say, "Other Israelites do not eat of its produce that grows during the sabbatical year."**

     G.   **The House of Hillel say, "They do eat produce of this field that grows during the sabbatical year. [Israelites who did not commit transgression of cultivating the field are not deprived of their right to eat produce of the sabbatical year.]**

H.   The House of Shammai say, "They do not eat produce of the sabbatical year when it was given by the owner of a field as a favor."

I.   The House of Hillel say, "They eat produce of the sabbatical year whether or not it was given by the owner of the field as a favor."

J.   R. Judah says, "The rulings attributed to the Houses are reversed, for this is among the lenient rulings of the House of Shammai and the stringent rulings of the House of Hillel" [M. Shebiit 4:2F-K (translation Louis Newman, *The Sanctity of the Seventh Year. A Study of Mishnah-Tractate Shebiit* [Chico, 1983: Scholars Press for Brown Judaic Studies] ad loc.).]

10. A.   "[The sabbath of the land shall provide food] for you":

B.   not for others.

11. A.   "food":

B.   not for presenting meal-offerings from that produce, nor for presenting drink-offerings from it.

12. A.   "for yourself and for your male and female slaves":

B.   What is the point of Scripture here?

C.   Since it is said, "[For six years you shall sow your land and gather in its yield, but the seventh year you shall let it rest and lie fallow,] that the poor of your people may eat; and what they leave the wild beasts may eat. You shall do likewise with your vineyard and with your olive orchard]" (Ex. 23:10-11),

D.   I might have supposed that produce of the seventh year may be eaten only by the poor alone.

E.   How do I know that even the rich may eat it?

F.   Scripture says, "for yourself and for your male and female slaves."

G.   Lo, wealthy landowners are covered, bondmen and bondwomen are covered.

H.   Then why is it written, "that the poor of your people may eat"?

I.   "The poor, but not the rich, may consume the available crop after the removal of stored crops from the household," the words of R. Judah.

J.   R. Yosé says, "All the same are the poor and the rich: all of them may consume the crop after the time for the removal of stored crops from the household has come."

13. A.   Another matter concerning the statement, "that the poor of your people may eat; [and what they leave the wild beasts may eat]":

B.   What is suitable for human consumption is given to human beings.

C.   What is suitable for animals is given to animals.

14. A.   "and for your hired servant and the sojourner":

B.   from among gentiles,

15. A.   " who lives with you":

B.   this serves to encompass guests.

16. A.   "for your cattle also and for the domesticated beasts":

B.   What is the point of Scripture here [for the point can be made without specifying both categories of beasts]?

C.   If a wild beast, which is not within your domain, lo, it may eat [produce of the seventh year],

D.   a domesticated cattle, which is within your domain, surely should eat produce of the seventh year!

E.   If that were the case, then I should say, let the farmer collect produce for his domesticated beast and let the beast consume that fodder without limit of time,

F.   in which case how am I to carry out the requirement of removing stored produce of the seventh year along with the produce that serves for human consumption?

G.   Then is the domesticated beast truly going to eat produce without limit [ignoring the limit imposed by the requirement of removal]?

H.   When Scripture says, therefore, "for your cattle also and for the domesticated beasts,"

I.   it draws an analogy between the domesticated beast and the wild beast, indicating,

J.   so long as a wild beast finds produce of a given sort growing wild in the field, a domesticated beast may eat produce of that same sort in the barn. But when the produce of that sort has disappeared from the field, then the produce of the same species is no longer to be made available to the domesticated beast in the barn. [The law requires people to remove produce of the sabbatical year from their homes when edibles of the same species are no longer available for people to gather from the field; once all vegetables of a certain type have been gathered or have dried up, people may not longer retain in storage similar vegetables in their homes (Newman, *op. cit.*, p. 179). This same rule extends to fodder.]

17. A.   "that are in your land [all its yield shall be for food]":

B.   what is in your land is for people to people eat.

C.   Food is not to be exported as Aqilas exported food for his workers in Pandos.

D.   Said R. Simeon, "I heard explicitly that they export produce to Syria but not abroad."

18. A.   "shall be for food":

B.   even for kindling a lamp, even for use as a dye.

19. A.   "all its yield":

B.   This teaches that only produce is eaten.

C.   In this connection sages have said:

D.   **After what time during the sabbatical year do they gather and eat the fruit of trees? [Gathering fruit too early in the ripening process is prohibited. By doing so the farmer would prevent fruit that grows during the sabbatical year from being used as food.]**

E.   **As regards unripe figs, from the time that they begin to glisten the farmer may eat them as a random snack together with his bread in the field.**

F.   **After they have ripened, he may gather them into his house and eat them.**

G.   **And similarly, when figs have ripened during the other years of the sabbatical cycle, they become liable to the separation of tithes.**

H.   **As regards unripe grapes, from the time that they produce liquid, the farmer may eat them with his bread in the field.**

I.   **After they have ripened, he may gather them into his house and eat them.**

J.   And similarly when the grapes have ripened during the other years of the sabbatical cycle, they become liable to the separation of tithes.

K.   As regards olives, from the time a seah of olives yields a quarter long of oil, the farmer may crush them and eat them in the field. When a seah of olives yields a half log of oil, he may press them and anoint himself in the field.

L.   When a seah of olives yields a third of its total eventual output, that is, a full log of oil, he may press the olives in the field and gather them into his house.

M.   And similarly, when the olives have reached a third of their eventual yield during the other years of the sabbatical cycle, they become liable to the separation of tithes.

N.   And as regards the fruit of all other trees, the season during other years when they become liable to the separation of tithes is the season during the sabbatical year when they may be eaten [M. Shebiit 4:7-9A-W, transl. and commentary by Newman, *op. cit.*, p. 106].

20. A.   "for food":

B.   and not to use it for aromatic sprinkling,

C.   not to make ointment with it,

D.   not to make poultices with it,

E.   and not to make an emetic with it.

The topical program derives from Scripture; and so far as there is interest in generalization, it is in the generalizations of the Mishnah and the Tosefta. Yet, while there is an ongoing interchange with the Mishnah and the Tosefta, I cannot predict what in those documents will capture the attention of our authorship and what will not. Nos. 1, 7, 9, 19 (which encompasses No. 18) all direct us to the prior documents. No. 4 presents a generalization without particulars. No. 5 alludes to a rule but does not cite it. No. 6 works out an exclusion. No. 8 makes an important point, which is that the prohibition of field labor ends at the conclusion of the year, even though produce that derives from the sabbatical year remains prohibited until mid-winter. The sequences of Nos. 10-11, 13-15, 17 and 20 go through the more conventional exclusionary process. Nos. 12, 16 then ask whether a logical argument will have yielded a conclusion without the detailed specifics of Scripture and proves that it will not (in saying so I follow Hillel's reading of the passage). Clearly, our authorship draws heavily upon the available documents, and when it does so, it has only limited interest in points of intersection or even contact. None of these statements yields generalizations susceptible to recapitulation in a coherent account and composition along with the statements fore and aft. Everything is particular to the base-verse and its topical program, which is to say, for the materials before us, our authorship has no topical program except that of Scripture, and little enough of a concrete proposition concerning the topical program of Scripture, except that of Mishnah and Tosefta.

247. Parashat Behar Parashah 2

CCXLVII:I

1. A. ["And you shall count for yourself seven weeks of years, seven times seven years, so that the time of the seven weeks of years shall be to you forty-nine years. Then you shall send abroad the ram's horn on the tenth day of the seventh month; on the day of atonement you shall send abroad the trumpet throughout all your land. And you shall hallow the fiftieth year and proclaim liberty throughout the land to all its inhabitants; it shall be a jubilee for you, when each of you shall return to his property and each of you shall return to his family. A jubilee shall that fiftieth year be to you; in it you shall neither sow nor reap what grows of itself, nor gather the grapes from the undressed vines. For it is a jubilee; it shall be holy to you; you shall eat what it yields out of the field" (Lev. 25:8-12).]

   B. "And you shall count for yourself":

   C. in a court.

2. A. "seven weeks":

   B. Might one suppose that at issue are seven weeks of days [that is, forty-nine days]?

   C. Scripture says, "seven weeks of years."

   D. If it is "seven weeks of years," then is the sense that one should count out seven sabbatical years in sequence and then observe the jubilee?

   E. Scripture says, "seven years seven times."

   F. Thus since Scripture makes the point through these two verses, [we can prove it,] but had Scripture not done so, we should not have been able to prove it.

3. A. And how do we know that one counts the years of the septennate?

   B. Scripture says, "[seven weeks of years, seven times seven years,] so that the time of the seven weeks of years shall be to you [forty-nine years]."

   C. How do we know that one counts the years of the jubilee?

   D. Scripture says, "forty-nine years."

   E. "And how do we know that one observes the seventh year without reference to the jubilee?

   F. "Scripture says, 'seven weeks of years.'

   G. "And how do we know that one observes the jubilee year without reference to the sabbatical cycle?

   H. "Scripture says, 'forty-nine years,'" the words of R. Judah.

   I. And sages say, "The seventh year applies without regard to the jubilee, but the jubilee applies only if the seventh year goes along with it."

4. A. And how do we know that the jubilee is announced with the ram's horn?

   B. Scripture says, "Then you shall send abroad the ram's horn."

   C. I know only that the ram's horn is used for the jubilee. How do I know that it also applies in the new year?

   D. Scripture says, "And how do we know that the sounding of the trumpets on the New Year is with the ram's horn?

E. Scripture says, "Then you shall send abroad the ram's horn for sounding [a quavering note] on the tenth day of the seventh month; on the day of atonement you shall send abroad the ram's horn throughout all your land" (Lev. 25:9).

F. Why does Scripture refer to the seventh month?

G. Lo, it is the sounding of the horn appropriate to the seventh month, and what is that? It is the ram's horn.

H. So too the sounding of the horn for the New Year is to be on the ram's horn.

I. And how do we know that before the quavering notes of the horn are to be notes on the same plane?

J. Scripture says, "Then you shall send abroad the ram's horn for sounding [a quavering note]."

K. And how do we know that after the quavering notes of the horn are to be notes on the same plane?

L. Scripture says, "Then you shall send abroad the ram's horn."

M. I know only that this applies to the proclamation of the Jubilee [to which Lev. 25 makes reference].

N. How do I know that the same rule applies to the New Year?

O. Scripture says, "Then you shall send abroad the ram's horn for sounding [a quavering note] on the tenth day of the seventh month; on the day of atonement" –

P. Why again does Scripture refer to the seventh month?

Q. Lo, the sounding of the horn throughout the entire seventh month is to be like this.

R. Just as the notes prior and after the wavering notes are to be on the same plane, so in connection with the quavering notes of the New Year, the notes prior and the notes after the quavering notes are to be on the same plane.

5. A. "on the [tenth] day":
    B. By day and not by night.

6. A. "on the day of atonement":
    B. even on the Sabbath.

7. A. "you shall send abroad the trumpet throughout all your land":
    B. this teaches that every individual is obligated in this regard.

8. A. Might one suppose that even the sounding of the ram's horn on the new year overrides the restrictions of the Sabbath "throughout your land"?

    B. Scripture says, "Then you shall send abroad the ram's horn on the tenth day of the seventh month."

    C. Since it is said, "on the day of atonement," do I not know that that is the tenth day of the month?

    D. If so, why is reference made to the tenth day of the month?

    E. Doing so on the tenth of the month overrides the restrictions of the Sabbath throughout your land, but the sounding of the ram's horn for the New Year does not override the restrictions of the Sabbath throughout your land but only in the court alone.

The expected restrictions ("this, not that") and inclusions and exclusions occupy Nos. 1-3. Of special note is the interest in how the proof is derived, not only on the upshot of the inquiry, at Nos. 2, 3. The rest covers familiar ground. The exercise of inclusion and exclusion forms the one recurrent and unifying mode of discourse; but it is, after all, a mode of thought: this, not that. Of modes of thought propositions are not composed.

248. Parashat Behar Pereq 2

CCXLVIII:I

1. A.   "And you shall sanctify the fiftieth year [and proclaim liberty throughout the land to all its inhabitants; it shall be a jubilee for you, when each of you shall return to his property and each of you shall return to his family. A jubilee shall that fiftieth year be to you; in it you shall neither sow nor reap what grows of itself, nor gather the grapes from the undressed vines. For it is a jubilee; it shall be holy to you; you shall eat what it yields out of the field]":

    B.   What is the point of Scripture?

    C.   Since it is said, "[Then you shall send abroad the ram's horn] on the tenth day of the seventh month,"

    D.   I might then have reached the conclusion that the year can be sanctified only on the tenth day, [so that if it was not proclaimed holy on that day, it would not be observed as holy].

    E.   So when Scripture says, "And you shall sanctify the fiftieth year," it teaches that the year had become consecrated from the New Year [and the rite only announced and confirmed that fact].

The "what is the point of Scripture"-passages ordinarily show that without Scripture, we should have reached false conclusions or should not have known the law. They form part of the larger methodical-analytical program of the document.

2. A.   Said R. Yohanan b. Beroqah, "Subjugated bondmen were not freed to return to their homes, nor were fields returned to their masters, but people ate, drank, and celebrated, with crowns on their heads,

    B.   "[from the New Year] until the Day of Atonement of that year arrived.

    C.   "Once the Day of Atonement had arrived, they would sound the ram's horn,

    D.   "then fields would revert to their original owners and bondmen would be freed to go home."

3. A.   "and proclaim liberty throughout the land to all its inhabitants":

    B.   "liberty" refers only to freedom.

    C.   Said R. Judah, "What is the sense of the word for freedom? [Since it shares consonants with the word for "go around,"] it is like a traveller who is licensed to go around and carry his goods through the whole district [Jastrow, p. 289]."

4. A.   "its inhabitants":

    B.   when they are actually living on the land, not when they have gone into exile from it.

C.   If they were living on it, but if the tribes of Judah were assimilated with the tribes of Benjamin, and of Benjamin in Judah, might one suppose that the Jubilee would still apply?

D.   Scripture says, "its inhabitants" – "to all its inhabitants,"

E.   meaning that, since the tribe of Reuben and Gad and the half-tribe of Manasseh, the Jubilee years have been annulled.

5.   A.   "'it shall be a jubilee':

B.   "even though there has been no release, even though the ram's horn has not been sounded.

C.   "Or might one suppose that there is a Jubilee even though the slaves have not been sent forth?

D.   "Scripture says, 'it...,'" the words of R. Judah.

E.   R. Yosé says, "'it shall be a jubilee':

F.   "even though there has been no release, even though the slaves have not been sent forth.

G.   "Then might one suppose that there is a Jubilee even though the ram's horn has not been sounded?

H.   "Scripture says, 'it....'"

I.   Said R. Yosé, "[Following GRA:] Since one verse of Scripture serves to include, and another one serves to exclude, how come I maintain that there can be a Jubilee without the sending forth of the slaves, but there cannot be a Jubilee without the sounding of the ram's horn?

J.   "Since a verse of Scripture makes the matter depend on the sounding of the ram's horn, while another verse of Scripture makes the matter depend on the sending forth of the slaves,

K.   "the sounding of the ram,'s horn depends upon the action of the court, while the sending forth of the slaves depends on the actions of each individual."

6.   A.   "when each of you shall return to his property and each of you shall return to his family":

B.   Said R. Eliezer b. Jacob, "Concerning what classification of slave does Scripture speak here?

C.   "If it concerns a [Hebrew slave] sold for six years, that of course has already been dealt with. And if it concerns a person sold for a year or two, that of course has already been dealt with.

D.   "The passage therefore addresses only the case of the slave who before the Jubilee has had his ear pierced to the door jamb so as to serve in perpetuity.

E.   "The Jubilee serves to release him."

7.   A.   Another teaching concerning the verse, "when each of you shall return to his property and each of you shall return to his family":

B.   "To the family that is assumed to be his family he returns [regaining their status, even if it is very exalted]," the words of R. Meir.

C.   R. Judah says, "To his property and his family he returns, and he does not return to the the status that is possessed by the family."

D.   And the same rule applies to the person guilty of manslaughter when he returns from his exile on the death of the high priest.

8.   A.   "shall return":

B.   encompassing a woman.

No. 1 makes the point that the Jubilee begins with the New Year, not the Day of Atonement. No. 2 explains what happens in the interval. No. 3 then provides an etymology for the word "freedom." None of this has any keen interest in the amplification of the rules at hand or can be called sustainedly propositional, or even exegetical. It is at No. 4 that the process of exclusion and inclusion gets underway. Then No. 5 raises the issue of what is essential to the rite, another component of the work of definition through inclusion and exclusion. The text is somewhat in disarray. Nos. 6, 8 conclude the work of inclusion. No. 7 raises an extraneous point.

249. Parashat Behar Pereq 3

CCXLIX:I

1. A.   ["A jubilee shall that fiftieth year be to you; in it you shall neither sow nor reap what grows of itself, nor gather the grapes from the undressed vines. For it is a jubilee; it shall be holy to you; you shall eat what it yields out of the field. In this year of jubilee each of you shall return to his property" (Lev. 25:11-13).]
   B.   "it shall be a jubilee for you":
   C.   Might one suppose that when the year begins, the sanctification should take effect from the New Year, and when the year comes to an end, it should be drawn out to the Day of Atonement,
   D.   for, after all, time is added from the profane to the consecrated spell?
   E.   Scripture says, "it shall be a jubilee for you.... A jubilee shall that fiftieth year be to you":
   F.   the sanctification lasts, therefore, only to the New Year.

This is the sort of ad hoc and episodic observation that provides intractable materials for reconstitution into a propositional statement. What follows has no bearing upon this statement.

2. A.   "in it you shall neither sow nor reap what grows of itself, nor gather the grapes from the undressed vines":
   B.   Precisely the rules that apply to the seventh year apply to the Jubilee year.
3. A.   "For it is a jubilee; it shall be holy to you":
   B.   Just as the holiness of a crop that is holy affects money that is paid for the crop, so the seventh year's holiness affects money that is paid for the crop of the seventh year.
   C.   Then might one say, just as what has been consecrated is so redeemed by the payment of money as to go forth into unconsecrated status while the money paid for it is held to be holy, so in the case of the produce of the seventh year the rule is the same?
   D.   Scripture states, "it [shall be holy to you]," meaning, it remains in its status of sanctification [even though exchanged for money].
   E.   One turns out to rule:
   F.   **[In the case of one who sold produce of the sabbatical year, used the money received to purchase some other produce, and then**

exchanged this produce, in turn, for still other produce,] the very last produce obtained in this manner is subjected to the laws of the Sabbatical year, and the produce itself [that is, the original produce of the Sabbatical year, remains] forbidden [and subject to the restrictions of the Sabbatical year] [M. Shebiit 8:7D-E [Newman, *The Sanctity of the Seventh Year*, p. 171].

G. How so?

H. If with produce of the seventh year one purchased meat, this and that [the produce, the meat] must be removed at the time of the removal of preserved crops in the seventh year.

I. If one purchased fish with the meat, the meat has dropped out and the fish has entered into consideration; if then for the fish, oil, the fish drops out and the oil is affected.

J. {Accordingly,] [in the case of one who sold produce of the sabbatical year, used the money received to purchase some other produce, and then exchanged this produce, in turn, for still other produce,] the very last produce obtained in this manner is subjected to the laws of the Sabbatical year, and the produce itself [that is, the original produce of the sabbatical year, remains] forbidden [and subject to the restrictions of the sabbatical year].

4. A. "you shall eat what it yields out of the field":

B. So long as ownerless produce of a given species is growing in the fields, people may continue to retain in their homes and eat produce of the same species that they have stored in their homes [M. Shebiit 9:4A, Newman, p. 187].

C. When ownerless produce of a given species has disappeared from the fields, people cease to retain in their homes and eat produce of the same species that they have stored in their homes.

D. In this connection sages have ruled:

E. One who pickles three types of vegetables of the sabbatical year together in a single jar –

F. R. Eliezer says, "They may continue to eat these vegetables by virtue of the fact that the vegetable which ordinarily is the first of the three to disappear from the field is still growing. [That is, once the first of these vegetables disappears from the field, all the vegetables in the jar are subject to removal.]"

G. R. Joshua says, "They may eat any of these vegetables even by virtue of the fact that the vegetable which ordinarily is the last to disappear from the field is still growing. [That is, only when the last of these vegetables has disappeared from the field are the contents of the jar as a whole subject to removal.]"

H. Rabban Gamaliel says, "As each type of vegetable disappears from the field, one must remove that type of vegetable from the jar."

I. And the decided law accords with Rabban Gamaliel's ruling.

J. R. Simeon says, "All vegetables are regarded as a single species of produce with respect to the laws of removal."

K. They may eat purslane of the sabbatical year anywhere in the land of Israel until all types of vegetables disappear from the valley of Beit Netofah [M. Shebiit 9:5A-G, Newman, op. cit., pp. 189-190].

5. A.   "In this year of jubilee [each of you shall return to his property]":

    B.   this year sets slaves free, but the seventh year does not set slaves free.

    C.   But is the opposite of that proposition not a matter of logical inference?

    D.   If the advent of the Jubilee year, which does not release monetary debts, releases slaves, the seventh year, which does release monetary debts, surely should release slaves!

    E.   Scripture states, "In this year of jubilee [each of you shall return to his property]":

    F.   this year sets slaves free, but the seventh year does not set slaves free.

    G.   Then there is an argument *a fortiori* that the Jubilee year also should release monetary debts:

    H.   if the seventh year, which does not set slaves free, does have the effect of releasing monetary debts, the Jubilee year, which does set slaves free, surely should have the effect of releasing monetary debts!

    I.   Scripture says, "[At the end of every seven years you shall grant a release.] And this is the manner of release: there shall release [every creditor what he has lent to his neighbor]" (Dt. 15:1-2).

    J.   it is the advent of the seventh year that remits monetary debts, but the Jubilee year does not remit monetary debts.

    K.   And the Jubilee year effects the release of slaves, while the advent of the seventh year does not effect the freeing of the slaves.

6. A.   "In this year of jubilee each of you shall return to his property":

    B.   this serves to encompass the case of one who sells a field, whose son then went and redeemed it [purchasing it from the buyer]. In the Jubilee year the field reverts to the father."

The clarification now draws heavily on already-spelled-out materials, which means that our authorship conceives its readership to be following their statement consecutively. That contradicts the conventional repetition of the same points in response to the same set of words in diverse passages. But No. 2 leaves no doubt of the expectation of our authorship in the matter, which means that where we have repetition, it is for formal and aesthetic reasons, not for the purpose of exposition of an important proposition. No. 3 then leads us to the program of the Mishnah, which allows us to give an example of 2.B's generalization. No. 4 then follows suit. The only important point comes with No. 5, which compares the Jubilee year and the seventh year, a matter that allows us also to touch base with Deut. 15:1ff., the counterpart passage, and (implicitly) to make the point that each passage contributes something fresh.

250. Parashat Behar Parashah 3

CCL:I

1. A.   ["And if you sell a property to your neighbor or buy from your neighbor":]

B. How do we know that, when one sells a property, one should sell only to "your neighbor"?

C. Scripture says, "And if you sell a property to your neighbor."

D. And how do we know that, when one buys a property, one should buy only from "your neighbor"?

E. Scripture says, "or buy from your neighbor."

F. I know only that these rules pertain to real estate transactions, concerning which Scripture speaks.

G. How do we know that the law encompasses movables?

H. Scripture says, "sell a property,"

I. which serves to encompass movables.

J. How do we know that **the claim of fraud for overcharge [above true value] does not apply to real estate transactions [M. Baba Mesia 4:9B]?**

K. Scripture says, "or buy from your neighbor...you shall not wrong" [meaning, there will be no claim of overcharge].

L. As to movables, there can be a claim of fraud through overcharge, but as to real estate there can be no such claim.

M. And how do we know that, **as to the sale of slaves, there can be no claim of fraud by reason of overcharge [M. Baba Mesia 4:9B]?**

N. Scripture says, "[You may also buy from among the strangers who sojourn with you and their families that are with you, who have been born in your land; and they may be your property.] You may bequeath them to your sons after you, to inherit as a possession for ever" (Lev. 25:45-46).

O. Just as inherited property is not subject to a claim of fraud by reason of overcharge, so slaves are not subject to a claim of fraud by reason of overcharge.

P. And how do we know that, **as to the redemption of things that have been consecrated to the temple, there can be no claim of fraud by reason of overcharge [M. Baba Mesia 4:9B]?**

Q. Scripture says, "you shall not wrong one another.," omitting reference to what has been consecrated to the temple. [If one overpays to redeem the dedicated object, there is no recourse.]

R. How do we know that **a claim of fraud by reason of overcharge does not apply to deeds [M. Baba Mesia 4:9B]?**

S. Scripture says, "sell a property" –

T. what is singular in such a thing is that one has sold the palpable object or bought the palpable object,

U. so excluded are deeds, in which case one has not bought or sold a palpable object, but only the evidence that these represent rea things.

V. Therefore if one has sold deeds for the purposes of using them for clothing, there can be a claim of fraud by reason of overcharge.

2. A. "you shall not wrong [here: defraud by reason of overcharge] one another":

B. this refers to fraud in monetary transactions.

C. Might one suppose that at issue is fraud in words?

D. When Scripture says, "You shall not wrong one another" (Lev. 25:17), lo, at issue is fraud accomplished through words.

E. Lo, how then am I to interpret, ""you shall not wrong [here: defraud by reason of overcharge] one another":

F. this refers to fraud in monetary transactions.

3. A. And how much of an overcharge is involved in fraud?

B. **Defrauding involves an overcharge of four pieces of silver for what one has brought for twenty-four pieces of silver to the sela –**

C. **a sixth of the purchase price of an object.**

D. **How long is it permitted to return a defective sela? For the length of time it takes to show to a storekeeper or an expert.**

E. **R. Tarfon gave instructions in Lydda: "Fraud is an overcharge of eight pieces of silver to a sela, one third of the purchase price," so the merchants of Lydda rejoiced.**

F. **He said to them, All day long it is permitted to retract."**

G. **They said to him, "Let R. Tarfon leave us where we were."**

H. **And they reverted to conduct matters in accord with the ruling of the sages [M. Baba Mesia 4:3A-K].**

4. A. **All the same are the buyer and the seller: both are subject to the law of fraud.**

B. **And just as fraud applies to an ordinary person, so it applies to a merchant.**

C. **R. Judah says, "Fraud does not apply to a merchant."**

D. **He who has been subjected to fraud – his hand is on top.**

E. **If he wanted, he says to him, "Return my money."**

F. **Or if he wanted he says to him, "Give me back the amount of the fraud" [M. Baba Mesia 4:4A-F].**

5. A. **How much may a sela be defective and still not fall under the rule of fraud?**

B. **R. Meir says, "Four issars, at an issar to a denar."**
   R. Judah says, "Four pondions, at a pondion to a denar."
   R. Simeon says, "Eight pondions, at two pondions to a denar" [M. Baba Mesia 4:5A-D].

6. A. **How long is it permitted to return a defective sela?**

B. **In large towns, for the length of time it takes to show the coin to a money-changer.**

C. **And in villages, up to the eve of the Sabbath [M. Baba Mesia 4:6A-C]**

D. **For so it is customary for the market to be held in large towns from one Friday to the next [T. Baba Mesia 3:20D].**

E. **But if the one who gave the coin refuses to take it back, he has no valid claim against the other except for resentment.**

F. **One may give such a coin in exchange for produce in the status of second tithe, for easy transportation to Jerusalem, and need not scruple, for it is only churlishness [to refuse a slightly depreciated coin] [M. Baba Mesia 4:6D-H].**

7. A. "you shall not wrong [here: defraud by reason of overcharge] one another":

B. I know then that the law covers men [since in the Hebrew "one another" is "a man, his brother'].

C. How do I know that a woman is not to be defrauded by a man?

D.   or a man by a woman?

E.   Scripture says, "...another" –

F.   covering all cases.

8. A.   **[All the same are the buyer and the seller: both are subject to the law of fraud.] Just as fraud applies to an ordinary person, so it applies to a merchant.**

    B.   **R. Judah says, "If an act of fraud is committed by a merchant against a common person, the latter may enter a claim of fraud. If it is committed by an ordinary person against a merchant, the latter may not enter a claim of fraud. [A claim of fraud by reason of overcharge over true value cannot be entered by a merchant]" [M. Baba Mesia 4:4A-C].**

9. A.   I know only that the law covers dealings between one merchant and another.

    B.   How do I know that as to dealings between a merchant and an ordinary person, an ordinary person and a merchant, an ordinary person and another ordinary person, [one may enter claims of fraud by reason of overcharge from true value]?

    C.   Scripture says, "...another" –

    D.   covering all cases.

The basic proposition of No. 1 is to prove on the basis of Scripture the inclusions and exclusions, as to a claim of fraud through overcharge, that the Mishnah lists, as indicated. No. 2 makes a distinction, important also in the Mishnah, between verbal and monetary fraud. Both are prohibited, but they represent different counts and are subjected each to its own sanction. Nos. 3-6, 8 are simply lifted from the Mishnah. No. 9 continues the program of No. 8. No. 7 provides a conventional proposition of an inclusionary order.

CCL:II

1. A.   ["According to the number of years after the jubilee, you shall buy from your neighbor, and according to the number of years for crops he shall sell to you. If the years are many you shall increase the price, and if the years are few you shall diminish the price, for it is the number of the crops that he is selling to you":]

    B.   How do we know that **he who sells his field of possession, that is, one received by inheritance, at the time of the Jubilee's being in effect, is not permitted to redeem it in less than two years [M. Arakhin 9:1A-]?**

    C.   Scripture says, "and according to the number of years for crops he shall sell to you."

    D.   What about a sale made after the Jubilee or near the Jubilee or at some time-span distant from the Jubilee?

    E.   Scripture says, "according to the number of years for crops he shall sell to you. If the years are many you shall increase the price, and if the years are few you shall diminish the price, for it is the number of the crops that he is selling to you."

2. A.   "number of crops":

B. if it was a year of blight or mildew or a seventh year, it does not count in the reckoning of the crop years.

C. If he only broke the ground or left it fallow, it does count in the reckoning of the crop years. [R. Eleazar says, "If he sold it to him before the New Year and it was full of produce, lo, this one enjoys the usufruct from it for three crops in a period of two years"] [M. Arakhin 9:1C-E].

D. R. Eleazar says, "If one left it and went forth prior to the New Year, and it is full of produce, might one suppose that he may so to him, 'Leave it before me full of fruit, just as I left it before you full of fruit?'

E. "Scripture says, 'for it is the number of the crops that he is selling to you.'

F. "There are times that one can enjoy the usufruct of it for three crops in a period of two years" [T. Arakhin 5:1E-H].

The entire program is borrowed from Mishnah-tractate Arakhin. If we look back at the biblical verses before us, we realize that our authorship has followed the program dictated by those verses and re-presented those verses in three ways. It has read into the presentation of those verses sizable tracts of the Mishnah and Tosefta. It has systematically imposed upon diverse verses a single systematic program of inquiry, e.g., exclusion/inclusion, the proof of the limitations of the Mishnah's logic of hierarchical classification, which ignores the classification of Scripture and focuses on the indicative traits of things in themselves (not a major theme in the illustration we have reviewed). And it has amplified the sense or meaning of various verses, very often by saying, "not this, but that," but "this, and also that." There is no prevailing viewpoint or premise, proposition or polemic, that I can identify from the details that have been considered.

2. A Test Case: Holiness in Leviticus 19:1-20 and in Sifra Qedoshim Chapters 195-200

Once more we begin with the biblical verses subject to discussion:

And the Lord said to Moses, Say to all the congregation of the people of Israel, You shall be holy, [for I the Lord your God am holy. Every one of you shall revere his mother and his father, and you shall keep my sabbaths; I am the Lord your God. Do not turn to idols or make for yourselves molten gods; I am the Lord your God]" (Lev. 19:1-4).

When you offer a sacrifice of peace-offerings to the Lord, you shall offer it so that you may be accepted. It shall be eaten the same day you offer it or on the morrow; [and anything left over until the third day shall be burned with fire. If it is eaten at all on the third day, it is an abomination; it will not be accepted, and everyone who eats it shall bear his iniquity, because he has profaned a holy thing of the Lord; and that person shall be cut off from his people" (Lev. 19:5-8).

When you reap the harvest of your land, you shall not reap your field to its very border, [neither shall you gather the gleanings after your harvest. And you shall not strip your vineyard bare, neither shall you gather the fallen grapes of your vineyard; you shall leave them for the poor and for the sojourner; I am the Lord your God" (Lev. 19:9-10).

You shall not steal [nor deal falsely nor lie to one another. And you shall not swear by my name falsely and so profane the name of your God; I am the Lord]" (Lev. 19:11-12).

You shall not oppress your neighbor [or rob him. The wages of a hired servant shall not remain with you all night until the morning" (Lev. 19:13).

You shall not curse the deaf [or put a stumbling block before the blind, but you shall fear your God: I am the Lord]" (Lev. 19:14).

You shall do no injustice in judgment; [you shall not be partial to the poor or defer to the great, but in righteousness shall you judge your neighbor. You shall not go up and down as a slanderer among your people, and you shall not stand forth against the life of your neighbor: I am the Lord]" (Lev. 19:15-16).

You shall not hate your brother in your heart, but reasoning, you shall reason with your neighbor, lest you bear sin because of him. You shall not take vengeance or bear any grudge against the sons of your own people, but you shall love your neighbor as yourself: I am the Lord" (Lev. 19:17-18).

You shall keep my statutes. You shall not let your cattle breed with a different kind; you shall not sow your field with two kinds of seed; nor shall there come upon you a garment of cloth made of two kinds of stuff" (Lev. 19:19-20).

Now that we know the topical program of the cited verses, we also have in hand a complete picture of precisely the subjects that will be discussed and the order in which they will make their appearance.

195. Parashat Qedoshim Parashah 1

CXCV:I

1. A. "And the Lord said to Moses, Say to all the congregation of the people of Israel, You shall be holy, [for I the Lord your God am holy. Every one of you shall revere his mother and his father, and you shall keep my sabbaths; I am the Lord your God. Do not turn to idols or make for yourselves molten gods; I am the Lord your God]" (Lev. 19:1-4):

   B. This teaches that this chapter was stated in the assembly of all Israel.

   C. And why was it stated in the assembly of all Israel?

   D. It is because most of the principles of the Torah depend upon its contents.

The interest in generalization, such as we noted above in Behar, is not followed up. It is the fact, all exegetes ancient and modern concur, that "most of the principles of the Torah" derive from the holiness code. But that proposition is not developed, explained, instantiated, even illustrated. What we have is an ad hoc comment on a particular verse, nothing more.

2. A.   "You shall be holy":
    B.   "You shall be separate."
3. A.   "You shall be holy, for I the Lord your God am holy":
    B.   That is to say, "if you sanctify yourselves, I shall credit it to you as though you had sanctified me, and if you do not sanctify yourselves, I shall hold that it is as if you have not sanctified me."
    C.   Or perhaps the sense is this: "If you sanctify me, then lo, I shall be sanctified, and if not, I shall not be sanctified"?
    D.   Scripture says, "For I...am holy," meaning, I remain in my state of sanctification, whether or not you sanctify me.
    E.   Abba Saul says, "The king has a retinue, and what is the task thereof? It is to imitate the king."

The introductory materials expand on the basic idea of Israel's imitating God by sanctifying God. The basic point is 1.E, the principles of the Torah are derived from the passage at hand. That a propositional program deriving from Sifra's reading of the book of Leviticus can have emerged seems to me demonstrated by this pericope. But it is simply one point among a plethora of points, not an organizing principle, let alone the foundation of a sustained composition that makes a point. Immediately following is simply another exercise of inclusion/exclusion.

CXCV:II

1. A.   "Every one [Hebrew: man] [of you shall revere his mother and his father, and you shall keep my sabbaths]":
    B.   I know only that a man [is subject to the instruction].
    C.   How do I know that a woman is also involved?
    D.   Scripture says, "...shall revere" [using the plural].
    E.   Lo, both genders are covered.
2. A.   If so, why does Scripture refer to "man"?
    B.   It is because a man controls what he needs, while a woman does not control what she needs, since others have dominion over her.
3. A.   It is said, "Every one of you shall revere his mother and his father," and it is further said, "The Lord your God you shall fear" (Dt. 6:13).
    B.   Scripture thereby establishes an analogy between the reverence of father and mother and the reverence of the Omnipresent.
    C.   It is said, "Honor your father and your mother" (Ex. 20:12), and it is further said, "Honor the Lord with your wealth" (Prov. 3:9).
    D.   Scripture thereby establishes an analogy between the honor of father and mother and the honor of the Omnipresent.
    E.   It is said, "He who curses his father or his mother will certainly die" (Prov. 20:20), and it is said, "Any person who curses his God will bear his sin" (Lev. 24:15).
    F.   Scripture thereby establishes an analogy between cursing father and mother and cursing the Omnipresent.

G. But it is not possible to refer to smiting heaven [in the way in which one is warned not to hit one's parents].

H. And that is entirely reasonable, for all three of them are partners [in a human being].

4. A. R. Simeon says, "Sheep take precedence over goats in all circumstances.

B. "Is it possible that that is because they are more choice?

C. "Scripture says, 'If he brings a sheep as his offering for sin' (Lev. 4:32), teaching that both of them are of equivalent merit.

D. "Pigeons take precedence over turtledoves under all circumstances.

E. "Might one suppose that that is because they are more choice?

F. "Scripture says, 'Or a pigeon or a turtledove for a sin-offering' (Lev. 12:6), teaching that both of them are of equivalent merit.

G. "The father takes precedence over the mother under all circumstances.

H. "Is it possible that the honor owing to the father takes preference over the honor owing to the mother?

I. "Scripture says, 'Every one of you shall revere his mother and his father,' teaching that both of them are of equivalent merit."

J. But sages have said, "The father takes precedence over the mother under all circumstances, because both the son and the mother are liable to pay respect to his father."

5. A. What is the form of reverence that is owing?

B. The son should not sit in his place, speak in his place, contradict him.

C. What is the form of honor that is owing?

D. The son should feed him, give him drink, dress him, cover him, bring him in and take him out.

6. A. Since it says, "Every one of you shall revere his mother and his father," might one suppose that if his father and mother told the son to violate one of any of the commandments that are stated in the Torah, he should obey them?

B. Scripture says, "and you shall keep my sabbaths; I am the Lord your God":

C. "All of you are liable to pay due respect to me."

7. A. "Do not turn to idols":

B. "do not turn aside to worship them."

C. R. Judah says, "Certainly do not turn aside even to look at them."

8. A. "[or make for yourselves] molten gods":

B. This is one of the ten names of a disparaging kind that are assigned to idolatry on account of the rites attendant to it.

C. They are called "molten gods" because they are empty [elil/halul];

D. icon, because they are invalid [pesel, nifsal];

E. molten because they are served by libations [masekah/nisokim];

F. a pillar, because they stand;

G. forms, because they are made limb by limb;

H. terafim, because they moulder;

I. abominations, because they are disgusting;

J. abominable things, because they are abhorrent;

K. solar columns, because they stand in the sun;

L. asherim, because they get rich through others.

9. A.   "Do not turn to idols or make for yourselves molten gods":
   B.   "To begin with, they are idols. But if you turn to them, you make them into gods."
10. A. "or make for yourselves molten gods":
   B.   Might one suppose that others may make molten gods for them?
   C.   Scripture says, "not...for yourselves."
   D.   Since it says, "not...for yourselves," might one suppose that they may make them for others?
   E.   Scripture says, "or make for yourselves...."
   F.   In this connection sages have said:
   G.   One who makes an idol for himself violates two admonitions, first, "you will not make," and second, "not...for yourselves."
   H.   R. Yosé says, "on three counts: first, 'you will not make,' and second, 'not...for yourselves,' and third, 'you will not have...' (Ex. 20:2)."

The exposition begins with an inclusionary exercise, No. 1, to make certain that both father and mother are revered. The secondary expansions, Nos. 2, 3, 4, 5, 6, are thematically cogent but establish no fresh point. Nos. 7-9 then present an anthology on idolatry. Only No. 10 provides an important inclusionary program, extending the prohibition to a variety of cases. In all, as to topics, we have nothing more than an anthology of this and that, and, as to propositions, none that joins with any other: sentences, but no paragraphs.

196. Parashat Qedoshim Pereq 1

Translated by Roger Brooks

CXCVI:I.

1. A.   "When you offer a sacrifice of peace-offerings to the Lord, you shall offer it so that you may be accepted. It shall be eaten the same day you offer it or on the morrow; [and anything left over until the third day shall be burned with fire. If it is eaten at all on the third day, it is an abomination; it will not be accepted, and everyone who eats it shall bear his iniquity, because he has profaned a holy thing of the Lord; and that person shall be cut off from his people" (Lev. 19:5-8).]
   B.   [Now in the cited verse], Scripture's intent is not to instruct [Israelites] about when [whole-offerings] must be eaten. [Sifra Sav 2:9 clearly states that all holy things must be consumed either within one day or two.] [Rather, Scripture] teaches about [the intention required when] sacrificing [the whole-offering]. [The point is that] even prior to the sacrifice itself, one must have the intention to consume it within two days.
2. A.   [On the basis of the cited verse], I can derive only that whole-offerings [must be sacrificed with the intention to consume them in two days]. From what [passage may I infer that the same rule applies] to all offerings that must be consumed within two days – [namely], that the act of sacrifice itself must be performed with the prior intention to consume the meat within the requisite two days?
   B.   Scripture states, "When you sacrifice a sacrifice of whole-offerings..." (Lev. 19:5). [The juxtaposition of] "When you sacrifice" and "you shall

sacrifice it" is taken to include all types of offerings that are to be eaten within two days. [Like the whole-offerings], these must be slaughtered with the prior intention to consume the meat within the requisite two-day period.

C. [In Lev. 19:5, the juxtaposition of] "When you sacrifice" and "you shall sacrifice it" implies that you may not slaughter two heads of cattle [as offerings] in one fell swoop. [Rather, since the phrase refers to a singular object, each act of sacrifice must be performed separately from others.]

3. A. "If it is eaten at all on the third day, [it is an abomination]" (Lev. 19:7a) –

B. [that is, after the second day, the meat falls into the category of] refuse, [which must not be eaten under penalty of extirpation].

C. "it will not be accepted..." (Lev. 19:7b).

D. [Now in the cited phrase], Scripture's intent is not to instruct [Israelites that the sacrifice must be consumed] within the proper interval of time. [That is clearly stated in the preceding phrase, "If it is eaten on the third day...." [Rather, the phrase "It will not be accepted..."] teaches that the offering may not be consumed outside of the proper place, [namely the Temple court]. [This too then is part of the concern as to the intention of the officiating priest; if he slaughters the beast with the intention of consuming the meat outside of the proper location, that too produces the effect of turning the sacrificial meat into an abomination.]

4. A. "And everyone who eats it [after two days or outside the Temple court] shall bear his iniquity, because he has profaned a holy thing of the Lord; and that person shall be cut off from his people" (Lev. 19:8).

B. This is the major principle [governing eating a portion of a sacrifice outside the proper time or location]: Those who consume even a minuscule amount of a holy thing [at the wrong time or place], are subject to extirpation for [this transgression].

The available concern is the proper intention of the officiating priest, that is, the principal theme of Mishnah-tractates Zebahim and Menahot Chapters One-Three (the two tractates match at that point). No. 1 then introduces the paramount consideration that our authorship wishes to impute to the statements at hand. The first consideration is not eating the meat beyond the alloted spell, so No. 1. No. 2 then expands the range of coverage of the principle established for the case at hand at No. 1. The second, No. 3, is not eating the meat outside the correct location. No. 4 then announces the sanction. This is a miniature of a type of exposition in which our authorship excels: imputing to Scripture considerations paramount in the Mishnah, then working out the range of applicability of the law. But we have nothing like the expositions that comprise the thirty-seven *parashiyyot*, each with its proposition, of Leviticus Rabbah.

CXCVI:II

1. A. "When you reap the harvest of your land, you shall not reap your field to its very border, [neither shall you gather the gleanings after your harvest. And you shall not strip your vineyard bare, neither shall you

gather the fallen grapes of your vineyard; you shall leave them for the poor and for the sojourner; I am the Lord your God" (Lev. 19:9-10).]

B. **[The emphasis on "when you harvest] excludes [the following cases from the requirement of setting aside peah]:**

C. **[a field that] (a) robbers harvested, (2) ants devastated, or that (3) the wind or cattle trampled [M. Peah 2:7A)]**

2. A. "When you harvest [the yield of your land, you shall not completely reap the corner of your field as you harvest]" (Lev. 19:9).

B. [The emphasis on "when you harvest"] excludes [a second sort of case, namely one in which] a gentile [owns and] harvests [the field].

C. On the basis [of the foregoing exegesis, the sages] said:

D. **[As regards] a gentile who harvested his field and afterward converted [to Judaism] –**

E. **[the produce that he had harvested is exempt from the restrictions of**

F. **(1) gleanings, (2) forgotten sheaves, and (3) peah.**

G. **R. Judah obligates [the convert] to [obey the law of] the forgotten sheaf, because [the law of] the forgotten sheaf [takes effect] only after [the conclusion of] the binding [process, which takes place after the gentile had converted (M. Peah 4:6. A-D)].**

3. A. [On the basis of Lev. 19:9's opening phrase, "When you reap your harvest of your field...,] I can derive only [that the obligation to set aside peah applies to produce] while one reaps [it].

B. From what [phrase, then, might I determine that the obligation likewise relates to produce] while one merely plucks [it for a random snack]?

C. Scripture states [at the end of Lev. 19:9, "...you shall not completely reap the corner of your field] as you harvest." [The repetition of the word "harvest" is taken to mean that the obligation of setting aside peah applies to all types of harvesting, both reaping and snacking.]

D. From what [phrase, then, might I determine that the obligation to set aside peah applies not only to grain as one reaps it, but also to grain] already harvested [and brought to the threshing floor, but from which peah was not set aside]?

E. Scripture states, "[When you reap] your harvest...," [thereby implying that peah must be set aside from all produce the Israelite harvests].

F. [On the basis of Lev. 19:9's phrase, "When you reap the harvest of your Land,"] I can discern only [that the obligation to set aside peah applies to] grain.

G. From what [phrase, then, might I determine that the obligation likewise applies to] legumes?

H. Scripture states, "[When you harvest] your Land...," [thereby implying that all produce of the Land of Israel is subject to the law of peah].

I. From what [phrase, then, might I determine that peah must also be set aside from groves of] trees?

J. Scripture states, "When you reap the harvest of your field...," [thereby implying that the produce of any field, even an orchard, is subject to the law].

K. [On the basis of Lev. 19:9's phrase, "the harvest of your field...,"] it is possible that vegetables, squash, gourds, melons, and cucumbers all are included in the [above stated] general rule [that all of the Land's yield is subject to the law of peah]. [From what phrase might I determine that this is not the case?]

L.   Scripture states, "[When you harvest] the yield [of your land]..."

M.   **Now the term "yield" is reserved only for [produce that is] (1) edible, (2) privately owned, (3) grown from the Land [of Israel], (4) harvested as a single crop, and (5) can be preserved in storage [M. Peah 1:4B-C].**

N.   **This [general rule likewise] excludes vegetables, for even though they are harvested as a crop, one cannot preserve them in storage [T. Peah 1:7A]**

O.   **This [general rule likewise] excludes dates, for even though one can preserve them in storage, they are not harvested as a crop [T. Peah 1:7B].**

P.   **Grain and legumes are included in this general principle [M.1:4C].**

Q.   **And among types of trees, the fruit of (a) a sumac tree, (2) carob trees, (3) walnut trees, (4) almond trees, (5) grape vines, (6) pomegranate trees, (7) olive trees, (8) and date palms is subject to designation as peah [M. Peah 1:5A-C].**

4. A.   "[When you reap your harvest of your land,] you shall not completely reap the corner of your field [as you harvest] (Lev. 19:9).

B.   Now "corner" must refer to the completion [of the harvesting of that field]. [This point is implied by the phrase "you shall not completely reap the corner..."].

C.   And "corner" must refer to [leaving unharvested the appropriate] specified [portion of the yield] (so Rabad). This point is implied by the phrase "you shall not completely reap the corner portion...".

D.   And "corner" must refer to the rear [of the field]. [This point is implied by the juxtaposition of the following two phrases: "you shall not completely reap... your field"].

E.   On the basis [of the foregoing interpretations, at B, C, and D, the sages] said:

F.   **[If] he designated [some produce as peah], whether at the beginning or at the middle [of the field], lo, this [grain] is peah, providing that he leaves at the rear [of the field] no less than one-sixtieth [of the crop] [M. Peah 1:3A-B].**

G.   **R. Simeon said, "For [the following] four reasons, a person must designate [produce as] peah only [while harvesting] the rear of his field:**

H.   **"On account of:**

I.   **"(1) robbery from the poor,**

J.   **"(2) the idleness of the poor,**

K.   **"(3) appearance's sake,**

L.   **"(4) and because [Scripture] states, 'You may not completely harvest the rear corner of your field' (Lev. 19:9).**

M.   **"Robbery from the poor – how so?**

N.   **"This assures that the farmer will not find an opportune moment and say to a poor relative, 'Come and collect [all of] this peah for yourself.' [If the farmer was allowed to designate all of the peah for his own family, the other poor people in the town** would not have fair access to the produce, thus robbing them of what rightfully is theirs (cf. M.8:6).]

O.   "The idleness of the poor – how so?

P.   "This assures that poor people will not be sitting around and watching [the farmer] all day, saying, 'Now he is designating peah!' Rather, since [the farmer designates produce as peah while harvesting the rear of his field, the poor person] may go and gather poor-offerings from another [person's] field, and may return to collect [the peah] at the end [of the harvest].

Q.   "Appearance's sake – how so?

R.   "This assures that passers-by will not say, 'Behold how so-and-so harvested his field and did not designate [any produce as] peah for the poor!'

S.   "Because [Scripture] states, 'You may not completely harvest the rear corner of your field' (Lev. 19:9) – [how so?].

T.   "Since the produce actually designated as peah will not have been collected before the farmer finishes harvesting his field, when he does finish it will appear that he never designated any produce] [T. Peah 1:6A-H with variations].

5.   A.   "[When you reap the harvest of] your field... (Lev. 19:9)."

B.   [The phrase "your field"] excludes [from the law of peah] the field of other people. [That is, each householder is required to set aside peah only from his own property.]

C.   R. Simeon b. Judah says in the name of R. Simeon, "[The phrase] 'your field' excludes [from the law of peah a field that is] jointly owned with a gentile."

D.   [The phrase] "your field" [is stated] to impose the obligation [to set aside a separate portion of produce as peah from] each and every field [owned by a single farmer].

The Sifra's authorship's program derives directly from Mishnah-tractate Peah, as Brooks shows in detail. The issue of No. 2 is typical, of course. But the consideration introduced at No. 3 derives directly from the principles of Mishnah-tractate Maaserot. This then is read into the simple verses before us. No. 4 likewise aims at linking a Mishnah-passage to Scripture. No. 5 goes over a point proved earlier, concerning joint ownership with a gentile. In all, we cannot have had this chapter without access to the Mishnah. Anyone who maintains that our authorship intended to set forth its own propositions, even with respect to an inherited program of topics, will have to tell us how and where it has done so in a coherent, not merely episodic, manner. The paramount position occupied by the Mishnah's and Tosefta's program and propositions surely stands as an enormous obstacle in the path of proving that position.

197. Parashat Qedoshim Pereq 2

Translated by Roger Brooks

CXCVII:I

1. A.   On the basis [of the foregoing conclusion that the phrase "your field" implies that each field is to have a separate portion of peah (Sifra Qed. 1:11D), sages] have said:

   B.   **And these [landmarks] establish [the boundaries of a field] for [purposes of designating] peah:**

   C.   **(1) a river, (2) pond, (3) private road, (4) public road, (5) public path, (6) private path that is in regular use both in the dry season and in the rainy season, (7) uncultivated land, (8) newly broken land, (9) and [an area sown with] a different [type of] seed.**

   D.   **"And [as regards] one who harvests unripe grain [for use as fodder] – [the area he harvests] establishes [the boundaries of a field, since it now may be deemed uncultivated land; see 7]," the opinion of R. Meir.**

   E.   **But sages say, "[The area he harvests] does not establish [the boundaries of a field], unless he also has ploughed [the stubble] under, [thereby creating newly broken ground; see 8] (M. Peah 2:1A-D)."**

2. A.   [As regards] an irrigation ditch that [divides a tract of land so that the tract] cannot be harvested as one –

   B.   R. Judah says, "[It] established [the boundaries of a field]."

3. A.   "And any hills that are hoed with a mattock [i.e., hills that divide tract of land and that are hoed manually] (Is. 7:25) –

   B.   **even though an ox cannot pass over them with its plough,**

   C.   **[the farmer] designates peah for the entire [tract of land, as one field] [M. Peah 2:2A-E].**

4. A.   **All [of the landmarks listed at M. Peah 2:1] establish [the boundaries of a field planted with] seeds,**

   B.   **but as for establishing [the boundaries of an orchard of] trees, only a fence [does so].**

   C.   **But if the branches [of several trees] are intertwined with each other, [even a fence] does not establish [a boundary between them].**

   D.   **Rather, [the farmer] designates [a single portion of produce as] peah on behalf of all [of the trees whose branches are intertwined] [M. Peah 2:3A-D)]**

5. A.   **And as regards carob trees, [which have extensive root systems that intertwine, as do the branches at D], all that are within sight of each other [constitute a single orchard, and a single portion of fruit is designated as peah on behalf of all of them together].**

   B.   **Said Rabban Gamaliel, "In my father's household they used to designate one [portion of produce as] peah on behalf of all the olive trees that they owned in every direction [i.e., all that they owned together].**

   C.   **"But as regards carob trees, all that are within sight of each other [constitute a single orchard, and a single portion of produce is designated as peah for all of them together]."**

D. **R. Eliezer bar Sadoq says in [Gamaliel's] name, "So too: [they designated one portion of produce as peah for all] of the carob trees that they owned in the locale, [whether or not they were in sight of each other]" [M. Peah 2:4E-H].**

6. A. "[You shall not gather] the gleanings after your harvest (Lev. 19:9)."

B. [This prohibition does] not refer to gleanings [dropped during] random plucking, [but only to those dropped during the harvest

C. it self gleanings of your harvest." [The juxtaposition of "gleanings" and "harvest" implies that gleanings can refer] only to that which falls due to the process of harvesting.

D. In this connection sages have said:

E. **What [produce is in the status of] gleanings?**

F. **That which falls [to the ground] during the harvest.**

G. **[If a householder] was harvesting [his field, and] harvested an armful, [or] plucked a handful,**

H. **[and] a thorn pricked him so that [the produce] fell from his hand to the ground –**

I. **lo, [this produce] belongs to the householder.**

J. **[Produce that falls from] within the [householder's] hand, or [from] within his sickle, [i.e., that which he already has taken into his possession], belongs to the poor.**

K. **[Produce that falls from] the back of the [householder's] hand, or [from] the back of his sickle, [i.e., the produce fell before the householder had taken possession of it], belongs to the householder.**

L. **[Produce that falls from] the tip of the [householder's] hand, or [from] the tip of his sickle –**

M. **R. Ishmael says, "[Such produce] belongs to the poor."**

N. **R. Aqiba says, "[It] belongs to the householder" [M. Peah 4:10A-L].**

7. A. "You shall not gather the gleanings [after your harvest]... [You shall leave them] for a poor person..." (Lev. 19:10).

B. [The juxtaposition of "You shall not gather" and "for a poor person" implies that] you may not help one poor person [rather than another]. [The householder must remain uninvolved in the distribution of poor-offerings; cf. M. Peah 4:1-4.]

C. [The juxtaposition of] "You shall not gather" [and "for a poor person" likewise implies that] one must warn a poor person regarding his own [field, that the poor person may not gather the poor-offerings from that field].

No. 1 links the cited Mishnah-pericope to Scripture, and so throughout. I see not the slightest explicit polemic that the law of the Mishnah must rest upon Scripture. That is implicit, and we know it is present because of the insistence, elsewhere, upon that very point: the Mishnah's mode of thought by itself does not suffice. Why not say so here? I should guess that our authorship has a polemic of a different sort in mind, not the one against the authorship of the Mishnah, but the one against those who maintain that the Mishnah's rules do not rest upon Scripture at all. So they frame what I conceive to be one of their paramount propositions, which takes up a middle position, addressing the Mishnah's authorship where the Mishnah and Tosefta are not cited verbatim, and addressing the contrary party, the one critical of the Mishnah, when the Mishnah or the Tosefta is cited verbatim. That theory accounts for the strikingly different character of the present passages and all others in which we have observed, this chapter cannot have been composed without access to the Mishnah (and the Tosefta). Only No. 7 does not cite a passage of the Mishnah in so many words, but its point is the same as the Mishnah's rule.

198. Parashat Qedoshim Pereq 3
Translated by Roger Brooks

CXCVIII:I

1. A.   "You shall not strip your vineyard bare of defective clusters" (Lev. 19:10).

    B.   On the basis [of this verse sages] said:

    C.   **[As regards] a vineyard [the produce of which] entirely is defective clusters –**

    D.   **R. Eliezer says, "[The fruit] belongs to the householder [i.e., the clusters do not fall into the category of defective clusters because the norm in that vineyard is clusters that are not well formed]."**

    E.   **R. Aqiba says, "[The fruit] belongs to the poor, [i.e., the clusters are deemed defective, because they lack the definitive characteristics of well-formed clusters]."**

    F.   **Said R. Eliezer, "[Scripture states], 'When you harvest the grapes of your vineyard, you shall not return to gather the defective clusters' (Deut. 24:21). "If there is no harvest [of normal clusters, because the entire yield is defective], how can there be defective clusters [left after the harvest]?"**

    G.   **Said to him R. Aqiba, "[Scripture also states], "And you shall not strip your field bare of defective clusters' (Lev. 19:10). "[This verse indicates that the law applies] even if [the] entire [yield of the vineyard] is defective clusters, [such that there is no harvest of normal clusters]."**

    H.   **[Aqiba continues:] "If that is the intent of Lev. 19:10], why does [Scripture] state, 'When you harvest the grapes of your vineyard, you shall not return to gather the defective clusters' (Deut. 24:21) [M. Peah 7:7A-H]?**

    I.   **"[Scripture states this] because it is possible that since the verse permits the poor [to gather the] defective clusters, they might come and take them at any time they wish, [even though the farmer has not yet harvested his portion of the crop]. Therefore Scripture states, 'When you harvest, you shall not strip your vineyard bare of defective clusters.'**

    J.   **"[This verse, i.e., Deut. 24:21, proves that] the poor may not claim the defective clusters before the harvest, [for the law of defective clusters takes effect only when the farmer claims the normal bunches for himself, by harvesting them]. [Before this time,** none of the grapes can enter the status of defective clusters]" [M. Peah 7:7I].

2. A. "You shall not gather the separated grapes of your vineyard" (Lev. 19:10).

    B. [Because of Lev. 19:9's opening phrase "When you harvest...," Lev. 19:10's phrase "separated" can refer only to [that which separates] because of the harvest, [but not to fruit that separates due to some external constraint].

    C. On the basis [of this interpretation sages] said:

    D. [If a householder] was harvesting, [and] cut an entire cluster, [and] it became entangled in the leaves [of the vine], [so that the cluster] fell from his hand to the ground, and separated [into individual grapes], lo, [the individual grapes, together with the remaining cluster], belong to the householder, [since the fruit fell due to some external constraint]. [Only produce that falls to the ground at random, for no apparent reason, enters the category of the separated grape.]

    E. One who places a basket under the vine while he harvests, [in order to catch the grapes that separate and fall, so that they will not enter the status of separated grapes], lo that man steals from the poor.

    F. Concerning him it is stated, "Remove not the landmark of the poor" (gbwl wlym). [This is a play on words on Prov. 22:28, which reads, "Remove not the ancient landmark." (gbwl wlm) [M. Peah 7:3A-H].

3. A. What [produce is subject to the law of] the defective cluster (wllt), [such that it belongs to the poor]?

    B. Any [cluster of grapes] that has neither a shoulder [i.e., a wide upper-part] nor a pendant [i.e., as cone-shaped lower-part].

    C. If [a cluster of grapes] has either a shoulder or a pendant, [or both], it belongs to the householder, [for it is deemed well formed].

    D. If it is uncertain [whether a cluster has at least one of these two definitive features, a shoulder or a pendant], [it is deemed a defective cluster and belongs] to the poor.

    E. [As regards] a cluster [that appears to be] defective, [for it grows] on the [portion of the vine that] lies [on the ground] (rkbh), [such a cluster cannot hang down, and so appears to have neither a shoulder nor a pendant, even though in fact it may possess these features] –

    F. if [the cluster] is harvested along with the [normal] clusters, lo, it belongs to the householder [i.e., it is deemed a well-formed cluster].

    G. But if [the cluster] is not [harvested with the normal clusters], lo, it belongs to the poor [i.e., it is deemed a defective cluster].

    H. [As regards] a single grape [i.e., one that does not grow within a cluster] –

    I. R. Judah says, "[It is deemed] a [normal] cluster, [and belongs to the householder]."

    J. But sages say, "[It is deemed] a defective cluster, [and belongs to the poor]" [M. Peah 7:4A-N].

4. A. "[You shall abandon them] for the poor" (Lev. 19:10).

B. Perhaps [one might infer from this phrase that poor-offerings must be given] to other poor people [i.e., non Israelites]?

C. Therefore Scripture states, "[You shall abandon them for the poor] and the sojourner." [The sojourner here referred to is taken to be an Israelite.]

D. If [poor-offerings must be given to] "sojourners," perhaps [this phrase is meant to include giving the offerings to] resident aliens?

E. [This cannot be the case because] Scripture states, "[You shall abandon them for the poor, the sojourner,] and to the Levite..."

F. Just as [the term] Levite clearly refers to a member of the covenant [i.e., an Israelite], so too [the term] sojourner, [in this context], refers to a member of the covenant.

5. A. Or: "[You shall abandon them] for the Levite and for the poor" (Lev. 19:10).

B. Perhaps [these two phrases indicate that one must give the poor-offerings to these people] whether or not they are in need.

C. [To prove this is not the case], Scripture states, "[You shall abandon them] *for the poor.*"

D. Just as [the term] "poor" refers to someone who is in need and a member of the covenant, so too all [those listed as recipients in Lev. 19:10] must be in need and members of the covenant.

E. "[When you reap the harvest of your field, you shall not reap it to its very corner, neither shall you gather the gleanings after your harvest.] You shall abandon [them for the poor] (Lev. 19:9)."

F. **The householder places the produce before them, and they divide it.**

G. **Even if ninety-nine [poor people] say that [the householder should harvest and] distribute [the produce], and [only] one [poor person] says that [the poor should harvest and] take [the produce by themselves] (M. Peah 4:1E),**

H. **even if the one who says the poor should divide the produce themselves is healthy and strong, [and will be able to take more than any other poor person],**

I. **they listen to the single individual, [who said that the poor should take the produce], for he has spoken according to the law (M. Peah 4:1F-G).**

J. **Perhaps in the case of produce suspended from a trellis or the produce of a palm tree (M. Peah 4:1H)** the same rule, that the poor should divide the offerings for themselves, hold true?

K. [To indicate that this is not the case, Scripture states, "you shall abandon] them [i.e. the offerings]." [The indirect object is taken to mean that the householder must abandon only those items that will benefit the poor. He has no right, by contrast, to leave for them produce that they will have to collect in dangerous situations.]

L. **[In this case, when collecting the produce is likely to endanger the poor], even if ninety-nine [poor people] say that [the poor should harvest and] take [the produce by themselves], and [only] one [poor person] says that [the householder should harvest and] distribute [it to the poor] (M. Peah 4:1I),**

     M.   **Peah: even if the one who says the householder should divide the produce is old and sickly, [and thus will gain more than he would be able to take for himself],**

     N.   **they listen to the single individual, [who said that the householder should divide the produce], for he has spoken according to the law (M. Peah 4:11-K).**

6.   A.   On what basis do you claim that [the householder] should divide produce on a trellis or a date palm, but that [the poor] should divide [for themselves] all other types of produce [set aside as poor-offerings] [cf. M. Peah 4:1-2]?

     B.   After Scripture made a general statement, ["When you harvest...", (Lev. 19:9)], it made a limiting statement, ["...the harvest of your Land", (Lev. 19:9)].

     C.   Scripture states, "...the harvest [of your Land]." Now what characterizes [the action of] "harvesting" is that a minor can reach up as easily as an adult. This excludes [the cases of produce on] a trellis or [the fruit of] a date palm, for [in these cases] a minor cannot reach up as easily as an adult.

     D.   **R. Simeon says, "[So too]: Smooth nut-trees [M. Peah 4:1D] are deemed like [produce on] a trellis or [the fruit of] a date palm, [because gathering the poor-offerings from these trees could endanger the poor].**

7.   A.   "You shall leave them for [the poor and for the sojourner]":

     B.   leave grain in its straw, fenugrec in its pod, dates on their palm twigs.

     C.   Might one say that that is the case even if the wind has blown them down?

     D.   Scripture says, "...them...."

     E.   If one separated them and afterward the wind blew them down, just as the poor have acquired ownership of them, so the poor have acquired ownership to their branches.

8.   A.   On what basis [may we determine that] **(1) produce about which there is a doubt [as to its status as] gleanings [is deemed to have the status of] gleanings, (M. Peah 4:11F) (2) produce about which there is a doubt [as to its status as] forgotten sheaves [is deemed to have the status of] forgotten sheaves, [and] (3) produce about which there is a doubt [as to its status as] peah [is deemed to have the status of peah]?**

     B.   Scripture states, "You shall abandon them for the poor." [The term "abandon" implies that the householder must leave behind even that produce which might belong to him].

9.   A.   "I am the Lord your God":

     B.   "I collect from you only souls [lives that your negligence has taken]."

     C.   For it is said, "Do not rob the poor, because he is poor, or crush the afflicted at the gate" (Prov. 22:22).

     D.   And so too: "For the Lord will plead their cause and despoil of life those who despoil them" (Prov. 22:23).

As before, virtually the entire program is particular to the Mishnah, and only a few initiatives are those characteristic of our authorship in general, e.g., No. 6.

199. Parashat Qedoshim Parashah 2

CXCIX:I

1. A. "You shall not steal [nor deal falsely nor lie to one another. And you shall not swear by my name falsely and so profane the name of your God; I am the Lord]" (Lev. 19:11-12).
   B. What is the point of Scripture here?
   C. Since with reference to stealing, it is said, "He shall pay double" (Ex. 20:4, 7), we know the penalty.
   D. But where do we find the admonition?
   E. Scripture says, "You shall not steal."

2. A. "You shall not steal" for the purpose of harassing the victim.
   B. "You shall not steal" for the purpose of paying double, or for the purpose of paying four or five fold [in line with the provisions of Ex. 22:1) [e.g., in order to help the poor man].
   C. Ben Bag Bag says, "'You shall not steal' what belongs to you from the thief, so that you will not appear to be stealing."

3. A. "nor deal falsely":
   B. What is the point of Scripture here?
   C. Since it is said, "...or has found what was lost and lied about it...he shall restore it in full..." (Lev. 5:22), we know the penalty.
   D. But where do we find the admonition?
   E. Scripture says, "nor deal falsely."

4. A. "to one another":
   B. [Since the Hebrew refers to "a man,"] I know only that prohibited is lying by one man to another man. How about lying by a man to a woman?
   C. Scripture says, "one another," meaning, under all circumstances.

5. A. "You shall not steal nor deal falsely nor lie to one another. And you shall not swear by my name falsely [and so profane the name of your God]":
   B. "Lo, if you steal, in the end you will deny, and in the end you will lie, and that will lead you to take a false oath by my name."

6. A. "And you shall not swear by my name falsely [and so profane the name of your God]":
   B. What is the point of Scripture?
   C. Since it is said, "You shall not take the name of the Lord your God in vain" (Ex. 20:7), I might have supposed that one incurs liability only if he takes in vain the ineffable name of God. How do I know that all of the euphemisms for God's name also are involved in a false oath?
   D. Scripture says, "[And you shall not swear] by my name [falsely [and so profane the name of your God],"
   E. encompassing all names that I have.

7. A. "...and so profane the name of your God":
   B. This teaches that a false oath is a profanation of God's name.

8. A. Another matter concerning "...and so profane the name of your God":
   B. You are turned into unconsecrated food for wild beasts and domesticated beasts.

C.   And so Scripture says, "Therefore a curse devours the earth and its inhabitants suffer for their guilt; therefore the inhabitants of the earth are scorched, and few men are left" (Is. 24:6).

There being no pertinent passages of the Mishnah at hand, our authorship reverts to its more routine inquiry. Here what is at stake is the repetition of materials in diverse passages of the Pentateuch, which precipitates the familiar appeal to the distinction between the pronouncement of the sanction or penalty and the announcement of the admonition not to perform such an action. That is what characterizes the matter at Nos. 1, 3, 6. The other passages form mere embellishments. No. 8 is tacked on, there being no clear reference in context at Is. 24 to the infraction under discussion here.

CXCIX:II

1. A.   "You shall not oppress your neighbor [or rob him. The wages of a hired servant shall not remain with you all night until the morning" (Lev. 19:13).

    B.   Might one think [that that sort of harassment does not involve] even one's saying, "Mr. So-and-so is a very powerful man," while he is not a powerful man, "Mr. So-and-so is a sage," while he is not a sage, "Mr. So-and-so is rich," while he is not rich?

    C.   Scripture says, "...or rob him." [Spreading lies, even to the man's advantage, is prohibited as harassment.]

2. A.   What is particular about robbery is that it involves money, so oppression in context must involve something that involves money.

    B.   What is then involved?

    C.   It is the case of one who holds back the wages of a hired servant.

3. A.   "The wages of a hired servant shall not remain with you all night until the morning":

    B.   I know only that the rule covers the fee owing to a human being. **How do I know that the rental-fee for a domesticated beast or for utensils is subject to the law, or the rent for use of real estate [M. Baba Mesia 9:12A]?**

    C.   Scripture says, The wages...shall not remain with you all night until the morning,"

    D.   meaning, the wages owing for any thing.

4. A.   "Until morning":

    B.   **One violates the law in his connection only [if he does not pay forthwith] only on account of the first night alone [T. Baba Mesia 10:2E].**

5. A.   Might one suppose that one violates the law **even if the worker does not come and lay claim for the fee [M. Baba Mesia 9:12F]?**

    B.   Scripture says, "with you,"

    C.   I have spoken of a case only in which the money remains with you at your pleasure. [But if it is at the pleasure of the other, you do not violate the law.]

6. A. Might one suppose that even **if the employer gave him a draft on a store-keeper or a money changer [M. Baba Mesia 9:12G-H]**, one might violate the law in question?

   B. Scripture says, "shall not remain *with you* all night."

7. A. "The wages of a hired servant shall not remain with you all night until the morning":

   B. I know only that **a day-worker collects his wage any time of the night [M. Baba Mesia 9:11A].**

   C. How do I know that **a night-worker collects his wage any time of the day [M. Baba Mesia 9:11B]**?

   D. Scripture says, "On his day you will pay his wage" (Dt. 24:15).

Here we see the contrast, namely, how a passage is treated when the authorship has a sizable and well-composed passage of the Mishnah at hand. Then the systematic interest lies in the clarification of the proofs for the Mishnah's positions; in this instance, Tosefta's authorship has pursued the same program, and the comparison shows how closely the two sets of authors have thought through their tasks in response to the Mishnah.

CXCIX:III

1. A. "You shall not curse the deaf [or put a stumbling block before the blind, but you shall fear your God: I am the Lord]" (Lev. 19:14):

   B. I know that the prohibition extends only to the deaf person. How do I know that the law applies to not cursing anybody?

   C. Scripture says, "You shall not execrate a ruler of your people" (Ex. 22:27).

   D. If so, why is it said, "You shall not curse the deaf"?

   E. Just as the deaf is particular in that he is alive, so excluded is a corpse, who is not among the living.

2. A. "or put a stumbling block before the blind":

   B. "The blind" refers to one who cannot see in that particular context,

   C. [for example,] if someone came along to you and said, "As to the daughter of Mr. So-and-so, what is her status as to her marrying into the priesthood,"

   D. do not say to him, "she is suitable," if she is simply unsuitable;

   E. or if someone came along to you and asked for advice, do not give him inappropriate counsel;

   F. do not say to him, "Go early in the morning," so that thugs will mug him;

   G. "Go at noon," so that he will faint from the heat;

   H. do not say to him, "Sell your field and buy an ass," and then lie in wait for him and take it from him.

   I. And might you say, "I'm really giving you good advice," while lo, the matter really depends on the intention,

   J. for it is said, "but you shall fear your God: I am the Lord."

No. 1 presents an inclusionary exercise, explaining also an exclusion as well. No. 2 glosses by extending the rule of Scripture to cases of not physical blindness but other kinds of ignorance as to the facts. But there is no proposition implicit here that related rules also have to be extended in the same way. Nor does the proposition at hand link to any other we have seen, so far as I can discern.

200. Parashat Qedoshim Pereq 4

CC:I

1. A. "You shall do no injustice in judgment; [you shall not be partial to the poor or defer to the great, but in righteousness shall you judge your neighbor. You shall not go up and down as a slanderer among your people, and you shall not stand forth against the life of your neighbor: I am the Lord]" (Lev. 19:15-16):

    B. This teaches that a judge who misjudges a case is called "unjust," "hated," "an abomination," "beyond all use," "an abhorrent."

    C. And he causes five things to happen: he imparts uncleanness to the land, he desecrates the divine name, he makes the Presence of God depart, he impales Israel on the sword, and makes Israel go into exile from its land.

2. A. "you shall not be partial to the poor":

    B. You should not say, "This man is a poor man. Since both this rich man and I are obligated to feed him, let me decide in his favor, so that he will turn out to gain his living in an easy way."

    C. That is why it is said, "you shall not be partial to the poor."

3. A. "or defer to the great":

    B. You should not say, "This man is a rich man. He is son of important people. I shall not humiliate him and be seen through his humiliation to impose humiliation upon him."

    C. Therefore it is said, "or defer to the great."

4. A. "but in righteousness shall you judge your neighbor":

    B. **This means that one party may not be permitted to speak as long as he needs, while to the other you say, "Cut it short."**

    C. **One should not stand while the other sits down.**

    D. **Said R. Judah, "I have heard a tradition that if they wanted to let both of them sit down, they let them sit down. What is prohibited is only that one of them should sit while the other is standing" [T. San. 6:2E-I].**

5. A. Another interpretation of the statement, "but in righteousness shall you judge your neighbor":

    B. **In judging everyone, give the benefit of the doubt [M. Abot 1:6].**

The amplification at Nos. 2, 3 poses no problems. Nos. 4, 5 draw on Mishnah-Tosefta to clarify Scripture's point.

CC:II

1. A. "You shall not go up and down as a slanderer among your people:

    B. You should not speak gently to one party and harshly to another.

    C. Another matter: You should not be like a peddler who gives a taste of things and then goes his way.

2. A. Said R. Nehemiah, "This is the customary procedure of the judges:

B.   "The litigants stand before them, and they listen to their presentations. Then they send them away and discuss the matter.

C.   **"When they have completed the matter, they bring them back in. The chief judge says, 'Mr. So-and-so, you are innocent,' 'Mr. So-and-so, you are guilty.'**

D.   **"Now how do we know that when one of the judges leaves the court, he may not say, 'I think he is innocent, but my colleagues think he is guilty, so what can I do? For my colleagues have the votes!'?**

E.   **"Concerning such a person, it is said, 'You shall not go up and down as a talebearer among your people' (Lev. 19:16).**

F.   **"And further: 'He who goes about as a talebearer and reveals secrets, but he that is faithful conceals the matter' (Prov. 11:13)"** [M. San. 3:6A-E].

3. A.   How do we know that if you know testimony for someone's case, you are not permitted to remain silent in that case?

B.   Scripture says, "and you shall not stand forth against the life of your neighbor."

C.   And how do we know that if one sees someone drowning in the river, or muggers coming to attack him, or a wild beast coming to attack him, one is liable to save the other [even at the risk of one's own life]?

D.   Scripture says, "and you shall not stand forth against the life of your neighbor."

E.   How do we know that [in the following cases, there are those who are to be saved from doing evil even at the cost of their lives:] **one who pursues after his fellow in order to kill him, after a male or after a betrothed girl [M. San. 8:7A-C]?**

F.   you are liable to save him, even at the cost of his life?

G.   Scripture says, "and you shall not stand forth against the life of your neighbor."

I am not sure how **1.**B illustrates the base-verse here. **2.**C is a play on the word at hand, which stands for both "slanderer" and "peddler."

CC:III

1. A.   "You shall not hate your brother in your heart, [but reasoning, you shall reason with your neighbor, lest you bear sin because of him. You shall not take vengeance or bear any grudge against the sons of your own people, but you shall love your neighbor as yourself: I am the Lord]" (Lev. 19:17-18).

B.   Might one suppose that one should not curse him, set him straight, or contradict him?

C.   Scripture says, "in your heart."

D.   I spoke only concerning hatred that is in the heart.

2. A.   And how do we know that if one has rebuked him four or five times, he should still go and rebuke him again?

B.   Scripture says, "reasoning, you shall reason with your neighbor."

C.   Might one suppose that that is the case even if one rebukes him and his countenance blanches?

D.   Scripture says, "lest you bear sin."

3. A. Said R. Tarfon, "By the temple service! I doubt that in this generation there is anyone who knows how to give a rebuke!"

    B. Said to R. Eleazar b. Azariah, "By the temple service! I doubt that in this generation there is anyone who knows how to receive a rebuke."

    C. Said R. Aqiba, "By the temple service! I doubt that in this generation there is anyone who knows just how a rebuke is set forth!"

    D. Said R. Yohanan b. Nuri, "I call to testify against me heaven and earth, if it is not so that four or five times Aqiba was given a flogging on my account on the authority of Rabban Gamaliel.

    E. "The reason is that I complained to him about him.

    F. "And through it all I knew that he loved me all the more on that account."

4. A. "You shall not take vengeance [or bear any grudge]":

    B. To what extent is the force of vengeance?

    C. If one says to him, "Lend me your sickle," and the other did not do so.

    D. On the next day, the other says to him, "Lend me your spade."

    E. The one then replies, "I am not going to lend it to you, because you didn't lend me your sickle."

    F. In that context, it is said, "You shall not take vengeance,"

5. A. "or bear any grudge":

    B. To what extent is the force of a grudge?

    C. If one says to him, "Lend me your spade," but he did not do so.

    D. The next day the other one says to him, "Lend me your sickle,"

    E. and the other replies, "I am not like you, for your didn't lend me your spade [but here, take the sickle]!"

    F. In that context, it is said, "or bear any grudge."

6. A. "You shall not take vengeance or bear any grudge against the sons of your own people":

    B. "You may take vengeance and bear a grudge against others."

7. A. "but you shall love your neighbor as yourself: [I am the Lord]":

    B. R. Aqiba says, "This is the encompassing principle of the Torah."

    C. Ben Azzai says, "It is 'This is the book of the generations of Adam' (Gen. 5:1) is a still more encompassing principle."

The reading at No. 1 tends to limit the applicability of the scriptural commandment. The important point is not repressing one's viewpoint. No. 2 then sets limits to this process of rebuke or reasoning with the other. No. 3 is parachuted down, because it intersects with the topic at hand. Nos. 4-5 provide a matched pair of illustrations which are quite germane. Nos. 6 reads "sons of your own people" as exclusionary; outsiders may be treated in a different way. No. 7 then stands on its own.

CC:IV.1-CC:IX.1 [Pereq 4:13-18]

Translated and Explained by Irving Mandelbaum

CC:IV

1. A. ["You shall keep my statutes. You shall not let your cattle breed with a different kind; you shall not sow your field with two kinds of seed;

nor shall there come upon you a garment of cloth made of two kinds of stuff" (Lev. 19:19-20)].

B.   Were it stated [only], "You shall not let your cattle breed" [Vatican Codices 31,66, B. B.M., Hillel, GRA omit: with a different kind] (*l' trby' bhmtk*) (Lev. 19:19), one might think that he should not take hold of the [female] domesticated animal and make it stand before the male [domesticated animal so that they may mate] [B. B.M.: I might say that a man should not hold [down] the [female] domesticated animal when the male [domesticated animal] mounts her].

C.   Scripture says, "With a different kind" –

D.   I have said [this] to you only on account of [the law of] diverse-kinds.

According to A the phrase *You shall not let your cattle breed* could be understood to mean that one may make a female animal stand before a male animal so that they may mate. B-C thus explains that the phrase *with a different kind* was included to prohibit not the holding of the female animal during mating, but the mating of animals of diverse-kinds.

CC:V

1. A.   ["You shall not let your cattle breed with a different kind" (Lev. 19:19).]

    B.   I know only [that you may not make] your [own] domesticated animal [mount] on your [own] domesticated animal.

    C.   Whence [do I know that you may not make] your [own] domesticated animal [mount] on a domesticated animal of others, [nor make] a domesticated animal of others [mount] on your [own] domesticated animal?

    D.   [GRA omits "whence," and so reads: [nor] your [own] domesticated animal on a domesticated animal of others, nor a domesticated animal of others on your [own] domesticated animal.]

    E.   Whence [do I know that you may not make] a domesticated animal of others [mount] on a domesticated animal of others?

    F.   Scripture says, "You shall keep my statutes" (Lev. 19:19).

B understands the phrase *your cattle* in Lev. 19:19 to mean that one is prohibited from mating animals of different kinds with one another only when both animals are one's own. C-E then takes the clause *You shall keep all my statutes* to imply that the prohibition covers all matings of animals of different kinds, including those instances in which either only one of the animals is one's own or both animals belong to someone else. Alternatively, according to GRA's reading *your cattle* is taken to include all cases in which at least one of the animals is one's own. The clause *You shall keep my statutes* is then understood to include the mating of another's animals of different kinds.

CC:VI

1. A.   ["You shall not let your cattle (*bhmh*) breed with a different kind" (Lev. 19:19).]

B. I know only that [one may not let] **a domesticated animal (*bhmh*)
    [mount] on a domesticated animal [= M. Kilayim 8:2A(1)].**

C. **Whence [do I know that one may not let] a domesticated animal
    [mount] on a wild animal, nor a wild animal [mount] on a
    domesticated animal? [GRA omits "whence" and so reads: (nor) a
    domesticated animal on a wild animal, nor a wild animal on a
    domesticated animal] [=M. Kilayim 8:2A(3)-(4)]?**

D. Whence [do I know that one may not let] **an unclean [animal mount]
    on a clean [animal], nor a clean [animal] on an unclean [one] [= M.
    Kilayim 8:2B(3)-(4)]?**

E. Scripture says, You shall keep my statues (Lev. 19:19).

Sifra cites M. Kilayim 8:2A(1) at B, M. Kilayim 8:2A(3)-(4) at C, and
M. Kilayim 8:2B(3)-(4) at D. Unlike M., however, Sifra concerns not the
joining of animals of different kinds to do work, but the mating of such
animals with one another. A-B takes Lev. 19:19, which refers to the *bhmh,*
to prohibit the mating of different kinds of domesticated animals alone.
C-E then understands the clause *You shall keep my statutes* to include in
the prohibition the mating of all animals of different kinds, and thus to
prohibit the mating of both domesticated with wild animals and clean with
unclean animals. Alternatively, according to GRA's reading A-C
understands Lev. 19:19 to refer to all matings which involve at least one
domesticated animal.

CC:VII

1. A. "Your field you shall not sow [with diverse-kinds]" (Lev. 19:19) –
    B. I know only that he should not sow [diverse-kinds].
    C. Whence [do I know that] he should not allow [diverse-kinds] to grow?
    D. Scripture says, "Not...diverse-kinds."
    E. [B. M.Q., B. Mak., B. A.Z., GRA omit:] I have said [this] only on
        account of [the law of] diverse-kinds.

Sifra deduces the prohibition of allowing diverse-kinds to grown in a
field from the word-order of Lev. 19:19. Since *not* precedes *diverse-kinds*
as well as *sow,* it is taken to be read with the former as well as with the latter
(D). The verse is thus understood to state not only that one may not sow
diverse-kinds (as it explicitly rules [A-B]), but also that one may not have
diverse-kinds in his field, i.e., allow diverse-kinds to grown (QA). E
explains that the point of the verse is to prohibit the growing of diverse-
kinds rather than the particular act of sowing them (QA). Sifra thus agrees
with M. Kilayim 8:1C's rule that one may not allow diverse-kinds of seeds
to grow.

CC:VIII

1. A. Whence [do I know] that they do not graft
    B. a barren tree upon a fruit tree,
    C. nor a fruit tree upon a barren tree,

D.   not a fruit tree upon a fruit tree [Y. adds: one kind upon one not of its kind]?

B.   Scripture says, "You shall keep my statutes" (Lev. 19:19).

A-B takes the clause *You shall keep my statutes,* which immediately precedes the prohibition concerning diverse-kinds of crops, to include the prohibition of grafting one kind of tree on another (which is not stated in Scripture). We note that unlike M. Kilayim 1:7B, which states simply that one may not graft one kind of tree on another, Sifra prohibits only the three possible grafts which involve at least one fruit tree.

CC:IX

1. A.   "Nor [shall] a garment of cloth made up of two kinds [of stuff come upon you]" (Lev. 19:19) –

    B.   Why does Scripture say so?

    C.   Since Scripture says, "You shall not wear a mingled stuff, wool and linen together" (Dt. 22:11), might I [not] think that one shall not wear pieces of shorn wool (*gyzy smr*) and bundles of flax-stalks (*'nysy pstn*) together?

    D.   Scripture says, "A garment."

    E.   I know [from this phrase] only [that the laws of diverse-kinds apply to] a garment.

    F.   Whence [do I know] to include felted stuffs [in the prohibition]?

    G.   Scripture says, "[A garment of cloth made up of two kinds] of stuff" (*sha'atnez*) – **something which is hackled, spun (*twwy*), or woven (*nwz*).**

    H.   **R. Simeon b. Eleazar says, "It [i.e., a fabric of diverse-kinds] is turned awry (*nlwz*), and turns (*mlyz*) his Father in Heaven against him [= M. Kilayim 9:8B-C].**

    I.   Since Scripture says, "Nor shall there come upon you [a garment of cloth made up of two kinds of stuff]" (Lev. 19:19), might I think that he shall not tie [a garment of diverse-kinds] in a bundle [and throw it] behind him [i.e., over his shoulder]?

    J.   Scripture says, "You shall not wear [a mingled stuff, wool and linen together]" (Dt. 22:11).

    K.   "You shall not wear" –

    L.   I know only that he shall not wear [a garment of diverse-kinds].

    M.   Whence [do I know] that he shall not cover himself [with such a garment]?

    N.   Scripture says, "Nor shall there come upon you."

    O.   [It follows that] you are permitted to spread it (*lhsy'w*) [i.e., a garment of diverse-kinds] under you.

    P.   But sages said, "You shall not do so, lest a single fringe (*nym'*) [of the garment of diverse-kinds] come upon (*thyh 'wlh*; B. Yoma, Bes., and Tamid: *tkrk* ["wind itself around"]) his [i.e., your] flesh."

A-B cites Lev. 19:19, asking why it is necessary for Scripture to state this verse, since Dt. 22:11 also prohibits one from wearing diverse-kinds (Hillel). C-D answers that Dt. 22:11, which states simply *You shall not wear a mingled stuff,* may be taken to mean that one may not wear anything which is composed of diverse-kinds, even pieces of shorn wool and stalks of flax which have been joined together. Lev. 19:19 therefore specifically mentions the word *garment*, and so includes in the prohibition only garments, and not other items composed of vegetable or animal fibers. E-F then takes the word *garment* to refer only to items which are woven, and thus asks whether the prohibition of Lev. 19:19 applies also to felted stuffs which are composed of wool and linen. G-H answers by citing the exegesis of *sha'atnez* (=M. Kilayim 9:8B-C), which rules that hackled fibers of wool and linen are also prohibited as fabrics of diverse-kinds. E-H thus agrees with the rule of M. Kilayim 9:9A-B, and directly links this rule to the exegesis of *sha'atnez* at 9:8B-C. I-N discusses why Scripture presents two prohibitions concerning diverse-kinds of garments (Lev. 19:19 and Dt. 22:11). According to I the phrase *Nor shall there come upon you* (Lev. 19:19) by itself implies that one may not bear diverse-kinds on his body in any way, so that one may not even tie his garments of diverse-kinds in a bundle and throw them over his shoulder. J therefore cites the phrase *You shall not wear* (Dt. 22:11), which serves to limit the prohibition of garments of diverse-kinds to concern only the act of wearing such garments. I-J thus agrees with M. Kilayim 9:5C, which states that the more scrupulous clothes-sellers would carry diverse-kinds in a bundle over their shoulders in order to avoid carrying them on their backs. K then states that the phrase *You shall not wear* by itself indicates that one is prohibited only from wearing garments of diverse-kinds. L-M therefore maintains that the rule of *Nor shall there come upon you* is necessary in order to include in the prohibition the act of covering oneself with diverse-kinds as well. The point of Sifra, then, is that the prohibitions of Lev. 19:19 and Dt. 22:11 serve to qualify one another. O then takes the phrase *Nor shall there come upon you* to imply that, while one is not permitted to cover himself with diverse-kinds, he is permitted to sit or lie on them. Sages, however, reverse this ruling in P, maintaining that one may not sit or lie on garments of diverse-kinds, for a fringe of one of the garments might come to rest upon him, and he would then be liable for covering himself with diverse-kinds. P thus presents a more stringent view than M. Kilayim 9:2C-D, which permits one to sit or lie on mattresses or cushions of diverse-kinds, provided that he does not allow his flesh to come into contact with them.

It remains to observe that the topical and propositional characteristics of the prior illustrative chapters recur here.

3. Does Sifra Set Forth Propositions?

For three reasons, we must conclude that Sifra does not set forth propositions in the way in which the Rabbah-compilations and Sifré to Deuteronomy do. First, In the sample of two sizable discussions of important passages in the book of Leviticus, I fail to see a topical program distinct from that of Scripture, nor do I find it possible to set forth important propositions that transcend the cases at hand. These materials of Sifra's that we have surveyed remain wholly within Scripture's range of discourse, proposing only to expand and clarify what it found within Scripture. Where they move beyond Scripture, it is not toward fresh theological or philosophical thought, such as we noted in the Rabbah-compilations and Sifré to Deuteronomy, but rather to a quite different set of issues altogether, concerning Mishnah and Tosefta. The blatant and definitive trait of our document therefore is simple: the topical program and order derive from Scripture. Just as the Mishnah defines the topical program and order for Tosefta, the Yerushalmi, and the Bavli, so Scripture does so for Sifra. It follows that Sifra takes as its structure the plan and program of the Written Torah, by contrast to decision of the framers or compilers of Tosefta and the two Talmuds.

Second, for sizable passages, the sole point of coherence for the discrete sentences or paragraphs of Sifra's authorship derives from the base-verse of Scripture that is subject to commentary. That fact corresponds to the results of Chapter Three. While, as we have noted, the Mishnah holds thought together through propositions of various kinds, with special interest in demonstrating propositions through a well-crafted program of logic of a certain kind, Sifra's authorship appeals to a different logic altogether. It is one which I have set forth as fixed-associative discourse. That is not a propositional logic – by definition.

The third fundamental observation draws attention to the paramount position, within this restatement of the Written Torah, of the Oral Torah. We may say very simply that, in a purely formal and superficial sense, a sizable proportion of our sample passages consists simply in the association of completed statements of the Oral Torah with the exposition of the Written Torah, the whole re-presenting as one whole Torah the Dual Torah received by Moses at Sinai (speaking within the Torah-myth). Even at the very surface we observe a simple fact. Without the Mishnah or the Tosefta, our authorship will have had virtually nothing to say about one passage after another of the Written Torah. A deeper knowledge of Sifra, set forth in my complete translation, will show, furthermore, that far more often than citing the Mishnah or the Tosefta verbatim, our authorship cites principles of law or theology fundamental to the Mishnah's treatment of a given topic, even when the particular passage of the Mishnah or the Tosefta that sets forth those principles is not cited verbatim.

It follows that even our preliminary survey highlights the three basic and definitive traits of Sifra, first, its total adherence to the topical program of the Written Torah for order and plan; second, its very common reliance upon the phrases or verses of the Written Torah for the joining into coherent discourse of discrete thoughts, e.g., comments on, or amplifications of, words or phrases; and third, its equally profound dependence upon the Oral Torah for its program of thought: the problematic that defines the issues the authorship wishes to explore and resolve. And yet, I shall now show, Sifra seen whole and complete does set forth an urgent and compelling set of propositions. Let me now explain what they are and how they are demonstrated.

4. The Position of Sifra

In detail we cannot reconstruct a topical program other than that of Scripture, nor does a propositional program attain explicit articulation in detail. But viewed in its indicative and definitive traits of rhetoric, logic, and implicit proposition, our document does take up a well-composed position on a fundamental issue, namely, the relationship between the Written Torah, represented by the book of Leviticus, and the Oral Torah, represented by the passages of the Mishnah deemed by the authorship of Sifra to be pertinent to the book of Leviticus.

In a simple and fundamental sense, Sifra joins the two Torahs into a single statement, accomplishing a re-presentation of the Written Torah in topic and in program and in the logic of cogent discourse, and within that rewriting of the Written Torah, a re-presentation of the Oral Torah in its paramount problematic and in many of its substantive propositions. Stated simply, the Written Torah provides the form, the Oral Torah, the content. What emerges is not merely a united, Dual Torah, but *The* Torah, stated whole and complete, in the context defined by the book of Leviticus. Here the authorship of Sifra presents, through its re-presentation, The Torah as a proper noun, all together, all at once, and, above all, complete and utterly coherent. In order to do so our authorship has constructed through its document, first, the sustained critique of the Mishnah's *Listenwissenschaft*, then, the defense of the Mishnah's propositions on the foundation of scriptural principles of taxonomy, hierarchical classification in particular.

Since I have already demonstrated the centrality, to Sifra, of the issue of hierarchical logic, as a principal formal pattern and a main logical principle of thought, I have now left no reasonable doubt that characteristic of Sifra in rhetoric, logic, and, as we have now seen, topic, is the disquisition on the logic of the Mishnah and the program of the Mishnah. In order to advance the argument, I have now to show two propositions, first, Sifra's authorship's defense of *Listenwissenschaft,* second, its critique of the Mishnah's mode of carrying out that science. First, we shall observe a sequence of cases in which Sifra's authorship demonstrates that *Listenwissenschaft* is a self-evidently valid mode of demonstrating the truth of propositions. Second, we shall note, in the same cases, that *the* source of the correct classification of things is Scripture and only Scripture. Without Scripture's intervention into the taxonomy of the world, we should have no knowledge at all of which things fall into which classifications and therefore are governed by which rules. Let us begin with a sustained example of the right way of doing things. Appropriately, the opening composition of Sifra shows us the contrast between relying on Scripture's classification, and the traits imputed by Scripture to the taxa it identifies, and appealing to categories not defined and endowed with indicative traits by Scripture.

Parashat Vayyiqra Dibura Denedabah Parashah 1

I:I

1. A. "The Lord called [to Moses] and spoke [to him from the tent of meeting, saying, 'Speak to the Israelite people and say to them']" (Lev. 1:1):

   B. He gave priority to the calling over the speaking.

   C. That is in line with the usage of Scripture.

   D. Here there is an act of speaking, and in connection with the encounter at the bush [Ex. 3:4: "God called to him out of the bush, 'Moses, Moses'"], there is an act of speaking.

   E. Just as in the latter occasion, the act of calling is given priority over the act of speaking [even though the actual word, "speaking" does not occur, it is implicit in the framing of the verse], so here, with respect to the act of speaking, the act of calling is given priority over the act of speaking.

2. A. No [you cannot generalize on the basis of that case,] for if you invoke the case of the act of speaking at the bush, which is the first in the sequence of acts of speech [on which account, there had to be a call prior to entry into discourse],

   B. will you say the same of the act of speech in the tent of meeting, which assuredly is not the first in a sequence of acts of speech [so there was no need for a preliminary entry into discourse through a call]?

   C. The act of speech at Mount Sinai [Ex. 19:3] will prove to the contrary, for it is assuredly not the first in a sequence of acts of speech, yet, in that case, there was an act of calling prior to the act of speech.

3. A. No, [the exception proves nothing,] for if you invoke in evidence the act of speech at Mount Sinai, which pertained to all the Israelites, will you represent it as parallel to the act of speech in the tent of meeting, which is not pertinent to all Israel?

   B. Lo, you may sort matters out by appeal to comparison and contrast, specifically:

   C. The act of speech at the bush, which is the first of the acts of speech, is not of the same classification as the act of speech at Sinai, which is not the first act of speech.

   D. And the act of speech at Sinai, which is addressed to all Israel, is not in the same classification as the act of speech at the bush, which is not addressed to all Israel.

4. A.   What they have in common, however, is that both of them are acts of speech, deriving from the mouth of the Holy One, addressed to Moses, in which case, the act of calling comes prior to the act of speech,

    B.   so that, by way of generalization, we may maintain that every act of speech which comes from the mouth of the Holy One to Moses will be preceded by an act of calling.

5. A.   Now if what the several occasions have in common is that all involve an act of speech, accompanied by fire, from the mouth of the Holy One, addressed to Moses, so that the act of calling was given priority over the act of speaking, then every case in which there is an act of speech, involving fire, from the mouth of the Holy One, addressed to Moses, should involve an act of calling prior to the act of speech.

    B.   But then an exception is presented by the act of speech at the tent of meeting, in which there was no fire.

    C.   [That is why it was necessary for Scripture on this occasion to state explicitly,] "The Lord called [to Moses and spoke to him from the tent of meeting, saying, 'Speak to the Israelite people and say to them']" (Lev. 1:1).

    D.   That explicit statement shows that, on the occasion at hand, priority was given to the act of calling over the act of speaking.

I:II

1. A.   ["The Lord called to Moses and spoke to him from the tent of meeting, saying, 'Speak to the Israelite people and say to them'" (Lev. 1:1)]: Might one suppose that the act of calling applied only to this act of speaking alone?

    B.   And how on the basis of Scripture do we know that on the occasion of all acts of speaking that are mentioned in the Torah, [there was a prior act of calling]?

    C.   Scripture specifies, "from the tent of meeting,"

    D.   which bears the sense that on every occasion on which it was an act of speaking from the tent of meeting, there was an act of calling prior to the act of speaking.

2. A.   Might one suppose that there was an act of calling only prior to the acts of speech alone?

    B.   How on the basis of Scripture do I know that the same practice accompanied acts of saying and also acts of commanding?

    C.   Said R. Simeon, "Scripture says not only, '...spoke,...,' but '...and he spoke,' [with the inclusion of the *and*] meant to encompass also acts of telling and also acts of commanding."

The exercise of generalization addresses the character of God's meeting with Moses. The point of special interest is the comparison of the meeting at the bush and the meeting at the tent of meeting. And at stake is asking whether all acts of God's calling and talking with, or speaking to, the prophet are the same, or whether some of these acts are of a different classification from others. In point of fact, we are able to come to a generalization, worked out at **I:I.5.A**. And that permits us to explain why there is a different usage at Lev. 1:1 from what characterizes parallel cases. **I:II.1-2** proceeds to generalize from the case at hand to other usages

entirely, a very satisfying conclusion to the whole. I separate **I:II** from **I:I**
because had **I:I** ended at 5, it could have stood complete and on its own,
and therefore I see **I:II** as a brief appendix. The interest for my argument
should not be missed. We seek generalizations, governing rules, that are
supposed to emerge by the comparison and contrast of categories or of
classifications. The way to do this is to follow the usage of Scripture, that
alone. And the right way of doing things is then illustrated.

I.III

1. A. Might one maintain that is also the case for free-standing statements
       [which do not commence with a reference either to speaking or to
       saying, as at Lev. 1:10, which opens, simply, "If his offering..."]?

   B. Scripture says, "...spoke...," meaning that on an occasion of an act of
       speech there was also an act of calling, but there was no act of calling
       prior to the setting forth of a free-standing statement.

2. A. What purpose was there in setting forth free-standing statements [such
       as those that commence without reference to speaking or saying]?

   B. It was so as to give Moses a pause to collect his thoughts between the
       statement of one passage and the next, between the presentation of
       one topic and the next.

3. A. And lo, that yields an argument *a fortiori:*

   B. If one who was listening to words from the mouth of the Holy One,
       and who was speaking by the inspiration of the Holy Spirit,
       nonetheless had to pause to collect his thoughts between one passage
       and the next, between one topic and the next,

   C. all the more so an ordinary person in discourse with other common
       folk [must speak with all due deliberation].

We proceed to a quite separate matter, at No. 1, asking about passages that
do not begin with "and he called, and he spoke," of which the writing
before us contains a great many. The fact that there are such is worked out
at No. 1, and these are explained at No. 2. No. 3 then provides a rule
applicable to ordinary folk. Again to revert to our point of interest, we see
that the traits of things viewed on their own, not in the context of
Scripture, prove null. Now we seek rules that emerge from Scripture's
classification.

I.IV

1. A. How on the basis of Scripture do we know that every act of speech
       involved the call to Moses, Moses [two times]?

   B. Scripture says, "God called to him out of the bush, 'Moses, Moses'"
       (Ex. 3:4).

   C. Now when Scripture says, "And he said," it teaches that every act of
       calling involved the call to Moses, Moses [two times].

2. A. And how on the basis of Scripture do we know, furthermore, that at
       each act of calling, he responded, "Here I am"?

   B. Scripture says, "God called to him out of the bush, 'Moses, Moses,' and
       he said, 'Here I am'" (Ex. 3:4).

C.   Now when Scripture says, "And he said," it teaches that in response to each act of calling, he said, "Here I am."

3. A.   "Moses, Moses" ((Ex. 3:4), "Abraham, Abraham" (Gen. 22:11), "Jacob, Jacob" (Gen. 46:2), Samuel, Samuel" (1 Sam. 3:10).

B.   This language expresses affection and also means to move to prompt response.

4. A.   Another interpretation of "Moses, Moses":

B.   This was the very same Moses both before he had been spoken with [by God] and also afterward.

The final unit completes the work of generalization which began with the opening passage. The point throughout is that there are acts of calling and speech, and a general rule pertains to them all. No. 3 and No. 4 conclude with a observations outside of the besought generalization. The first of the two interprets the repetition of a name, the second, a conclusion particular to Moses personally. These seem to me tacked on. The first lesson in the rehabilitation of taxonomic logic is then clear. Let me state the proposition, which is demonstrated over and over gain in rhetoric and logic: *Scripture provides reliable taxa and dictates the indicative characteristics of those taxa.*

The next step in the argument is to maintain that Scripture *alone* can set forth the proper names of things: classifications and their hierarchical order. How do we appeal to Scripture to designate the operative classifications? Here is a simple example of the alternative mode of classification, one that does not appeal to the traits of things but to the utilization of names by Scripture. What we see is how by naming things in one way, rather than in another, Scripture orders all things, classifying and, in the nature of things, also hierarchizing them.

Parashat Vayyiqra Dibura Denedabah Parashah 4

VII:V

1. A.   "...and Aaron's sons the priests shall present the blood and throw the blood [round about against the altar that is at the door of the tent of meeting]":

B.   Why does Scripture make use of the word "blood" twice [instead of using a pronoun]?

C.   [It is for the following purpose:] How on the basis of Scripture do you know that if blood deriving from one burnt-offering was confused with blood deriving from another burnt-offering, blood deriving from one burnt-offering with blood deriving from a beast that has been substituted therefor, blood deriving from a burnt-offering with blood deriving from an unconsecrated beast, the mixture should nonetheless be presented?

D.   It is because Scripture makes use of the word "blood" twice [instead of using a pronoun].

2. A.   Is it possible to suppose that while if blood deriving from beasts in the specified classifications, it is to be presented, for the simple reason

that if the several beasts while alive had been confused with one another, they might be offered up,

B.   but how do we know that even if the blood of a burnt-offering were confused with that of a beast killed as a guilt-offering, [it is to be offered up]

C.   I shall concede the case of the mixture of the blood of a burnt-offering confused with that of a beast killed as a guilt-offering, it is to be presented, for both this one and that one fall into the classification of Most Holy Things.

D.   But how do I know that if the blood of a burnt-offering were confused with the blood of a beast slaughtered in the classification of peace-offerings or of a thanksgiving-offering, [it is to be presented]?

E.   I shall concede the case of the mixture of the blood of a burnt-offering confused with that of a beast slaughtered in the classification of peace-offerings or of a thanksgiving-offering, [it is to be presented], because the beasts in both classifications produce blood that has to be sprinkled four times.

F.   But how do I know that if the blood of a burnt-offering were confused with the blood of a beast slaughtered in the classification of a firstling or a beast that was counted as tenth or of a beast designated as a passover, [it is to be presented]?

G.   I shall concede the case of the mixture of the blood of a burnt-offering confused with that of a beast slaughtered in the classification of firstling or a beast that was counted as tenth or of a beast designated as a passover, [it is to be presented], because Scripture uses the word "blood" two times.

H.   Then while I may make that concession, might I also suppose that if the blood of a burnt-offering was confused with the blood of beasts that had suffered an invalidation, it also may be offered up?

I.   Scripture says, "...its blood," [thus excluding such a case].

J.   Then I shall concede the case of a mixture of the blood of a valid burnt-offering with the blood of beasts that had suffered an invalidation, which blood is not valid to be presented at all.

K.   But how do I know that if such blood were mixed with the blood deriving from beasts set aside as sin-offerings to be offered on the inner altar, [it is not to be offered up]?

L.   I can concede that the blood of a burnt-offering that has been mixed with the blood deriving from beasts set aside as sin-offerings to be offered on the inner altar is not to be offered up, for the one is offered on the inner altar, and the other on the outer altar [the burnt-offering brought as a freewill-offering, under discussion here, is slaughtered at the altar "...that is at the door of the tent of meeting," not at the inner altar].

M.   But how do I know that even if the blood of a burnt-offering was confused with the blood of sin-offerings that are to be slaughtered at the outer altar, it is not to be offered up?

N.   Scripture says, "...its blood," [thus excluding such a case].

In place of the rejecting of arguments resting on classifying species into a common genus, we now demonstrate how classification really is to be carried on. It is through the imposition upon data of the categories dictated by Scripture: Scripture's use of language. That is the force of this powerful exercise. No. 1 sets the stage, simply pointing out that the use of the word "blood" twice encompasses a case in which blood in two distinct classifications is somehow confused in the process of the conduct of the cult. In such a case it is quite proper to pour out the mixture of blood deriving from distinct sources, e.g., beasts that have served different, but comparable purposes. We then systemically work out the limits of that rule, showing how comparability works, then pointing to cases in which comparability is set aside. Throughout the exposition, at the crucial point we invoke the formulation of Scripture, subordinating logic or in our instance the process of classification of like species to the dictation of Scripture. I cannot imagine a more successful demonstration of what the framers wish to say.

From this simple account of the paramount position of Scripture in the labor of classification, let us turn to the specific way in which, because of Scripture's provision of taxa, we are able to undertake the science of *Listenwissenschaft,* including hierarchical classification, in the right way. What can we do because we appeal to Scripture, which we cannot do if we do not rely on Scripture? It is to establish the possibility of polythetic classification. We can appeal to shared traits of otherwise distinct taxa and so transform species into a common genus for a given purpose. Only Scripture makes that initiative feasible, so our authorship maintains. What is at stake? It is the possibility of doing precisely what the framers of the Mishnah wish to do. That is to join together masses of diverse data into a single, encompassing statement, to show the rule that inheres in diverse cases.

In what follows, we shall see an enormous, coherent, and beautifully articulated exercise in the comparison and contrast of many things of a single genus. The whole holds together, because Scripture makes possible the statement of all things within a single rule. That is, as we have noted, precisely what the framers of the Mishnah proposed to accomplish. Our authorship maintains that only by appeal to The Torah is this feat of learning possible. If, then, we wish to understand all things all together and all at once under a single encompassing rule, we had best revert to The Torah, with its account of the rightful names, positions, and order, imputed to all things.

Parashat Vayyiqra Dibura Denedabah Parashah 11

XXII:I

1.   A.   **[With reference to M. Men. 5:5:] There are those [offerings which require bringing near but do not require waving, waving but not bringing near, waving and bringing near, neither waving nor bringing near: These are offerings which require bringing near but do not require waving: the meal-offering of fine flour and**

the meal-offering prepared in the baking pan and the meal-offering prepared in the frying pan, and the meal-offering of cakes and the meal-offering of wafers, and the meal-offering of priests, and the meal-offering of an anointed priest, and the meal-offering of gentiles, and the meal-offering of women, and the meal-offering of a sinner. R. Simeon says, "The meal-offering of priests and of the anointed priest – bringing near does not apply to them, because the taking of a handful does not apply to them. And whatever is not subject to the taking of a handful is not subject to bringing near,"] [Scripture] says, "When you present to the Lord a meal-offering that is made in any of these ways, it shall be brought [to the priest who shall take it up to the altar]":

B. What requires bringing near is only the handful alone. How do I know that I should encompass under the rule of bringing near the meal-offering?

C. Scripture says explicitly, "meal-offering."

D. How do I know that I should encompass all meal-offerings?

E. Scripture says, using the accusative particle, "the meal-offering."

2. A. I might propose that what requires bringing near is solely the meal-offering brought as a freewill-offering.

B. How do I know that the rule encompasses an obligatory meal-offering?

C. It is a matter of logic.

D. Bringing a meal-offering as a freewill-offering and bringing a meal-offering as a matter of obligation form a single classification. Just as a meal-offering presented as a freewill-offering requires bringing near, so the same rule applies to a meal-offering of a sinner [brought as a matter of obligation], which should likewise require bringing near.

E. No, if you have stated that rule governing bringing near in the case of a freewill-offering, on which oil and frankincense have to be added. will you say the same of the meal-offering of a sinner [Lev. 5:11], which does not require oil and frankincense?

F. The meal-offering brought by a wife accused of adultery will prove to the contrary, for it does not require oil and frankincense, but it does require bringing near [as is stated explicitly at Num. 5:15].

G. No, if you have applied the requirement of bringing near to the meal-offering brought by a wife accused of adultery, which also requires waving, will you say the same of the meal-offering of a sinner, which does not have to be waved?

H. Lo, you must therefore reason by appeal to a polythetic analogy [in which not all traits pertain to all components of the category, but some traits apply to them all in common]:

I. the meal-offering brought as a freewill-offering, which requires oil and frankincense, does not in all respects conform to the traits of the meal-offering of a wife accused of adultery, which does not require oil and frankincense, and the meal-offering of the wife accused of adultery, which requires waving, does not in all respects conform to the traits of a meal-offering brought as a freewill-offering, which does not require waving.

J.   But what they have in common is that they are alike in requiring the taking up of a handful and they are also alike in that they require bringing near.

K.   I shall then introduce into the same classification the meal-offering of a sinner, which is equivalent to them as to the matter of the taking up of a handful, and also should be equivalent to them as to the requirement of being drawn near.

L.   But might one not argue that the trait that all have in common is that all of them may be brought equally by a rich and a poor person and require drawing near, which then excludes from the common classification the meal-offering of a sinner, which does not conform to the rule that it may be brought equally by a rich and a poor person, [but may be brought only by a poor person,] and such an offering also should not require being brought near!

M.   [The fact that the polythetic classification yields indeterminate results means failure once more, and, accordingly,] Scripture states, "meal-offering,"

N.   with this meaning: all the same are the meal-offering brought as a freewill-offering and the meal-offering of a sinner, both this and that require being brought near.

The elegant exercise draws together the various types of meal-offerings and shows that they cannot form a classification of either a monothetic or a polythetic character. Consequently, Scripture must be invoked to supply the proof for the classification of the discrete items. The important language is at H-J: *these differ from those, and those from these, but what they have in common is....* Then we demonstrate, with our appeal to Scripture, the sole valid source of polythetic classification, M. And this is constant throughout Sifra.

XXII:II

1. A.   R. Simeon says, "'[When you present to the Lord a meal-offering that is made in any of these ways,] *it shall be brought* [to the priest who shall take it up to the altar]' – that statement serves to encompass under the rule of waving also the sheaf of first grain,

    B.   "for it is said, 'When you come into the land which I give you and reap its harvest, *you shall bring* the sheaf of the first fruits of your harvest to the priest, [and he shall wave the sheaf before the Lord, that you may find acceptance]' (Lev. 23:10).

    C.   "'...who shall take it up to the altar' serves to encompass the meal-offering of the wife accused of adultery, that that too requires being brought near: 'who shall take it up to the altar' [parallel to Num. 5:25].

This discussion continues in the immediately following pericope, continuous with Chapter 22.

23. Parashat Vayyiqra Dibura Denedabah Pereq 13

XXIII:I

1. **A.**   [Continuing the foregoing: R. Simeon says, '"When you present to the Lord a meal-offering that is made in any of these ways, *it shall be brought* [to the priest who shall take it up to the altar' – that statement serves to encompass under the rule of waving also the sheaf of first grain, for it is said, 'When you come into the land which I give you and reap its harvest, *you shall bring* the sheaf of the first fruits of your harvest to the priest, [and he shall wave the sheaf before the Lord, that you may find acceptance]' (Lev. 23:10), '...who shall take it up to the altar' serves to encompass the meal-offering of the wife accused of adultery, that that too requires being brought near: 'who shall take it up to the altar' (parallel to Num. 5:25)]":

B.   is that proposition not a matter of logic?

C.   if the meal-offering brought by a sinner, which does not require waving, does require drawing near, the meal-offering of a wife accused of adultery, which does require waving, surely should require drawing near.

D.   No, if you have invoked that rule in the case of the sinner's meal-offering, which derives from wheat, will you invoke the same rule in the case of the meal-offering of an accused wife, which does not derive from wheat [but from barley, and therefore falls into a different genus]?

E.   The meal-offering of the sheaf of first grain will prove the contrary, for it too does not derive from wheat [but rather from barley] and yet it does require being brought near!

F.   No, if you have invoked that rule in the case of the meal-offering of the sheaf of first grain, which requires also oil and frankincense, will you place into that same category and subject to that same rule the meal-offering of an accused wife, which does not require oil and frankincense?

G.   Lo, you must therefore reason by appeal to a polythetic analogy [in which not all traits pertain to all components of the category, but some traits apply to them all in common]:

H.   The sinner's meal-offering, which derives from wheat, is not in all respects equivalent to the meal-offering of the sheaf of first grain, which after all does not derive from wheat, nor is the meal-offering of the sheaf of first grain, which requires oil and frankincense, equivalent in all respects to the meal-offering of the sinner, which does not require oil and frankincense. But the common trait that pertains to them both is that they both require the taking up of a handful, and, furthermore, they both require being brought near.

I.   So I shall invoke the case of the meal-offering of an accused wife, which is equivalent to them in that the taking up of a handful is required. It should also be equivalent to them in being brought near.

J.   Or perhaps what they have in common is that they are not valid if they derive from coarse meal and they require drawing near. Then that would exclude the meal-offering of the accused wife, which indeed is valid when it derives from coarse meal, and which, therefore, should not require drawing near.

K.   [Accordingly, Scripture is required to settle the matter, which it does when it states,]"..who shall take it up to the altar,"

L.   which then serves to encompass the meal-offering of the wife accused of adultery, and indicates that that too requires being brought near.

Precisely the same mode of argument worked out in **XXII:I** now applies to Simeon's proposition, with the same satisfactory result.

XXIII:II

1.   A.   R. Judah says, "'When you present [to the Lord a meal-offering that is made in any of these ways, it shall be brought to the priest who shall take it up to the altar]:

     B.   'That phrase serves to encompass also the meal-offering of an accused wife, indicating that it too requires being brought near, as it is said, 'And he will present her offering in her behalf' (Num. 5:15)."

2.   A.   But perhaps when Scripture says, "When you present...," the implication is only to mean that an individual is permitted to present as a freewill-offering a variety of meal-offering other than those that are listed in the present context?

     B.   And that is a matter of logic:

     C.   The community at large presents a meal-offering deriving from wheat and brought as a matter of obligation, and the individual may present a meal-offering deriving from wheat and brought as a freewill-offering.

     D.   If the community, which presents a meal-offering deriving from wheat and brought as a matter of obligation, also may present a meal-offering deriving from barley and brought as a matter of obligation, so the individual, who may bring a meal-offering deriving from wheat and brought as a matter of a freewill-offering, also may present as a freewill-offering a meal-offering deriving from barley.

     E.   [That incorrect conclusion is forestalled by Scripture, when it says,] "[When you present to the Lord a meal-offering that is made in any of] these ways, it shall be brought [to the priest who shall take it up to the altar],"

     F.   you have the possibility of bringing only these.

3.   A.   Or perhaps the sense of "these" is only as follows:

     B.   One who says, "Lo, incumbent on me is a meal-offering" must bring all five types?

     C.   Scripture says, "*of* these ways,"

     D.   there is he who brings only one of the types, and there is he who brings all five types. [If someone made explicit which one he has in mind, he brings that one, but if he does not remember what he did specify the type of meal-offering, then he may bring all five types.]

I see no close tie between No. 1, which can stand fully worked out on its own, and No. 2. The issue of No. 2, complemented by No. 3, serves to show that the logic of classification leads to false results.

XXIII:III

1. A. R. Simeon says, "'[When you present to the Lord a meal-offering [that is made in any of these ways,] *it shall be brought* to the priest who shall take it up to the altar' – that statement serves to encompass all meal-offerings under the rule of bringing near."

   B. Might one suppose that that requirement pertains to the two loaves of bread and the show bread?

   C. Scripture says, "[When you present to the Lord a meal-offering that is made] in any of these ways" [which then excludes the specified bread].

2. A. Why then have you encompassed under the rule of being brought near all manner of meal-offerings but then excluded from the rule the two loaves and the show bread?

   B. After Scripture has used inclusionary language, it has further used exclusionary language.

   C. What distinguishes these meal-offerings is that part of any one of them is tossed onto the altar fires, then excluding the two loaves of bread and the show bread, which yield nothing at all to the altar fires [but which the priests consume entirely on their own].

   D. But then the meal-offering that accompanies the drink-offerings [specified at Num. 15:1ff.], which is wholly tossed onto the altar fires, also should require bringing near!

   E. Scripture states, "[And it shall be brought [to the priest] who shall take it up to the altar."

3. A. Why then have you encompassed all varieties of meal-offerings but excluded the meal-offerings that accompany drink-offerings?

   B. After Scripture has used inclusionary language, it has further used exclusionary language.

   C. What distinguishes these meal-offerings is that they come in their own account, which then excludes meal-offerings that accompany drink-offerings, for these do not come in their own account at all.

   D. But is it not the fact that the meal-offering of priests and the meal-offering of a priest that is anointed come on their own account.

   E. Is it possible that they too require being brought near?

   F. Scripture says, "who shall take it up to the altar."

4. A. Why then have you encompassed all meal-offerings and at the same time excluded the meal-offering of priests and the meal-offering of the anointed priest?

   B. After Scripture has used inclusionary language, it has further used exclusionary language.

   C. What distinguishes these meal-offerings is that part of them is tossed on the altar fires, and, further, they come on their own account, and they yield a residue for the priests.

   D. That then excludes the two loaves and the show bread, none of which is put on the fire, and it further excludes the meal-offering that accompanies drink-offerings, which does not come on its own account, and, finally, it excludes the meal-offering of priests and the meal-offering of the high priest, none of which yields a residue for the priests to eat.

The exquisite exercise reaches a conclusion, having encompassed every possible meal-offering and shown the relationships of the one to the next throughout.   I cannot imagine a more comprehensive exercise of classification – all in the service of the proposition that classification by itself does not yield valid results, while classification in accord with Scripture's system makes possible not only taxonomy but a polythetic taxonomy. Most impressive, in my view, is the power of taxonomic logic to draw together all manner of data and to set them into relationship with one another.

And, in that context, the strength of argument of our authorship is manifest: the capacity to demonstrate how diverse things relate through points in common, so long as the commonalities derive from a valid source. And that leads us to the central and fundamental premise of all: Scripture, its picture of the classifications of nature and supernature, its account of the rightful names and order of all things, is the sole source for that encompassing and generalizing principle that permits scientific inquiry into the governing laws to take place. This tripartite subject of [1] the transformation of case to rule in Leviticus through the exercise of exclusion and inclusion; [2] the movement from rule to system and structure, hence the interest in taxonomy based on Scripture's classification-system; and [3] the reunification of the two Torahs into a single statement, effected in part through commentary, in part through extensive citation of passages of the Mishnah and of the Tosefta, – this is what I take to be the topic addressed by Sifra, together with its simple problematic: the relationship of the two Torahs not only in form but at the deepest structures of thought.

VIII. CONTRASTS AND COMPARISONS: ALIKE AND NOT ALIKE

Beyond doubt each document of midrash-compilations follows its distinctive topical and propositional program, as much as a particular rhetorical and logical one. And the correspondence between the topical-propositional program and the rhetorical and logical choices is established, at least, for some of the compilations, clearly including this one. If we now ask ourselves a simple question: is the message of Sifra or Sifré to Numbers the same as that of Leviticus Rabbah or Genesis Rabbah? the answer is obvious. No, these are four different books. The former two make distinct points of their own, respectively. The latter produce a coherent statement, but each with its own emphases. So, in all, the several documents make different points in answering different questions. In plan and in program they yield more contrasts than comparisons. Since these *are* different books, which *do* use different forms to deliver different messages, it must follow that there is nothing routine or given or to be predicted about the point that an authorship wishes to make. Why not? Because it is not a point that is simply "there to be made." It is a striking and original point. How, again, do we know it? The reason is that, when the sages who produced Genesis Rabbah read Genesis, they made a different point from the one that the book of Leviticus precipitated for the authorships of Sifra and, as a matter of fact, also Leviticus Rabbah. So contrasting the one composition with the other shows us that each composition bears its own distinctive traits – traits of mind, traits of plan, traits of program.[8]

The conclusion is a simple one. Sifra and the other documents we have reviewed do not merely assemble this and that, forming a hodgepodge of things people happen to have said: scrapbooks. In the case of each document we can answer the question of topic as much as of rhetoric and logic: Why this, not that? That is to say, why discuss this topic in this pattern of language and resort to this logic of cogent discourse, rather than treating some other topic in a different set of language-patterns and relying on other modes of making connections and drawing conclusions? These are questions that we have now answered for Sifra, and, in the contrasts already drawn, for the other writings as well.

The writings before us, seen individually and also as a group, stand not wholly autonomously but also not everywhere forming a continuity of discourse, whether in rhetoric, or in logic, or in topic and problematic. They are connected. They intersect at a few places but not over the greater part of their territory. For they are not compilations but free-standing compositions. They are not essentially the same, but articulately differentiated. They are not lacking all viewpoint, serving a single undifferentiated task of collecting and arranging whatever was at hand. Quite to the contrary, these documents emerge as sharply differentiated from one another and clearly defined, each through its distinctive viewpoint and particular polemic, on the one side, and formal and aesthetic qualities, on the other. And that raises once more the difficult problem of how these documents relate: not autonomously but also not continuously, rather connectedly. To invoke a theological category, that fact tells me that we deal with a canon, a canon made up of highly individual documents. A canon comprises separate books that all together make a single statement. In terms of the Judaism of the Dual Torah, the canon is what takes scriptures of various kinds and diverse points of origin and turns scriptures into Torah, and commentaries on those scriptures into Torah as well, making them all into the one whole Torah – of Moses, our rabbi. But what are the doctrines of that canon, the

---

[8]My comparison of Genesis Rabbah and Leviticus Rabbah, in *Comparative Midrash: The Plan and Program of Genesis Rabbah and Leviticus Rabbah* [Atlanta: Scholars Press for Brown Judaic Studies, 1986] underscores this result.

traits of intellect and the program, that encompasses these diverse writings and many others? At issue now is not the answer to the question, but at the least, a mode of finding the answer.

Part Three

TOWARD THE COMPARISON OF MIDRASH-
COMPILATIONS

Chapter Five

Sifra in Context

I. IN THE CONTEXT OF SCRIPTURE:
CLASSIFYING MIDRASH-COMPILATIONS THROUGH COMPARISON
OF RELATIONSHIPS TO SCRIPTURE:
A PRELIMINARY EXERCISE

Scripture defines the context of all Judaic systems, hence also of their canonical writings of all kinds and classifications. Sages in the writings of the Judaism of the dual Torah appealed to Scripture not merely for proof-texts as part of an apologia but for a far more original and sustained mode of discourse. In the midrash-compilations, it was in constant interchange with Scripture that sages found ways of delivering their own message, in their own idiom, and in diverse ways. Verses of Scripture therefore served not merely to prove but to instruct. Israelite Scripture constituted not merely a source of validation but a powerful instrument of profound inquiry, whether, as in Leviticus Rabbah, into the rules of society, or, as in Sifra, into the modes of correct logical analysis and argument. And the propositions that could be proposed, the statements that could be made, prove diverse. Scripture served as a kind of syntax, limiting the arrangement of words but making possible an infinity of statements. The upshot is that the received Scriptures formed an instrumentality for the expression of an authorship responsible for a writing bearing its own integrity and cogency, an authorship appealing to its own conventions of intelligibility, and, above all, making its own points. Our authorship did not write *about* Scripture, creating, e.g., a literature of commentary and exegesis essentially within the program of Scripture. Rather, they wrote *with* Scripture.[1] And that they did in many ways.

All authorships worked out for their documents a relationship with Scripture. Each turned to Scripture not for proof-texts, let alone for pretexts, to say whatever they wanted, anyhow, to say. They used Scripture as an artist uses the colors on the palette, expressing ideas through and with Scripture as the artist paints with those colors and no

---

[1]The conception of "writing with Scripture" comes to me from Professor William Scott Green. Our jointly-authored book under that title will appear in due course.

others. Sages appealed to Scripture not merely for proof-texts, as part of an apologia, but for a far more original and sustained mode of discourse. Verses of Scripture served not merely to prove but to instruct. Israelite Scripture constituted not merely a source of validation but a powerful instrument of profound inquiry. The framers of the various midrash-compilations set forth propositions of their own, yet in dialogue with Scripture. Scripture raised questions, set forth premises of discourse and argument, supplied facts, constituted that faithful record of the facts, rules, and meaning of humanity's, and Israel's, history that, for natural philosophy, derived from the facts of physics or astronomy. Whether or not their statement accorded with the position of Scripture on a given point, merely said the simple and obvious sense of Scripture, found ample support in proof-texts – none of these considerations bears material consequence. These authorships made use of Scripture, but they did so by making selections, shaping a distinctive idiom of discourse in so doing. True, verses of Scripture provided facts; they supplied proofs of propositions much as data of natural science proved propositions of natural philosophy. Writing with Scripture meant appealing to the facts that Scripture provided to prove propositions that the authorships at hand wished to prove, forming with Scripture the systems these writers proposed to construct.

As I said, authorships entered into a more complex and profound relationship with Scripture than is suggested by the rubric "proof-texts." To suggest that authorships intended to prove propositions by appealing to Scripture obscures the nuances and depths of the conversation which they undertook with Scripture. What then are the classifications of the relationships between Scripture and the diverse midrash-compilations? With reference to Sifra, a brief survey suffices to show what our document has in common with other midrash-compilations, and how all those documents differ from the Mishnah.

One such taxonomic system visible to the naked eye instructs us to look for evidence that a verse of the Israelite Scriptures illustrates theme, that is to say, provides *information* on a given subject. In the context of the statement of a document, that information is systemically inert. That is characteristic of Sifra. But, then, Scripture occupies an odd position in Sifra, dominant for everything, definitive, as to the message of the document, of nothing. A second will tell us that a verse of the Israelite Scriptures defines a *problem* on its own, in its own determinate limits and terms. In the setting of a document, the problem will be identified and addressed because it is systemically active. Sifra for its part takes a keen interest in verses and their meanings. Yet in doing so, its authorship weaves a filligree of holy words over a polished surface of very hard wood: a wood of its own hewing and shaping and polishing. My sense is that the recurrent allusion to verses of Scripture forms an aesthetic surface rather than a philosophical foundation, for our book. Yet a third points toward *that utilization of Israelite Scriptures in the formation and expression of a proposition independent of the theme or even the facts contained within – proved by – those Scriptures.* That is surely the relationship established between Scripture and the fundamental program of our document, which is not extra-scriptural but meta-scriptural. Scripture in this function is systemically essential yet monumentally irrelevant. Sifra in that way addresses and disposes of Scripture by rewriting it in ways of Sifra's authorship's design. That is the wonder of this marvelous writing: its courage, its brilliance, its originality, above all, its stubbornness.

Let me expand on these possible "relationships" to, or modes of utilization of, Scripture, which, we now know, were not so much relationships as modes of the utilization of Scripture, modes that left in the distant past the conception of scriptural authority, true, a given, but also a useless fact. Where, to take up the first classification, a given theme requires illustration, the ancient Scriptures provide a useful fact. That is assuredly the case not only for Sifra but for all other midrash-compilations. Indeed, those Scriptures may well form the single important treasury of facts. But the amplification of the verses of Scripture will take second place to the display of the facts important to the topic at hand; the purpose of composition is the creation of a scrapbook of materials relevant to a given theme. The verse of received Scripture will serve not to validate a proposition but only to illustrate a theme. In the sense in which Sifra's great theme is the critique of classification without Scripture, Scripture serves forever to validate the proposed mode of taxonomy. Where, second, the sense or meaning or implications of a given verse of Scripture defines the center of discourse, then the verse takes over and dictates the entire character of the resulting composition, and that composition we may call exegetical (substituting "eisegetical" is a mere conceit). That is surely the case in those many passages in which we conduct the inclusionar/exclusionary exercise. And when, finally, an authorship proposes to make a strong case for a given proposition, appealing to a variety of materials, there Israelite Scriptures take a subordinate position within discourse determined by a logic all its own. When we consider the principal points of our compilation, we realize that that relationship to Scripture does characterize the document as a whole. In a word, we have in our compilation each of the three theoretically conceivable relationships – and, I am inclined to think, a variety of others presently beyond our conceptual capacity to discern.

I shall now show, in much more concrete terms, that precisely the same relationships to Scripture characterize Sifré to Deuteronomy. For that purpose we consider three *pisqaot,* or completed statements, as signified by the received textual tradition. One of these shows us Israelite Scripture in its role as illustrative of a theme, in a larger composition to be categorized as an anthology or a scrapbook. The second presents us with an instance in which the exegesis of a given verse defines the center of interest and dictates the principle of cogent discussion. That is to say, if we wish to understand the point of an exegetical composition, what holds that composite together and renders it intelligible, we find ourselves required to focus upon the verse at hand, its meanings, whether actual or merely potential, its context and focus and address. The upshot is to establish for both Sifra and Sifré to Deuteronomy pretty much the same taxonomy: a shared relationship of relationships to Scripture.

The first mode of relationship is to develop an anthology on a theme, an unusual address to Scripture in our document, a common one in Sifré to Deuteronomy. One way of forming a comprehensible statement is to draw together information on a single theme. The theme then imposes cogency on facts, which are deemed to illuminate aspects of that theme. Such a statement constitutes a topical anthology. The materials in the anthology do not, all together, add up to a statement that transcends detail. For example, they do not point toward a conclusion beyond themselves. They rather comprise a series of facts, e.g., fact 1, fact 2, fact 3. But put together, these three facts do not yield yet another one, nor do they point toward a proposition beyond themselves. They generate no generalization, prove no point, propose no proposition. Here is an example of a writing that forms an anthology, the theme being the righteous in the firmament or in the Paradise.

Sifré to Deuteronomy

X:I

1. A.   "...The Lord your God has multiplied you until you are today as numerous as the stars in the sky" (Dt. 1:9-13):

   B.   "Lo, you are established as is the day."

All we have is the amplification of the "today" of the cited verse. Next comes a completely independent statement, joined to the foregoing by meaningless joining-language, 2.A. Then we have a set of facts about classes of the righteous in paradise, each established by a fact constituted by a verse of Scripture. The point for our larger inquiry is that the verse of Scripture constitutes not proof of a proposition but a simple fact.

2. A.   On this basis they have said:

   B.   There are seven classes of righteous in the Garden of Eden, one above the last.

   C.   First: "Surely the righteous shall give thanks to your name, the upright shall dwell in your presence" (Ps. 140:14).

D.   Second: "Happy is the man whom you choose and bring near" (Ps. 65:5).

E.   Third: "Happy are those who dwell in your house" (Ps. 84:5).

F.   Fourth: "Lord, who shall dwell in your tabernacle" (Ps. 15:1).

G.   Fifth: "Who shall dwell upon your holy mountain" (Ps. 15:1).

H.   Sixth: "Who shall ascend the mountain of the Lord" (Ps. 24:3).

I.   Seventh: "And who shall stand in his holy place" (Ps. 24:3).

The seven facts are coextensive with the seven verses of Scripture. Were we to deal with atomic weights or facts of history, such as, on July 4, 1776, the colonies declared their independence, we should have in hand nothing different from the facts before us. The source, Scripture, validates the facts, which are revealed truths to be sure – but which function, as is clear, as nothing more than data. The following component of the larger composition on the righteous in Paradise or heaven or the age to come follows suit. It has no proposition in common with the foregoing; it makes no point beyond itself; it is a simple statement of fact, formed of a set of other facts that are drawn together for the purpose of establishing the generalization given at 1.A following.

X:II

1.   A.   R. Simeon b. Yohai says, "Like seven sources of joy will the faces of the righteous appear in the age to come:

B.   "the sun, moon, firmament, stars, lightning, lilies [*shoshannim*], and candelabrum of the Temple.

C.   "How do we know that that is the case for the sun? 'But they who love him shall be as the sun when it goes forth in its might' (Jud. 5:31);

D.   "the moon: 'Fair as the moon' (Song 6:10);

E.   "the firmament: 'And they who are wise shall shine as the brightness of the firmament' Dan. 12:3);

F.   "the stars: And they who turn the many to righteousness as the stars' (Dan. 12:3);

G.   "the lightning: 'They run to and fro like lightnings (Nah. 2:5);

H.   "the lilies: 'For the leader, upon shoshannim" (Ps. 45:1);

I.   "the candelabrum of the temple: 'And two olive trees by it, one on the right side of the bowl, the other on the left side thereof (Zech. 4:3).

Now to see the exercise as a whole: because of the use of the comparative, "as at this day," No. 1 amplifies the comparison of Israel to the day, then No. 2 picks up on the theme of the stars, hence the firmament, and **X:II** is tacked on for the same thematic connection to form an anthology on a theme. There is no intersection with the verse at hand, and no point of interest in the substance of the passage. This composition was formed with its own principle of topical cogency, not in relationship to the exegetical interests, if any, of the framers of a compilation concerning the book of Deuteronomy.

Another relationship is the focus of interest on the exegesis of Scripture. As we already realize from our analysis of the logics of intelligible discourse, in Sifra and Sifré to Deuteronomy we have composites of materials which find cogency solely in the words of a given verse of Scripture but in no other way. These materials string together, upon the necklace of words or phrases of a verse, diverse comments; the comments do not fit together or point to any broader conclusion; they do not address a single theme or form an anthology. Cogency derives from the (external) verse that is cited; intelligibility begins – and ends –in that verse and is accomplished by the amplification of the verse's contents. Without the verse before us, the words that follow form gibberish. But reading the words as amplifications of a sense contained within the cited verse, we can make good sense of them. That then is an example of explaining ("exegeting") Scripture.

Sifré to Deuteronomy

XXI:I

1. A. "I approved of the plan and so I selected twelve of your men, one from each tribe. They made for the hill country, came to the wadi Eshcol, and spied it out. They took some of the fruit of the land with them and bright it down to us. And they gave us this report, 'It is a good land that the Lord our God is giving to us'" (Dt. 1:22-25):

   B. "I approved of the plan," – but the Omnipresent did not.

2. A. But if he approved the plan, then why was it written along with the words of admonition?

   B. The matter may be compared to the case of someone who said to his fellow, "Sell me your ass."

   C. The other said, "All right."

   D. "Will you let me try it out?"

   E. "All right. Come along, and I'll show you how much it can carry in the hills, how much it can carry in the valley."

   F. When the purchaser saw that there was nothing standing in the way, he said, "Woe is me! It appears that the reason he is so obliging is to take away my money."

   G. That is why it is written, "I approved of the plan."

I see two distinct views of the cited verse. No. 1 finds a "no" in Moses's "yes," and No. 2 shows Moses's true intent. He did not really approve what the people wanted to do, but he went along in order to get what he wanted. We can read no. 1 without no. 2, but not no. 2 without no. 1. The upshot is that no. 1 forms a cogent statement only within the framework of the cited verse, and no. 2 gains intelligibility only as an amplification of what is said in no. 1 – hence a two-stage exegesis, first, of the cited verse, second, of the exegesis itself.

Sifré to Deuteronomy

XXI:II

1. A. "...and so I selected twelve of your men":

   B. ...from the most select among you, from among the most seasoned among you.

2. A. "...one from each tribe":

   B. Why tell me this? Is it not already stated, "...I selected twelve of your men"? [So I know that there was one from each tribe.]

   C. It is to indicate that a representative of the tribe of Levi was not among the spies.

The phrase-by-phrase clarification continues to underline Moses's dubiety about the project. But there is no effort at generalization or a statement, in the form of a proposition, of an idea. Nor can we suppose that the authorship at hand has put these matters together to make a simple point, introduced, e.g., at No. 1, expanded at No. 2, then amplified at No. 3. Since that fact is self-evident – that is, there is no cogency to the whole, beyond the verse upon which all materials comment – it follows that we have not a propositional statement nor even a topical anthology but solely an exegesis, that is, a set of exegeses upon a cited verse. Such compositions do occur in the document at hand, but they are uncommon.

This brief survey shows that pretty much the same relationships to Scripture characterize both Sifra and Sifré to Deuteronomy.[2] That those relationships prove distinctive becomes clear when we turn our attention to the Mishnah's relationships with Scripture. The Mishnah rarely cites a verse of Scripture, refers to Scripture as an entity, links its own ideas to those of Scripture, or lays claim to originate in what Scripture has said, even by indirect or remote allusion to a Scriptural verse of teaching. Formally, therefore, the Mishnah is totally indifferent to Scripture. The very redactional structure of Scripture, found serviceable by the framers of Sifra and Sifé to Deuteronomy is of no interest whatever to the organizers of the Mishnah and its tractates, except in a very few cases (Leviticus 16, Yoma; Exodus 12; Pesahim). It goes without saying, therefore, that all midrash-compilations bear in common a relationship to Scripture that differs from the relationship of the Mishnah to Scripture. And, for the present purpose, it is the simple fact that Sifra is in some ways like Sifré to Deuteronomy (and the other Sifré as well) and different from the Rabbah-compilations. Now to the final phase of our search for an appropriate context for Sifra.

---

[2]The relationships of the Rabbah-compilations to Scripture form a separate set of problems, with which I do not deal in this context. It suffices to say the contrast drawn in this paragraph applies with equal force to those compilations as much as to Sifra and Sifré to Deuteronomy.

II. IN THE CONTEXT OF MIDRASH-COMPILATIONS:
THE SINGULARITY AND PARTICULARITY OF SIFRA.:
A SIMPLE CONCLUSION

We may give short shrift to this question. For each analytical exercise has produced the same result as all others. Sifra is like but also unlike every other writing with which we make comparisons. Sifra is like Sifré to Numbers and Sifré to Deuteronomy in rhetoric and logic, but different from them in its topic. In many important ways, as to rhetoric and logic, moreover, Sifra differs from the other two even in its rhetorical and logical classification. For although the same repertoire of forms occur in the two Sifrés and Sifra, they appear in different proportions, and we are able to explain the formal preferences of Sifra. We furthermore can account for the logics that particularly well serve Sifra's authorship: why this, not that. Sifra's principal messages prove congruent, but not wholly similar, to those of Sifré to Numbers, but still quite distinctive to its authorship. If what seems to me important in Sifré to Numbers stands up under examination when the document is read whole,[3] then the two documents are by no means wholly symmetrical. Its topical program and propositional repertoire is simply out of phase with those of Sifré to Deuteronomy.

As to the Rabbah-compilations Sifra is like Leviticus Rabbah in its topic, the book of Leviticus, but utterly out of phase with Leviticus Rabbah in its treatment of its topic. What concerns our authorship is a range of issues that is utterly outside of the perspective of Leviticus Rabbah. While, one may surmise, our authorship will have concurred in the propositions that are set forth by Leviticus Rabbah, Genesis Rabbah, and Pesiqta deRab Kahana, in point of fact not a single paramount proposition in those documents plays a sustained role in ours. So, seen in context, Sifra is a remarkably singular document, in which rhetoric and logic are so framed as to serve the expression of a statement highly particular to this piece of writing.

Like some compilations in rhetoric, but unlike those same compilations in topic and proposition, congruent with others in logic, but not in rhetoric and certainly unlike in proposition, Sifra presently appears to be singular in its classification, midrash-compilations. Sifra bears some traits in common with a variety of documents, but proves identical to none of them. It seems to me self-evident that the same judgment pertains to all midrash-compilations. We appear to stand at an impasse in the effort to define a genus into which all of the species may be

---

[3]This rereading will take place after William Scott Green completes the translation of the final third of Sifré to Numbers. At that point a topical and programmatic restudy of the document will be required.

classified. To use theological language, we have holy books but cannot define the way in which they all together form components of a canon in common.

III. WHY, WHILE SINGULAR, SIFRA IS NOT "UNIQUE":
A STEP TOWARD SOLVING THE PROBLEM OF
"THE JUDAISM BEYOND THE TEXTS"

The solution to the problem of classifying the diverse midrash-compilations in such wise as to form of the species a common genus, and to define that genus, derives from the authorship of Sifra itself. The solution self-evidently will derive from the approach of polythetic classification, to which reference has already been made. We recall that mode of classification that came to expression as follows:

G.   Lo, you must therefore reason by appeal to a polythetic analogy [in which not all traits pertain to all components of the category, but some traits apply to them all in common]:

H.   The sinner's meal-offering, which derives from wheat, is not in all respects equivalent to the meal-offering of the sheaf of first grain, which after all does not derive from wheat, nor is the meal-offering of the sheaf of first grain, which requires oil and frankincense, equivalent in all respects to the meal-offering of the sinner, which does not require oil and frankincense. But the common trait that pertains to them both is that they both require the taking up of a handful, and, furthermore, they both require being brought near.

I.   So I shall invoke the case of the meal-offering of an accused wife, which is equivalent to them in that the taking up of a handful is required. It should also be equivalent to them in being brought near.

J.   Or perhaps what they have in common is that they are not valid if they derive from coarse meal and they require drawing near. Then that would exclude the meal-offering of the accused wife, which indeed is valid when it derives from coarse meal, and which, therefore, should not require drawing near.

K.   [Accordingly, Scripture is required to settle the matter, which it does when it states,]"..who shall take it up to the altar,"

L.   which then serves to encompass the meal-offering of the wife accused of adultery, and indicates that that too requires being brought near.

Polythetic classification accomplishes its goal of discovering the genus common to several disparate species, so Sifra's authorship claims, when Scripture defines the indicative traits that, held in common, define the genus and distinguish that genus from others.

But what foundation can we locate for polythetic classification of documents? and how shall we know when we have found those shared traits that form a genus out of species that differ in many ways but cohere in some? We therefore ask ourselves where shall we look for a paradigm that will serve in our context, like Scripture in its context, to clarify for us what holds together these diverse writings and makes of them what, in theological language, we call a canon, or, in more secular terms, we call a single genus of writing. Scripture solves the problem of polythetic classification because it establishes controls, a fixed and factual court of final appeal. To what category or trait of documents can we look for decisions of polythetic classification that will allow us on the basis of solid literary evidence to define that "Judaism," that set of shared traits? We seek to define what draws together all writings within the canon of the Judaism of the dual Torah – and also distinguishes all writings within that canon from all writings of other Judaisms of the same time and place.[4] Let us review the four categories – rhetoric, logic, topic (inclusive of proposition), and relationship to Scripture, that I have now fully demonstrated (for the first three) or set forth in a preliminary way (for the fourth). These four classifications of indicative traits of a document impart particular and distinctive, definitive traits to writings: rhetoric, logic, topic inclusive of proposition, relationship to Scripture.

As I see it, for reasons particular to each classification, rhetoric, topic inclusive of proposition, and relationship to Scripture will not serve in our quest for that polythetic taxonomy that will include all canonical writings and exclude all other Judaism's writings: the Judaism presupposed by these texts and not by any other texts.

1. *Rhetoric:* In my judgment we cannot find much use for shared formal traits, sufficiently similar so that, despite differences, we may impute to all canonical writings certain indicative qualities in common. The reason is that some canonical writings appeal for structure to Scripture, others to the Mishnah. That consideration all by itself suffices to dismiss the possibility that common rhetorical preferences form out of diverse species a genus based on polythetic classification.

2. *Topic inclusive of proposition:* As to shared doctrinal conceptions, e.g., topics and propositions, such as many have claimed to discern, if the documents we have reviewed are indicative, then what is in common also is trivial, on the one side, or systemically inert, on the other. A simple example makes the point. Trivial is the fact that all documents appeal to Scripture, that is, to Sinai; or all participants to the canon believe in one God; and similar genuinely uninteresting matters. Systemically inert are important shared convictions, e.g., concerning covenant, history and salvation, law and sanctification, that surely animate all authorships but play an active role in the systems put forth by

---

[4]In the appendix I shall spell out the urgency of this problem.

no authorship. Relationships to Scripture seem to me a hopelessly general indicator.[5]

Then what? I should anticipate that it is in the deep structure of logic, which is to say, in the processes of thought, that we may constructively search out traits of mind, modes of thought, both common to all our documents and also uncommon to all non-canonical writings in the Judaic framework.

3. *Logic, broadly construed:* I do conceive the modes of intelligible thought and cogent discourse characteristic of these writings and, in the Judaic context, of no others, to form and define the "Judaism out there" that holds the whole together and makes of diverse writings a canon – and that distinguishes all these writings, as a group, from the writings identified as canonical by any other Judaism. Why do I think that it is in the shared modes of thought – logics, in the terminology of this book or modes of cogent and intelligible discourse – that we shall find what holds together all writings of this classification and also distinguishes them from all writings of other Judaisms?

To account for the shared and public, common character of the logic of intelligible discourse as the basis for polythetic classification of documents, I appeal to the very basic trait of religion: its public and shared character. Religion begins with the possibility of intelligible discourse and cogent, comprehensible thought. That accounts for its capacity to hold together and to express the world view, the way of life, the social entity, that all together constitute the definition of the social group. Where cogent discourse (in context) takes place, there we find the social entity of which a religion speaks, the way of life and world view of which a religion sets forth and explains. Where cogent discourse ceases, there we find some other world, heretical or simply different. The modes of cogent and intelligible discourse then form the intellectual statement of the social reality that the religious group, the social entity, constitutes – and that by definition. The reason is that, as people generally recognize, an on going social entity inculcates in age succeeding age modes of thought that, shared by all, impart self-evidence and enduring sense to transient propositions. Minds may change on this and that. But *mind* does not, mind meaning modes of patterned thought on ephemera.

Accordingly, while the social entity undergoes change, rules of deliberation dictate the range of permissible deed, and the realm of choice honors limits set by sense deemed common. *How* people think dictates the frontiers of possibility. The mind of Judaism, in the medium

---

[5]But that is because no one has systematically classified relationships to Scripture exhibited by a range of documents. The very taxonomy has yet to be defined, and my preliminary effort in section I of this chapter only means to raise the question.

of writing, specifically, the logics of cogent and intelligible discourse, that is to say, *the process*, is what will define the Judaism that is presupposed or taken for granted in all the writings of a given Judaism. That is where we may locate, for a given system, the Judaism in age succeeding age, so long as that Judaic system endures. And that is as long as the social entity coheres; and the holding together is in speech and thought that these people understand, and share uniquely, by contrast to everybody else. That principal part of the religious, the Judaic, system is therefore that locus for the shared traits that constitute the (necessary) monothetic denominator of the polythetic comparison. When we know the logics and how they work, we know what all writings take for granted and hold in common: the Judaism beyond the texts, the Judaism out there, the Judaism presupposed and everywhere acknowledged within the systemic details of an encompassing system.[6]

Why neglect doctrines or propositions? The reason is simple. *What people think* – exegesis in accord with a fixed hermeneutic of the intellect – knows no limit. *How they think* makes all the difference. When we can describe the mind of a social entity through sorting out the rules governing the reaching of discrete and disparate conclusions, then we can claim to understand how the mind of a society of like-minded people is formed, those generative rules of culture and regulations of intellect that succeeding generations receive from infancy and transmit to an unknowable future. Attitudes shift. Values and beliefs change. One generation's immutable truths come to the coming age as banalities or nonsense. But processes of reflection about the sense of things, modes of thought concerning how we identify and solve problems, above all, the making of connections between this and that – these endure like oceans and mountains. Shifting only in tides and currents so vast as to defy the grasp of time, so that, when they do quake, the whole earth moves, these processes and modes of mind in the end dictate structure and establish order, the foundations of all social life, the framework of all culture.

---

[6]I claim to describe that mode of thought without alleging no other group of writers thought that way, let alone that all writers within Judaism from then to now thought that way and no other way. Describing traits characteristic of one set of writings requires showing that people made choices, not that their choices were unique to them. Still, as a matter of fact, I tend to think that the Bavli forms an instrument of cultural expression and continuity without significant parallel in the history of the literate cultures of humanity – though each, self-evidently, has had its equivalent to the Bavli, that is, something unique to itself. But comparisons of a global nature lie far beyond the distant horizons of this proposed protracted exercise, even though, I do believe, the time will come, also, for comparison, even of considerable dimensions indeed. That is the comparison of rationalities.

The fundamental premise of this prescription for the search for the commonalities of disparate writings, on which all else rests, is simple. It is that intellect endures in language, modes of thought in syntax and sentence structure, which realize in concrete ways abstract processes of reasoning. The enduring and public, shared and ubiquitous mind of a given Judaism reaches us only in its results, and the results lie in the always discrete exegeses of thought: the sentences formed into paragraphs, the paragraphs into chapters, the chapters into books: the truths deemed self-evidently valid, the propositions held beyond all debate, yielding the intense disagreement on this and that that serves as the wherewithal of everyday thought. If therefore we wish to understand what people think and how they bring their ideas to expression in discrete documents that share a common fundament of intellect, we had best first ask how they think, and to know how people think, we analyze their writing.

What then requires description, then analysis and even interpretation? It is the modes of making up sentences and joining them together into paragraphs, manner of composing paragraphs into chapters, chapters into books – all translated into the abstractions of knowledge, from fact to proposition, from proposition to encompassing theory. That means explaining the ways in which they choose the problems they find urgent, know that one set of data pertains and another does not. So we have to account for how the writers of authoritative documents make connections between this and that. All of these abstracts come to immediate and concrete expression not in sentences but in paragraphs, that is to say, in the composition of two or more sentences. These points of union, the joining of two facts into a proposition that transcends them both, the making of a whole that exceeds the sum of the parts – these acts of intellectual enchantment wonderfully form the smallest whole units of propositional thought. When, therefore, we know why this, not that, why a paragraph looks one way, rather than some other, we find ourselves at the very center of the working of a mind: its making of sense out of the nonsense presented by the detritus of mere information.

I know no studies that demonstrate for us the claim that there is a distinctively "Jewish-ethnic" way of thought, characteristic of all Jews and no gentiles. But there was, and is, a religious system, a Judaism, with its own rules of intellect and conduct, its integrity, its definitive (and therefore, to itself) unique traits. That religious system did find coherence in modes of thought found distinctive to those who thought in one way and not in some other and deemed to form the premise of all thought and discourse in which, in detail, various writings found their locus. And in the canonical writings of that Judaism coming work must aim to show that there was, and is, a distinctively (but none can claim, uniquely) Judaic mode of thought.[7] For as a matter of description of the logic of connection, the canonical writings of Judaism do reach and express conclusions in one way and not in some other, and I therefore can provide an account of the making of the mind of not the Jews but Judaism: the canonical writings, seen whole and complete, that constitute the statement of Judaism, its world-view, way of life, and address to the social entity, "Israel," of its invention.

People who form the authorships of canonical writings – textual communities, in the matrix of social worlds – did make choices and did determine in one way and not in some other to form their cogent statements of connection, to draw conclusion from discerned connection. What is characteristic of a group of writings tells us how those writers thought.[8] And – as a matter of hypothesis – how writers thought tells us how they assumed their readers would think too: an unbroken circle of shared intelligence, a society formed of cogent discourse, a word understood, in its season, by those to whom it was entrusted for all eternity. God (in context: a Judaism) lives in the deep structures of the social processes of thought.

---

[7]To begin with, of course, *The Making of the Mind of Judaism* (Atlanta, 1987: Scholars Press for Brown Judaic Studies) and *The Formation of the Jewish Intellect* (in press) provide some elementary stages of work. But I have a separate program which I hope will secure entry into this set of problems on a much broader front. The first (in my mind) break-through is in my *Economics of Judaism. The Initial Statement* (Chicago, 1989: The University of Chicago Press). This will be followed by *The Politics of Judaism. The Initial Statement* and *The Philosophy of Judaism. The Initial Statement*. I presently attempt to think through *The Law of Judaism. The Initial Statement*. In these several studies I mean to place into the context of the thought-world beyond the Judaic framework principal components of the contents of the thought-world of the Judaism of the dual Torah in its initial statement. For the systematic exercise of comparison and contrast seems to me to begin at the outer limits of the system. True, I have already begun the work at the deepest structure of that same system. But I stumbled into the problem before I realized its full logical requirements.

[8]I stress that I of course do not allege that the principal repertoire of logics characteristic of the canonical authorships is distinctive to that canon, for that is something I cannot show and therefore do not know. I suspect that we may point to other religious systems that appeal for cogency and order to those same principles that operate in Judaism. I have the impression that the peculiar mode of dialectical argument to which I appeal in the end is uncommon in modes of thought overall.

APPENDICES

Appendix One

Explaining the Problem of
"the Judaism Beyond the Texts"

The problem of identifying and defining what I have called "the Judaism beyond the texts" proves urgent in contemporary scholarly debate. That is why it seems to me worth some effort to spell out what makes the problem important just now. We consider first of all the positions of critics of an earlier work of mine, *Judaism: The Evidence of the Mishnah*, as they advance the claim of a Judaism presupposed or affective in the Mishnah, of which we have knowledge other than through and in the pages of the Mishnah. Then we turn to the interesting critique of my claim that each document is to be read not only in the context of other documents but also, and to begin with, on its own. Both of these chapters of the ongoing debate contain important implications for the consideration of Sifra in context.

Building their proposition on sound theological foundations, some scholars claim that there is a "Judaism out there," a "Judaism beyond the texts," that is to say, a set of doctrines and beliefs, a world-view, a way of life fully spelled out, a definition of the social entity, "Israel," that exist beyond any one document. To that "Judaism beyond the texts" or "Judaism out there," in some way or other all documents in various ways and proportions are supposed to refer and, of course, it is that Judaism, and not the sherd or component of that Judaism in a given finite statement comprising a document, that every document is meant to attest. That position, as I said, is entirely valid, indeed, it is required as a theological premise, since, as in any religious system, so the Judaism of the Dual Torah treats all canonical writings as authoritative and makes no material distinctions among them. Hence all canonical writings contribute to the picture of a single Judaism.

Not only so, but that "Judaism" is held to be present prior to, and to serve as premise of, all canonical writings. Accordingly, that Judaism "out there," prior to, encompassing, assumed by, all documents, each with its "Judaism in here" imposes its judgment upon our reading of every sentence, every paragraph, every book "in here," as a hermeneutical

judgment. A reading of a single document therefore is improper. If the
Bavli (for instance) not only may be, but must be, read in its own terms so
as to present its distinct and distinctive statement, then that hermeneutic
that appeals to an ever-present and prevailing "Judaism out there" must be
set aside, except, once more, for what I regard as fully legitimate
theological purposes. But then it is a theological, *not a hermeneutical*
judgment, and certainly not a judgment of how things ever actually were.
That theological judgment then is to be set forth and defended in its own
terms and context. To that theological position the question that so
troubles me, how to find points of commonality among diverse midrash-
compilations, is immaterial, indeed, absurd. Let me explain.

A considerable debate concerning the Judaism supposedly implicit
in, and beyond, any given document of that Judaism, presently enlivens
all scholarship on the literature of formative Judaism. Specifically,
people wonder whether and how we may describe, beyond the evidence
of what an authorship has given us in its particular piece of writing, what
that authorship knew, had in mind, took for granted, and otherwise
affirmed as its larger "Judaism." I precipitated matters in my *Judaism:
The Evidence of the Mishnah*. Specifically, I proposed to describe the
system and structure of a given document and ask what "Judaism" – way of
life, world view, address to a defined "Israel" – emerged from that
document. The notion that documents are to be read one by one and not
as part of a larger canonical statement – the one whole Torah of Moses,
our rabbi, for example – troubled colleagues, and not without reason. For
reading the literature, one book at a time, and describing, analyzing, and
interpreting the system presented by a document that to begin with invited
systemic analysis set aside received notions in three ways.

First, as is clear, the conception of the document as part of a prior
and encompassing tradition now met competition.

Second, I dismissed the prevailing notion that we may describe on the
basis of whatever we find in any given document a composite, "Judaism"
(or some qualification thereof, e.g., classical, rabbinic, Talmudic,
normative, what-have-you-Judaism).

Third, I treated as merely interesting the received and hitherto
commanding tradition of exegesis, imputing to the ancient texts
meanings not to be tampered with.

For example, I translated fully half a dozen tractates of the Bavli
without referring in any systematic way (or at all) to Rashi's interpretation
of a single passage, let alone accepting at face value his reading and sense
of the whole. I dismissed as pertinent only to their own times the
contributions of later authorships to the description of the Judaism
attested by earlier documents. These things I did for good and substantial
reason, which Western academic learning has recognized since the

Renaissance: the obvious fallacy of anachronism being the compelling and first one, utter gullibility as to assertions of received writings, an obvious second. But, further, I maintain, along with nearly the whole of academic secular learning, that each document derives from a context, and to begin with is to be read in that context and interpreted, at the outset, as a statement of and to a particular setting. Constructs such as -*isms* and -*ities* come afterward (if they are admitted into discourse at all). Not only so, but in the case of ancient Judaism, a mass of confused and contradictory evidence, deriving from Jews of a broad variety of opinion, requires not harmonization but sorting out. The solution to the disharmonies – a process of theological selection, e.g., of what is normative, classical, Talmudic, rabbinic, or, perhaps, Jewish-Christian, Hellenistic-Jewish, and the like – no longer solved many problems.

From this quest for "the Judaism beyond" the documents, so familiar and so much cherished by the received scholarly and theological tradition, with no regret I took my leave. My absence was soon noticed – and vigorously protested, as is only right and proper in academic discourse. One statement of the matter[1] derives from the British medievalist, Hyam Maccoby:

> Neusner argues that since the Mishnah has its own style and program, nothing outside it is relevant to explaining it. This is an obvious fallacy. The Mishnah, as a digest, in the main, of the legal...aspect of rabbinic Judaism, necessarily has its own style and program. But to treat it as something intended to be a comprehensive compendium of the Oral Torah is simply to beg the question. Neusner does not answer the point, put to him by E. P. Sanders and myself, that the liturgy being presupposed by the Mishnah, is surely relevant to the Mishnah's exegesis. Nor does he answer the charge that he ignores the aggadic material within the Mishnah itself, e.g., Avot; or explain why the copious aggadic material found in roughly contemporaneous works should be regarded as irrelevant.

Nearly all scholarship recognizes that tractate Avot, while printed with the Mishnah, in no way forms part of the Mishnah, having reached redaction a generation or so after the (rest of the) Mishnah. The "roughly contemporaneous works" to which Maccoby alludes are surely the so-called halalkhic Midrashim, such as Sifra and the two Sifrés. It is perfectly clear that Sifra is not "roughly contemporaneous," but a work produced in the aftermath of, and in response to, the Mishnah. Let us now return to Maccoby's conclusion:

---

[1]The debate with Eliezer Schweid, presented in Appendix Two, is another, and I think, more productive statement of the same matter.

> Instead he insists that he is right to carry out the highly artificial project of
> deliberately closing his eyes to all aggadic material, and trying to explain
> the Mishnah without it.[2]

Maccoby exhibits a somewhat infirm grasp upon the nature of the inquiry
before us. If one starts with the question, "What does the authorship of
this book mean to say, when read by itself and not in light of other, *later*
writings?" then it would be improper to import into the description of the
system of the Mishnah in particular (its "Judaism" – hence "Judaism: The
evidence of the Mishnah") conceptions not contained within its pages.[3]
Tractate Abot, for one instance, cites a range of authorities who lived a
generation beyond the closure of the (rest of the) Mishnah and so is
ordinarily dated[4] to about 250, with the Mishnah dated to about 200. On
that basis how one can impute to the Mishnah's system conceptions first
attaining closure half a century later I do not know. To describe the
Mishnah, for example, as a part of "rabbinic Judaism" is to invoke the
premise that we know, more or less on its own, just what this "rabbinic
Judaism" is and says.

But what we cannot show we do not know. And, as a matter of
established fact, many conceptions dominant in the final statements of
Rabbinic Judaism to emerge from late antiquity play no material role
whatsoever in the system of the Mishnah, or, for that matter, of Tosefta
and Abot. No one who has looked for the conception of "the Oral Torah"
in the Mishnah or in the documents that succeeded it, for the next two
hundred years, will understand why Maccoby is so certain that the
category of Oral Torah, or the myth of the Dual Torah, applies at all. For

---

[2]Writing in the symposium, "The Mishnah: Methods of Interpretation," *Midstream*,
October, 1986, p. 41. Maccoby's deplorable personal animadversions may be
ignored.

[3]I stated explicitly at no fewer than six points in the book my recognition that
diverse ideas floated about, and insisted that the authorship of the Mishnah can
have entertained such ideas. But the statement that they made in the Mishnah did
not contain them, and therefore was to be read without them. Alas, the few
reviews that the book did receive contained no evidence that the reviewers
understood that simple, and repeated cavest. Jakob J. Petuchowski in *Religious
Studies Review* for July, 1983, subjected the book to a savage attack of trivializing
and with vast condescension imputed to the book precisely the opposite of its
message, as, we see, does Maccoby.

[4]I take responsibility for not a single date in any writing of mine, culling them all
from available encyclopaedia articles, in the notion that those articles, e.g., the
splendid one by M. D. Heer in *Encyclopaedia Judaica* s.v. *Midrash*, represent the
consensus of learning at this time. I do not know why Maccoby and Sanders
reject the consensus on Avot, since, to my knowledge, neither of them has
published a scholarly article on the dating of the document. But I believe my
position accords from what is presently "common knowledge." If it does not, I
should rapidly correct it.

the mythic category of "Oral Torah" makes its appearance, so far as I can discern, only with the Yerushalmi and not in any document closed prior to that time, although a notion of a revelation over and above Scripture – not called "Oral Torah" to be sure – comes to expression in Avot. Implicitly, moreover, certain sayings of the Mishnah itself, e.g., concerning rulings of the Torah and rulings of sages, may contain the notion of a secondary tradition, beyond revelation.

But that tradition is not called "the Oral Torah," and I was disappointed to find that even in the Yerushalmi the mythic statement of the matter, so far as I can see, is lacking. It is only in the Bavli, e.g., in the famous story of Hillel and Shammai and the convert at b. Shab. 30b-31a, that the matter is fully explicit. Now, if Maccoby maintains that the conception circulated in the form in which we know it, e.g., in the Yerushalmi in truncated form or in the Bavli in complete form, he should supply us with the evidence for his position.[5] As I said, what we cannot show we do not know. And most secular and academic scholarship concurs that we have no historical knowledge *a priori*, though in writing Maccoby has indeed in so may words maintained that we do. In fact the documents of formative Judaism do yield histories of ideas, and not every idea can be shown to have taken part in the statement of each, let alone all, of the documents. But those who appeal to a Judaism out there, before and beyond all of the documents, ignore that fact.

Sanders and Maccoby seem more certain of the content of the liturgy than the rest of scholarship, which tends to a certain reserve on the matter of the wording and language of prayer. Maccoby's roughly contemporaneous aggadic works cite the Mishnah as a completed document, e.g., Sifra and the two Sifrés, and so therefore are to be dated in the period beyond the closure of the Mishnah.[6] Unless we accept at face value the attribution of a saying to the person to whom a document's editorship assigns it, we know only that date of closure for the contents of a document. True, we may attempt to show that a saying derives from a period prior to the closure of a document; but we cannot take for granted that sayings belong to the age and the person in whose name they are given. These are simple truisms of all critical learning, and, once we understand and take them to heart, we find it necessary to do precisely

---

[5]Maccoby may not have read my *Torah: From Scroll to Symbol in Formative Judaism* (Philadelphia, 1985: Fortress Press). There I survey the materials that stand behind the statements made here.

[6]My next work will address Mekhilta deR. Ishmael. I have neglected that work because of the important article by Ben Zion Wacholder on the date of the document, published in 1969 in *Hebrew Union College Annual.* But with the replies to Wacholder now in print, particularly that of Günter Stemberger in *Kairos,* 1981, it is time to return to that document.

what I have done, which is to read each document first of all on its own and in its framework and terms.[7]

At stake are not merely literary, but also cultural and religious-historical *(religionsgeschichtlich)* conceptions. So let us return to this matter of "the Judaism beyond the texts" or "the Judaism out there" to explain the connection between a narrowly hermeneutical debate and the much broader issue of culture and the nature of religion. When I speak of "the Judaism beyond," I mean a conception of a very concrete character. To define by example, I invoke the definition of this "Judaism out there" operative in the mind of E. P. Sanders when Sanders describes rabbinic writings. In my debates with Sanders[8] I have complained that his categories seem to me improperly formed, since the rabbinic texts do not conform to the taxonomy Sanders utilizes. They in other words are not talking about the things Sanders wants them to discuss. That complaint is turned against me, as we see, in Maccoby's critique of my picture of how we may describe (not "explain," as Maccoby would have it) the system of the Mishnah in particular.

Commenting on this debate with Sanders, William Scott Green says, Sanders "reads rabbinic texts by peering through them for the ideas

---

[7]Maccoby further seems not to have read a variety of scholarship. He says that it is aburd to say that "the Mishnah is not much concerned with justice, or with repentance, or with the Messiah." He does not seem to realize the way in which the Messiah-theme is used in the Mishnah, by contrast to its use in other documents, as demonstrated in my *Messiah in Context. Israel's History and Destiny in Formative Judaism* (Philadelphia, 1983: Fortress Press). I am genuinely puzzled at who has said that the Mishnah is not much concerned with justice or with repentance. I look in vain for such statements on the part of any scholar, myself included. Mishnah-tractate Yoma on repentance and Mishnah-tractate Sanhedrin on the institutions of justice have not, to my knowledge, been ignored in my account of the Mishnah and its literature and system. It would appear that Maccoby reads somewhat selectively.

[8]These begin in my review of his *Paul and Palestinian Judaism,* in *History of Religion* 1978, 18:177-191. I reprinted the review in my *Ancient Judaism: Debates and Disputes* (Chico, 1984: Scholars Press for Brown Judaic Studies), where I review more than a score of modern and contemporary books in the field in which I work and also present several bibliographic essays and state of the question studies. I also reworked parts of my Sanders' review in essays on other problems. To my knowledge he has not reviewed my *Judaism: The Evidence of the Mishnah,* and if he has in print responded to my questions of method addressed to his *Paul and Palestinian Judaism,* I cannot say where he has done so. Quite to the contrary, in his *Paul, The Law, and the Jewish People* (Philadelphia, 1985: Fortress), which I review also in my *Ancient Judaism,* where he claims to reply to critics of the original book, he not only ignores my review, and also that of Anthony J. Saldarini in *Journal of Biblical Literature,* cited in my review of *Paul, The Law, and the Jewish People,* which makes the same point, but he even omits from his list of reviews of the original work Saldarini's review as well as mine. This seems to me to impede scholarly debate.

(presumably ones Jews or rabbis believed) that lie beneath them." This runs parallel to Maccoby's criticism of my "ignoring" a variety of conceptions I do not find in the Mishnah. Both Maccoby and Sanders, in my view, wish to discuss what *they* think important – that is, presentable in terms of contemporary religious disputation[9] – and therefore to ignore what the texts themselves actually talk about, as Green says, "the materials that attracted the attention and interest of the writers."[10] In my original review I pointed out that Sanders' categories ignore what the texts actually say and impose categories the Judaic-rabbinic texts do not know. Sanders, in Green's judgment, introduces a distinct premise:

> For Sanders, the religion of Mishnah lies unspoken beneath its surface; for Neusner it is manifest in Mishnah's own language and preoccupations.[11]

Generalizing on this case, Green further comments in those more general terms that bring us into a debate on the nature of religion and culture, and that larger discourse lends importance to what, in other circumstances, looks to be a mere academic argument. Green writes as follows:

> The basic attitude of mind characteristic of the study of religion holds that religion is certainly in your soul, likely in your heart, perhaps in your mind, but never in your body. That attitude encourages us to construe

---

[9]Maccoby makes this explicit in his contribution to the symposium cited above, "The Mishnah: Methods of Interpretation," *Midstream,* October, 1986, p. 41, "It leads to Neusner's endorsement of 19th-century German anti-Jewish scholarship...[Neusner] admires the Mishnah for the very things that the New Testament alleges against the Pharisees: for formalism, attention to petty legalistic detail, and for a structuralist patterning of reality in terms of 'holiness' rather than of morality, justice, and love of neighbor." Here Maccoby introduces the bias of Reform Judaism, with its indifference to "petty legalistic detail." But I (among millions of Jews) find intensely meaningful the holy way of life embodied, for one example, in concern for what I eat for breakfast, along with love of neighbor, and the conception that the Judaic way of life leads to a realm of holiness is hardly my invention. It is contained in the formula of the blessing, ...*who has sanctified us by the commandments and commanded us to....* I can treat with respect Maccoby's wish to describe as his Judaism some other system than the received one, but the "very things" that the New Testament alleges against the Pharisees are recapitulated by the Reform critique of the way of life of the Judaism of the dual Torah, today embodied in Orthodoxy and Conservative Judaism, to which I adhere. It follows that not all of the "other side" are Orthodox, although, as to intertextuality, that seems to be the sector from which the principal advocates derive. Maccoby is unable to criticize a book without descending to personal animadversions, but that does not mean he does not have interesting criticisms to set forth.

[10]Personal letter, January 17, 1985.

[11]William Scott Green in his Introduction, *Approaches to Ancient Judaism* (Chicago, 1980: Scholars Press for Brown Judaic Studies) II, p. xxi.

religion cerebrally and individually, to think in terms of beliefs and the believer, rather than in terms of behavior and community. The lens provided by this prejudice draws our attention to the intense and obsessive belief called "faith," so religion is understood as a state of mind, the object of intellectual or emotional commitment, the result of decisions to believe or to have faith. According to this model, people have religion but they do not do their religion. Thus we tend to devalue behavior and performance, to make it epiphenomenal, and of course to emphasize thinking and reflecting, the practice of theology, as a primary activity of religious people....The famous slogan that "ritual recapitulates myth" follows this model by assigning priority to the story and to peoples' believing the story, and makes behavior simply an imitation, an aping, a mere acting out.[12]

Now as we reflect on Green's observations, we of course recognize what is at stake. It is the definition of religion, or, rather, what matters in or about religion, emerging from one reading of Protestant theology and Protestant religious experience.

For when we lay heavy emphasis on faith to the exclusion of works, on the individual rather than on society, on conscience instead of culture, and when, as in the language of Maccoby, we treat behavior and performance by groups as less important, and present as more important the matters of thinking, reflecting, theology and belief – not to mention the abstractions of "love of neighbor" and "morality," to which Reform theologians in the pattern of Maccoby adhere, we simply adopt as normative for academic scholarship convictions critical to the Lutheran wing of the Protestant Reformation. And that accounts for the absolutely accurate instinct of Maccoby in introducing into the debate the positions of the Lutheran New Testament scholars who have dominated New Testament scholarship in Germany and the USA (but not Britain or France).

This brings us back to the discussion with which I conclude the treatment of Sifra in context: the social foundations of religious systems, and the intellectual principles that preserve, and are preserved by, the social entity that realizes a religious system. Judaism and the historical, classical forms of historical Christianity, Roman Catholic and Orthodox, as well as important elements of the Protestant Reformation, however, place emphasis on religion as a matter of works and not faith alone, behavior and community as well as belief and conscience. Religion is something that people do, and they do it together. Religion is not something people merely have, as individuals. Since the entire civilization of the West, from the fourth century onward, has carried forward the convictions of Christianity, not about the individual alone but about politics and culture, we may hardly find surprising the Roman

---

[12]Personal letter, January 17, 1985.

Catholic conviction that religion flourishes not alone in heart and mind, but in eternal social forms: the Church, in former times, the state as well.

At stake in the present debate therefore is the fundamental issue of hermeneutics and history of religion, rightly carried out. For claims as to the character of the literature of Judaism entail judgments on the correct hermeneutics, down to the interpretation of words and phrases. We can read everything only in light of everything else, fore and aft. That is how today nearly everyone interested in these writings claims to read them – citing the Bavli as proof for that hermeneutics. Or we can read each item first of all on its own, a document as an autonomous and cogent and utterly rational, syllogistic statement, a unit of discourse as a complete and whole composition, entire unto itself, taking account, to be sure, of how, in the larger context imposed from without, meanings change(d). That is how – and not solely on the basis of the sample we have surveyed – I maintain any writing must be read: in its own context, entirely on its own, not only in the one imposed by the audience and community that preserved it.

For whatever happens to thought, in the mind of the thinker ideas come to birth cogent, whole, complete – and on their own. Extrinsic considerations of context and circumstance play their role, but logic, cogent discourse, rhetoric, – these enjoy an existence, an integrity too. If sentences bear meaning on their own, then to insist that sentences bear meaning only in line with friends, companions, partners in meaning contradicts the inner logic of syntax that, on its own, imparts sense to sentences. These are the choices: everything imputed, as against an inner integrity of logic and the syntax of syllogistic thought.[13] But there is no compromise between what I argue is the theologically grounded hermeneutic, taken as a given by diverse believers, and the descriptive and historical, utterly secular hermeneutic which I advocate. As between the philosophical heritage of Athens and any other hermeneutics, I maintain that "our sages of blessed memory" demonstrate the power of the philosophical reading of the one whole Torah of Moses, our rabbi. And, further, I should propose that the reason for our sages' remarkable success in persuading successive generations of Israel of the Torah's ineluctable truth lies not in arguments from tradition, from "Sinai," so much as in appeals to the self-evidence of the well-framed argument, the

---

[13]No one can maintain that the meanings of words and phrases, the uses of syntax, bear meanings wholly integral to discrete occasions. As I argue in the concluding chapter, syntax of thought is always social, by definition; that is why it works, and it also is why it endures. Syntax works because it joins mind to mind, and no mind invents language. But that begs the question and may be dismissed as impertinent, since the contrary view claims far more than the social foundation of the language.

well-crafted sentence of thought. And it is in society, the social entity, that the sentence of thought is shared, hence intelligible, vivid and effective.

Let us conclude, then, with a restatement of the necessarily historical hermeneutic that I set forth, by which we do not read everything as continuous with everything else, but all things as, first, autonomous and free-standing, then connected, and, only when demonstrated in some concrete way, continuous: I think, in modes of thought. Reading what authorships wrote – a problem of textual analysis and interpretation – undergoes distortion of we impose, to begin with, the after-the-fact interpretation of the audience that received the writing. We err if we confuse social and theological with literary and hermeneutical categories, and the religious system at the end constitutes a social and theological, not a literary classification. Hermeneutics begins within the text and cannot sustain definition on the basis of the (later, extrinsic) disposition of the text. Nor should we miss the gross anachronism represented by the view that the way things came out all together at the end imposes its meaning and character upon the way things started out, one by one. Reading the Mishnah, ca. 200, as the framers of the two Talmuds read it two hundred, then four hundred years later, vastly distorts the original document in its own setting and meaning – and that by definition. But the same must be said, we now see, of the Bavli: reading the Bavli as if any other authorship but the Bavli's authorship played a part in making the statement of the Bavli is simply an error.[14] A mark of the primitive character of discourse in the field at hand derives from the need to point to self-evident anachronism in the prevailing hermeneutics.

Much is at stake. On the one side I identify a heuristic system, with a hermeneutic built out of theology and anachronism, yielding a chaotic and capricious, utterly atomistic reading of everything in light of everything else, all together, all at once. In such a situation no test of sense limits the free range of erudition, and erudition transforms

---

[14]Critics of my translations of the Bavli and the Yerushalmi into English prove the necessity of making this simple point, because they invariably fault me for translating not in accord with the received hermeneutics, e.g., the medieval interpreter, Solomon Isaac (1040-1105), "Rashi." They accuse me not of ignoring Rashi, to which I plead guilty, but not understanding Rashi. But I consistently translate the words before me, as best I can, without reference to Rashi's interpretation of them – except – for reason, not for piety – as an interesting possibility. I point to the world of biblical scholarship, which manages to translate the Hebrew Scriptures without consistently accepting the interpretation of the medieval commentators. Why should the Talmuds be treated differently? There are other approaches to the sense and meaning, other criteria, other definitions of the problem. But we cannot expect a hearing from those who know in advance that Rashi has said the last word on the matter.

discourse into political contest: who can make his judgment prevail against whom. Against that I offer an orderly and systematic reading of the documents, one by one, then in their second-order connections, so far as they intersect, finally, as a cogent whole – thus a genuinely secular reading of documents, one by one, in connection with others, as part of a continuous whole, each in its several contexts, immediate and historical, synchronic and diachronic.

Appendix Two

Identifying the Correct Context of a Text:
The Debate with Eliezer Schweid

THE SELF-INTERPRETING MISHNAH
Review of Jacob Neusner's *Judaism: The Evidence of the Mishnah*

By Eliezer Schweid, The Hebrew University of Jerusalem
[Translated by David A. Weiner]

The originality and interest of Professor Jacob Neusner's *Judaism: The Evidence of the Mishnah* stem primarily from the author's bold approach to the Mishnah. As the basic document of the Oral Torah literature, the Mishnah was studied and interpreted by successive generations of students and scholars. Professor Neusner's innovation is his effort to examine the text critically using its internal evidence alone. He sets out to study the Mishnah as an independent document.

Neusner's methodological project bears an astonishing resemblance to the project of biblical criticism set forth by Spinoza in his *Tractatus-Theologico-Politicus*. Spinoza's essential innovation was his demand to liberate our understanding of the Bible from the domination of traditional, rabbinic, and scholastic interpretations. Spinoza sought to examine the biblical books in their own right and to place them in their immediate historical context – inasmuch as this context was identifiable. The very fact that modern scholarship has not yet applied Spinoza's method to Mishnaic studies indicates the radical nature – and indeed the problematic nature – of Jacob Neusner's courageous scholarly innovation. Neusner's work advances beyond both traditional Talmudic scholars as well as his predecessors in the discipline of historical-textual criticism. But it is one thing to see the Bible as a text independent of later interpretations. It is quite another thing to view the Mishnah as a work outside the interpretive tradition that eventually, over many generations, came to be seen as directly emerging from the Mishnah itself, from its style, and indeed from its internal evidence.

Let us first examine Neusner's scholarly methodology and the results it produces.

I. Jacob Neusner suggests, first of all, that we view the Mishnah in its existing form[1] as a complete literary document that is unitary in content, style, and structure. He asks us to regard the Mishnah as a book composed and redacted by Judah the Patriarch in the Land of Israel at the outset of the third century.

II. As a complete and unitary literary document, the Mishnah should be subjected to structural-phenomenological scrutiny. In order to treat the Mishnah as an important document in its own right the scholar must delineate its distinctive subject-matter, structure, and style. In this manner the scholar may learn the book's purpose, message, and audience.

III. By assuming that the Mishnah constitutes a complete and unitary literary document, we do not rule out the possibility that its materials initially accumulated long before its redaction. It is even possible that parts of the Mishnah were composed earlier under different headings. This question, Neusner believes, is worth investigating. But once again, he insists that the issue should be addressed through an analysis of the internal evidence of the text. We must examine the internal constitution of the document. To the extent that the document still retains traces of its layers, we must reconstruct its form at the various stages of its constitution, in order to reveal the independent history of the document. At the same time we must examine the Mishnah's relation to other sources, especially the Bible. Once again, the methodological emphasis is placed on the internal evidence of the Mishnah. The question is: How and what did the Mishnah borrow from other sources? In other words, what were the factors and criteria that influenced the Mishnaic redactors' approach to previous authoritative documents?

IV. The evidence of other sources suggests that the Mishnah was created at a specifiable time by particular people within a given historical context. It follows that we should examine the following question: To what extent and in what way can the Mishnah be regarded as a response to existential and spiritual questions that stirred the Jewish people and its leaders at the time of the Mishnah's composition, the era following the Temple's destruction and the Bar-Kokhbah debacle.

---

[1]Neusner does not devote a chapter to the critical versions and manuscripts of the Mishnaic text. It must be assumed that in this matter he relies upon the philological-historical work of his predecessors. But unfortunately this is only a logical deduction. It would have been appropriate to address, however briefly, this issue, and it certainly would seem appropriate to mention the philological enterprise of his predecessors.

We are thus dealing with a complex scholarly method that begins with history, advances to phenomenological-literary analysis, and returns finally to history. The results are as follows:

I. The Mishnah is a literary creation designed to deliver a theological message concerning the relation between God and the people of Israel. This message is conveyed in a halakhic medium that shapes and ritualizes behavior of the family and community. Neusner rejects the prevalent scholarly view that the Mishnah contains direct or indirect historiographical materials. In other words, he rejects the common view that the Mishnah can be used as an immediate source of historical evidence regarding the period of its creation. In opposition to the dominant viewpoint Neusner insists that the Mishnah does not at all intend to provide historical testimony about the period of its constitution. Therefore, Neusner claims, the Mishnaic text, including the stories relating to persons and their deeds, should not be used as immediate historiographical evidence.[2] The historical information in the Mishnah can be gleaned only be delineating the document's theological message and relating it to the existential and political circumstances at the time of its composition. In this way we can derive historical information regarding the ideas and attitudes of a certain social class in the Land of Israel during the time of the Mishnah.

II. The Mishnah bases itself upon the Written Torah and faithfully appropriates large sections of Scripture. But it also selects, according to its own interests and criteria, the sections it requires. The Mishnah relates primarily to the Priestly Code and to the ritualistic laws applying to Priests. Moreover, the Mishnah attributes special importance to the priestly meals and to the rules of purity and uncleanness.

III. As for the Mishnah's process of constitution, Neusner's process of constitution, Neusner believes that the document's internal construction reveals three clearly distinct redactional and conceptual stages. But we should emphasize that, in Neusner's opinion, the final stage utilizes the earlier two by integrating them into a unified, consistent, and monolithic creation. Although Neusner offers a detailed description of the structure and content of the Mishnah at each state of its constitution, he finally describes the Mishnah as a unitary document.

IV. Through its detailed halakhic norms, the Mishnah describes a life of ritual purity in the realm of family and society. This description applies to a particular group of Jewish scholars and householders, not necessarily Priests or Levites, who adopted the Priestly rules of purity outside the Sanctuary. This group acted as if they were Priests.

---

[2]Neusner devotes to this issue a special appendix to his book. See the third appendix, "Story and Tradition in Judaism."

V. Underlying this way of life is the view that God imparts holiness through laws and commandments, while man, through his own will and choice, activates holiness through the intention reflected in his interpretation and performance of divine commandments. Consequently, the holy life is the telos of the people of Israel and its individual members. This goal's realization does not depend on external circumstances. It depends, on the one hand, on the God who commands and sanctifies, and on the other hand, on the Israelite who willfully chooses to obey and to incline his heart to God.

VI. Let us emphasize that this theological outlook is not elaborated in the form of an explicit intellectual discourse. Rather, it is contained implicitly in the comprehensive network of detailed halakhic norms. The Mishnah is the product of scribes who use rigid, formalized, and measured prose to depict norms of ritualized behavior. The Mishnah expects its readers to understand by themselves the principles and considerations that led to the determination of its specific norms.

VII. In sum, the Mishnah offers an ideal-normative depiction of the ritualized religious life of a rural class of Jews in the Land of Israel. Neusner regards this depiction as one of the typical modes of Jewish response to the existential, national, and spiritual situation created after the Temple's destruction and the Bar Kokhbah debacle. The group places itself beyond history. The group exists in the mundane world. But nevertheless, it suspends the enslaving, depressing reality of Israel's existence, by realizing, in a sanctified daily life, the chosenness and religious freedom of the people of Israel. Despite destruction and calamity, and despite the prohibition against entering Jerusalem, Israel remains a people who choose to live a holy life in compliance with God's will. To repeat, the Mishnah is one source of evidence concerning one particular group. There are other sources pertaining to other attitudes among the people. But it appears that this particular position attained a foundational status and shaped the character of Judaism through many generations of exile.

It is hard to refrain from pointing to the enormous similarity between the world view that Neusner finds underlying the Mishnah and the conception of Judaism provided by one of the great Jewish theologians of the first half of the twentieth century: Franz Rosenzweig.[3] Rosenzweig also believes that the Second Temple's destruction and Bar Kokhbah's failure represent a major watershed in Jewish history. Rosenzweig refers to this shift as the people's "exodus from history". From this point on Israel lives as a holy people, anchored as a group in its familial-tribal existence, living in its fixed cycle of Sabbaths, New Months, and Festivals, and

---

[3]See especially the essay, "The Spirit and Periods of Jewish History," in Franz Rosenzweig, *Naharaim* (Hebrew), Jerusalem: Bialik Foundation, 1961.

performing its rituals in its holy community. In this way the people of Israel anticipate the eternal life that God bestowed through the Torah. The essence of Israel's life remains indifferent to the changes taking place in political history. In his book, *The Star of Redemption,* Rosenzweig offers a deep and fascinating phenomenological description of the people of Israel's ritualized way of life. Rosenzweig pays much attention to the "sociology" of the praying and feasting community. He also notes that the Jew continually renews his gesture of accepting God's commandments, thereby drawing holiness into his mundane life. One may, of course, argue that Neusner's scholarly efforts parallel Rosenzweig's socio-theological characterizations simply because the sources of Oral Torah truly support this interpretation. But it is hard to suppress the intimation that Neusner's characterization of Mishnaic Judaism's reflection on its era is also a testimony to a conception of Judaism held by a particular stratum of Jews in the twentieth century Jewish diaspora.

Let us now turn to a critical examination of the methodology and its results. At first Neusner seems entirely right to insist that we study the Mishnah as a complete literary unit. Neusner seems justified in demanding that we examine the Mishnah's substance, structure, and style in order to elicit the document's theological message. This is the way we should treat any literary work that bears the authoritative seal of an author, or of an editor who imprinted his personality and world view upon the materials at his disposal. We must ask ourselves: Does the work shape a world view by selecting specific themes and placing them in a certain order and form? Indeed Neusner's answers to this question provides revealing insights concerning the theological reasons and meanings of ritualistic ordinances. The problems with this approach arise only later, when we reflect on the testimony of the post-mishnaic tradition and the literary constitution of the Mishnah itself. Do they confirm the assumption that the Mishnah is a complete unitary document that should be interpreted solely by its own internal evidence? In other words, is this truly the Mishnah's sole testimony about itself? Or perhaps the Mishnah's relation to the Talmudic tradition reveals something of its very nature as a literary work? And if so, we will have to place many of the points raised by Neusner in his innovative study in a different perspective and a different context. These new contexts and perspectives will significantly alter the meaning that Neusner attributes to his findings.

Indeed, several of Neusner's parenthetical remarks suggest that his work is open to the type of criticism suggested above. First of all, we noted that Neusner sees fit to examine the Mishnah's own relation to the Written Torah. But in the section dealing with the Mishnah's relation to the source called "The Written Torah", we confront a loaded and inconclusive argument. Neusner mentions two divergent opinions. According to the first, the interpretations of Oral Torah are entirely subordinate to the Written Torah. The second opinion is that the Oral Torah is an independent source parallel to the Written Torah. But the rub of the matter is this: Neusner divorces these opinions from the Mishnah itself, and attributes them to the tradition of post-Mishnaic interpreters. He believes that the Mishnah itself is not involved in this debate and does not raise the question except in one place, the first pericope of Tractate *Avot*. The Mishnah presents its views as normative dictates and it appropriates the Scriptural commandments selectively. The Mishnah assumes for itself an authority that it does not bother to substantiate. But even if we agree to view the evidence of Mishnah Tractate *Avot* as distinct from the wide array of Mishnaic Orders and Tractates, the question still remains: How can we understand such an assumption of authority within the Mishnah's own theological context?

Is such an assumption of authority intelligible without the supposition that we are in fact dealing here with "Oral Torah" that derives its authority from the Torah or from a parallel revelation? We must now reconsider Neusner's recurrent claim that the Mishnah does not announce its theological assumptions. Such assumptions, Neusner believes, are contained in the Mishnah's legal detail. Neusner believes that we must extract from these details some underlying principle, reason, or meaning. To use Neusner's expression, the Mishnah "compliments" its students by assuming that they understand many things that it does not explain, but that nevertheless, are essential to a basic understanding of the book.

If this is truly the way matters stand, then we are right to argue that even without expressing itself explicitly, the Mishnah takes for granted an existing authoritative tradition that sustains it and through which it is interpreted. The Mishnah can compliment its students to such an extent only because it can rely on such a tradition, which is passed on from teacher to student as they study Torah together. The Mishnah fails to refer directly to this tradition and to its theological assumptions precisely because such testimony was provided explicitly by the tradition itself. By its own testimony the Mishnah was fundamentally a text for the Talmudic Academy. This text was to be studied through the talmudic deliberations between student and teacher, that is, between the student and a person whose extratextual knowledge authorized him to convey and interpret the words of the Mishnah. It follows that we are dealing here with a text whose life-context is within the tradition that runs through it.

Let me emphasize that this conclusion is the basic assumption of the Mishnah's traditional interpreters. It is also the basic assumption of the philological-historical school of Mishnaic studies. In this sense the modern philological-historical school accepts the assumptions of traditional exegesis. This makes modern scholars the target of Neusner's sharp critique. However, in light of the foregoing discussion, can we accept Neusner extremely radical critique and his extremely radical conclusions? As for us, we tend to respond negatively to this question. The Mishnah does not proclaim itself as an independent, self-interpreting document that provides an exhaustive treatment of its subject-matter. Indeed we can learn much from the Mishnah by striving to understand it from its own internal evidence. In this regard Neusner has achieved a distinctive success worthy of much gratitude. But a discussion focused on the Mishnah alone leaves much to be said. Indeed, the Mishnah itself does not directly confront political issues, historical events and processes, or the people's crucial existential concerns. But this fact does not indicate that the sages, whose halakhic opinions are recorded in the Mishnah, ignored these questions intentionally. In other words, It is wrong to try to derive from the Mishnah, whether from its explicit statements or its conspicuous omissions, a comprehensive theological world view. Such an effort is especially unjustified, because other sources teach us that these same sages devoted attention to the very issues that are not addressed in the Mishnah. It would be more exact to say that certain matters are not discussed in the Mishnah, because the Mishnah was designed from the outset to treat certain subjects and not others. But what the Mishnah says about its chosen subject matter must be interpreted also by reference to sayings appearing in other literary sources.

If this argument is sound, it follows that we should accept with qualification Neusner's critique of the scholars who used the Mishnah to derive historiographical information. He is right in claiming that stories and legends about sages and their actions should be examined first as stories with a specific structure and style. In this way we can extract their intended conceptual message. Nevertheless, the fact that modern historians endeavored to extract from these stories a kernel of historical testimony was not the result of complete blindness to their literary character and religious-moral message. These messages were understood and, for the most part, taken into account. Nevertheless, the interpretive tradition that dealt with these stories apparently attached great significance to the fact that the stories concern the actual deeds of specific persons whose status as believers and scholars made them leaders and teachers. The actions of these personages, as well as their words, were Torah. Accordingly, the traditional exegetes were morally committed to the view that the stories were not fictitious fairy tales, but rather accounts of the actual deeds of real people. We will surely be right to claim that these stories are not biographical or historiographical accounts that should be accepted as factual historical records. For, the stories were related in a manner that highlights their moral message and meaning.

Moreover, they were edited and reformulated for this purpose several times, because each successive generation of interpreters applied its own scale of values to the protagonists' actions. But it is wrong to argue that these stories are not designed to attest to the actual deeds of historical persons whose actions are Torah. It is thus right to search for a kernel of biographical-historical testimony in these stories. To deny this is to ignore their role and meaning.

Moreover, traditions anchored in historical testimony play an important role in substantiating the authority behind the sages' opinions. If we evaluate this tradition properly, we will conclude that the literature of Oral Torah, including the Mishnah itself, is quite conscientious about the precision of historical testimony. This is at least true with regard to the sages' chain of generations and their roles and status as teachers, bearers of tradition, interpreters and legislators who lead the society of contemporary adherents of divine commandments. We are dealing here with historiographical testimony of the highest religious significance. It seems that in the end Jacob Neusner must also accept it as credible and rely upon it. But he ignores this fact's significance for assessing the importance of historical testimony as an important Mishnaic theme.

Neusner's scholarly work on the Mishnah appears, in the light of these criticisms, as a decisive step toward an "exodus from history", not only in regard to the Mishnah's interpretation, but also in regard to the historical understanding of traditional exegesis and modern scholarship. Of course the overall goal is to return to that same history in a new way that characterizes the spiritual orientation of a new generation. Modern scholarship bitterly criticized the traditional exegetes and their attitude to history, but nevertheless relied upon their testimony and tried to continue it in its own distinctive fashion. In the same manner Neusner and his students direct bitter attacks against the historical scholarship of their predecessors, but nevertheless they rely upon it and seek to continue it in a new way. Once again we are reminded of the remarkable parallels between Neusner's approach to the Mishnah and Spinoza's approach to Scripture, as well as the surprising resemblance between the theology that Neusner attributes to the Mishnah and the modern exilic theology of Franz Rosenzweig. It seems that we are dealing here with a classic example of research that throws a new and exciting light upon the past, but testifies more to the present than to the past. In other words, Neusner's work exemplifies the endeavors and expectations of Jewish thinkers who search for their roots in the sources, and in the process, discover a reflection of themselves and their Jewish world view.

Indeed, we have here a fascinating study, not only in the history of Judaic scholarship, but also in the history of modern Jewish thought. But to substantiate this claim we must take account of Jacob Neusner's prolific work. He has written many scores of books, and hundreds of articles dealing with Judaism throughout the generations. These books also deal directly with the basic contemporary issues of the Jewish people's life, culture, and religion. Jacob Neusner is not only an important scholar in the history of Jewish historical and Talmudic scholarship. He is also one of the thinkers who represent the conceptual trends of the Jewish people's contemporary spiritual leadership. There is a very close, conscious connection between his scholarship and his political-religious outlook. but in order to deal adequately with the connection between his Jewish world view and his historical-literary scholarship, we must grapple with his books on contemporary issues. Let us hope that we can engage in such a deliberation soon, when the Israeli reader can read additional books on Neusner in the Hebrew language. He deserves it, and the educated Israeli public deserves it. If we are interested in deepening the relationship between the Jewish people in Israel and in the diaspora, it is important that the policy of ignoring Neusner and his students should be abandoned. To date Israeli scholars and thinkers have generally neglected Neusner and his enterprise. This attitude should give way to a comprehensive and open debate that includes criticism, sustained argument, but also dialogue that contributes to the deepening of learning and the renewal of understanding.

RESPONSE

Jacob Neusner

Professor Schweid proposes to read the Mishnah not only in its own terms but also in light of its reception later on. No one can differ. But if we want to know what the document meant to the people who made it up and put it together, then the way in which later authorships received and revised the writing is not relevant. To an account of the later history of the Mishnah, of course, the reading of those subsequent writers forms the center of interest. But that is a different matter. The Mishnah, after all, is no different from Scripture. No one working in the study of the Hebrew Scriptures claims that Rashi tells us what the author of J or E or JE or P or D had in mind in the age before 586 B.C.E., but only how Judaic exegetical tradition received and interpreted the pentateuchal mosaic in 1100 C.E. Why accept in reading Scripture what we are supposed to deny in addressing a writing in the canon of the Judaism of late antiquity? The reception of any document a century or two later tells us only what happened later on.

The Mishnah as read later on is not the document as written. For if we were to accept Professor Schweid's proposed hermeneutics, then we should, to begin with, have to excise from the Mishnah the divisions of Holy Things and Purities for the Yerushalmi's Mishnah, and the divisions of Agriculture and Purities for the Bavli's. Not only so, but we should have to include in the Mishnah vast tracts of the Tosefta, the compilers of which impute to the Mishnah readings and whole passages unknown to the Mishnah as present manuscript evidence presents that writing.[4] The Mishnah's authorship indeed presents us with the Mishnah's sole testimony about itself and what was in its mind, and any proposition that the talmudic tradition tells us about "its very nature as a literary work" has to be set aside as, at best, beyond all test of falsification, therefore also insusceptible to verification.[5]

The claim that there was a "tradition" beyond the pages of the Mishnah in which the Mishnah's authorship found its sustaining place is both self-evident but also beside the point. It is self-evident, because, after all, all Judaisms of antiquity addressed their systemic statements to an encompassing revelation of Sinai, the Hebrew Scriptures or, in the fully realized system of Judaism, the Written Torah. Not only so, but all Judaic writings make ample use of facts of life and thought commonplace in the Near East for three thousand years, for example, the distributive economics of Leviticus and of the Mishnah. It is beside the point, because, in the absence of evidence of the content of that tradition, its morphology, structure, and focus, what are we to say about it, beyond what is implicit within the document we propose to read? That is to say, whatever we know we know, and what we do not know, we do not know. The "Judaism beyond the texts" that Professor Schweid invokes is whatever we make of it, until we subject ourselves to the discipline of the document in hand. And then it is the system of the document in hand, its implicit affirmations, its explicit propositions, its generative tensions, its self-evident truths in response to its urgent and critical questions.

At the same time, I concur with Professor Schweid's view that, even in the context in which the Mishnah was set forth and received, and even by those who made up the document, other important issues demanded attention. No one claims that the Judaism that rests, for its first statement, upon the Mishnah, derives only from the Mishnah. All the more so, none can imagine that that Judaism, even in the time of the Mishnah, consisted only of the program of the Mishnah. That simple premise of all discourse explains why I asked the obvious question, what is the evidence of the Mishnah in particular for the Judaism to which the authorship of the

---

[4]And, by the same token, exclude those vast passages that Tosefta's framers ignore. Rabbi Yaakov Elman, Yeshiva University, has documented that fact for Pesahim.

[5]When we come to the history of the reception of the Mishnah, we deal with documents that cite passages of the Mishnah verbatim, as we find in Sifra and the two Sifrés, and that simple and well-known fact renders highly improbable the notion that implicit in the Mishnah is the reading of those who received it.

Mishnah, through that document, made so formidable a contribution? Had I stopped there, Professor Schweid would have reason to find me disingenuous. But I have, after all, proceeded since 1981, to a variety of other writings and asked precisely the same question of those documents: Avot, the Tosefta, the Yerushalmi, Genesis Rabbah, Leviticus Rabbah, the Bavli, Sifré to Numbers, Sifré to Deuteronomy, The Fathers According to Rabbi Nathan, Pesiqta deRab Kahana, Pesiqta Rabbati, and I in the present work complete my study of Sifra in particular.[6] In each instance I have tried to read the document at hand in its own terms and also in relationship to other writings of its time. Accordingly, reading the Mishnah by itself forms only one step on a fairly protracted journey.

But having made that point clear, I do have to affirm that the Mishnah's authorship does place in our hands a closed system, not an open one, in that, explicitly for the most part, implicitly in part, they do provide us, in form, in language, in logic, in rhetoric, and, I think, in their entire topical program, whatever they think we need to know to build the kind of world and society for Israel that they think Israel should constitute. In that way they have created a writing for Western civilization that compares with Plato's *Republic* and Aristotle's *Politics,* that is to say, a utopian statement, a *Staatsroman,* covering politics, economics, social structure, relationships within the polity and with the sheltering world beyond, the family, the role of all components of society, men, women, children, slaves and free persons, everything a world-ruler, whether Alexander or Aristotle or the regnant collegium of sage, priest, and householder, for the Mishnah, would need to know to make a world. Once more, I have read not only the Mishnah, but an entire sequence of later writings in the same line of tradition, as systemic statements, standing both on their own and also in relationship to prior ones with which each is, if not wholly continuous, at least demonstrably connected.[7]

I take as an unearned, therefore much appreciated, compliment Professor Schweid's conclusion, that scholarship, including my scholarship, proceeds not in dessicated, disembodied mind, to whom it may concern (and that is, nobody, including the originating scholar) but in the intellects of real people, solving real problems in a trying time. Any other conception denies the iron fact of the sociology of knowledge,

---

[6]In the preface I list the other relevant works.

[7]Among the three possible relationships, [1] autonomy, [2] connection, and [3] continuity, no document, including the Mishnah, is autonomous of all others in its context. At stake in this debate is whether any document is wholly continuous with any other, and, further, whether and how all documents are continuous with all others. That is what is at stake in *Canon and Connection* and in *Literature and Midrash,* cited above.

that all learning speaks for a particular time and place, even while, honorably and with integrity, proposing to speak from eternity to eternity. The notion, for example, that we can, and therefore should, find out *precisely how things were,* paramount in nineteenth century European scholarship, derived from a prior claim and premise. It was that, if we can determine what really happened, we also know what really should now take place as well. The premise, of course, is that we *can* indeed find out what really happened on that one day – even with sources that depict rules and principles, not singular events. Hence the "historical Jesus" formed a centerpiece for theological debate in the nineteenth century. Nowadays we frame matters in other terms, because the world at hand and ahead forms a different program of inquiry for us.

Accordingly, I have asked how our sages of blessed memory identified paramount human questions and answered them, devising self-evidently valid answers to urgent and unavoidable issues. My premise, therefore, is that a Judaic system is formed of an inexorably correct answer to an inescapable question, and does so by presenting a complete and whole system, comprising a world view, a way of life, and a definition of the social entity that realized the one and embodied the other: ethos, ethics, in society.[8] Issues of theology, philology, lower criticism of texts, even the much-maligned travesty on learning we designate "positivism" (as in the famous Bar Ilan seminar, "locks and keys in Talmudic sources"), all make their contribution. None is ignored. But the center has shifted, as it did before, as it will again. But I hope to gain the gravity to affect the orbit.

Who in my position could fail to give thanks for so engaging and compelling a critic as Professor Eliezer Schweid, who has taken the trouble to read and to form a position on the center of discourse? No book of mine has ever received so purposeful and so pertinent a critique, and, as issues move onward, as they have and will continue to for me, I can only look forward to that ongoing dialogue that transforms scholarship into learning, and, should we enjoy sufficient merit, in *yeshiva shel maalah,* learning even into Torah. But not now, not here, not yet: only in the coming time.

---

[8]I have spelled out the method and terms of systemic analysis in my *First Principles of Systemic Analysis: The Case of Judaism* (Atlanta: Scholars Press for Brown Judaic Studies, 1987).

Index